Young Israel Of Woodmere

43RD ANNUAL DINNER

Honoring

SHAYNEE AND MARTIN KESSLER

Guests of Honor

ZENA AND NORMAN DACHS

Amud Avodah Award

AILEEN AND ERIC GELLMAN

New Leadership Award

March 1, 2003 ❖ 28 Adar I, 5763

Dedicated by the Friends of Zena and Norman Dachs

MYRNA AND CHARLES ALPERT

SHELLY AND HARVEY DACHS

ESTHER AND HARVEY FELSEN

MYRNA MILLER

DASSIE AND DAVID SCHREIBER

Women in the Talmud

נשים בתלמוד

Women

Published by the

ORTHODOX UNION
תורה ומצוות

זרעים • מועד
Zeraim • Moed

in the Talmud

נשים בתלמוד

An Anthology of the Talmud's stories about women, as explained by the classic commentators.

Rabbi Aaron Eli Glatt, M.D.

WOMEN IN THE TALMUD

FIRST EDITION
First Impression ... February 2003

Published and Distributed by
MESORAH PUBLICATIONS, Ltd.
4401 Second Avenue / Brooklyn, N.Y 11232

Distributed in Europe by
LEHMANNS
Unit E, Viking Industrial Park
Rolling Mill Road
Jarow, Tyne & Wear, NE32 3DP
England

Distributed in Australia and New Zealand by
GOLDS WORLD OF JUDAICA
3-13 William Street
Balaclava, Melbourne 3183
Victoria, Australia

Distributed in Israel by
SIFRIATI / A. GITLER — BOOKS
6 Hayarkon Street
Bnei Brak 51127

Distributed in South Africa by
KOLLEL BOOKSHOP
Shop 8A Norwood Hypermarket
Norwood 2196, Johannesburg, South Africa

ISBN:
1-57819-710-4 (hard cover)

Printed in the United States of America by
Noble Book Press Corp., New York, NY

ISRAEL MEIR LAU
Chief Rabbi of Israel
President of The Great Rabbinical Court

ישראל מאיר לאו
הרב הראשי לישראל
נשיא בית הדין הרבני הגדול

בס״ד, י׳ טבת, תשס״ב
25 דצמבר, 2001
ספחי- 391.סב

לכבוד
הרב אהרון גלאט שליט״א
ניו יורק, ארה״ב.

השלום והברכה
מציון ומירושלים,

עלים מספרך ״נשי התלמוד״, הגיעוני. בספר זה אסופה ״כעמיר גרנה״ של כל מאמרי חז״ל המובאים בש״ס בסדר ״זרעים״ ו״מועד״, שעניינם נשים בכלל, והאישה בפרט.

שלמה המלך בדבריו היטיב להגדיר את מעמד האם בישראל ״שמע בני מוסר אביך ואל תטוש תורת אמך״. נשאלת השאלה, מדוע ייחס את עניין השמיעה של ענייני המוסר – לאב, ואילו את שמירת המסורת ואי נטישתה – לאם. מאמר זה הוא הדגל לשלימות היחסים בין אב ואם ותפקידם בעיצוב הבית. האב מכוון את הדרך, בתוכחות מוסר מנווט את חינוך ילדיו. לעומת זאת, האם המגדלת את ילדיה, היא זו המטביעה בנפשם את ערכי התורה והמצוות, ולאו דווקא בדברי מוסר, אלא בעצם הנהגתה.

לצערי, בתקופתנו ניטשטשו הגבולות והגדרים. כחלק מהניסיון לפריקת העול מנסים גם לפגוע במבנה הבית ובערכיו. הניסיונות הללו כוללים גם שינוי מהותי בהגדרת תפקידי ההורים. כשם שלכל אחד ואחד מן הברואים - תכלית לבריאתו, כן חייבת להיות חלוקה בין בעל ואישה ובין אם לאב.

רחש לבך דבר טוב להציג בפני הלומדים והכמהים לידע, את עמדת תורתנו הקדושה. הבאת את דברי חז״ל, כלשונם, מן המקורות, ומהם ילמדו לעצב בית נאמן בישראל.

מברכך בכל לב,

ישראל מאיר לאו
הרב הראשי לישראל

ELIYAHU BAKSHI-DORON
RISHON-LEZION CHIEF RABBI OF ISRAEL

אליהו בקשי-דורון
הראשון לציון הרב הראשי לישראל

ב״ה, כ״ד תשרי, תשס״ב
ס״ב/16-18-1

מכתב ברכה

חכמת נשים בנתה ביתה

שלא כשאר הנבראים האדם נברא לבדו ובדידותו הוגדרה כ״לא טוב היות האדם לבדו״, ורק לאחר שנבראה האשה שהוגדרה ״עזר כנגדו״ נאמר על הבריאה והנה טוב מאוד, ללא אשה הוגדר האדם לא רק כחסר אלא כלא טוב, ועל כך אמרו חז״ל ״כל השרוי בלא אשה שרוי בלא טובה בלא שמחה בלא ברכה בלא תורה בלא חומה ובלא שלום״, מבואר בדברי חז״ל שהחסרון בלא אשה הוא לא בצרכי הגוף ולא רק העזר הגשמי חסר, אלא חסר הוא במושגים הרוחניים והנעלים שבו, לפי שהאשה משלימה את הטובה, השמחה, הברכה והתורה שבאדם, לא להכפיל את הלא טוב נבראה האשה, אלא להשלים את החסר לו, כדי ליצור את הטוב מאוד כאחד, על כן שונים האיש והאשה במזגם ותכונותיהם ותפקידם, שעיקר יצירתם היא להשלים זה את זו, מכאן שהדרישה לשויון גמור בכל התחומים נוגדת את עצם הבריאה ומחטיאה את המטרה של והנה טוב מאוד.

בתקופה האחרונה דגל השויון נשא בכל מקום, גם במקום שאינו אלא מדומה, עד כדי השוואה גמורה בין המינים בכל התחומים האפשריים, לצערנו השקפה זו מחלחלת גם בקודש פנימה, ויש המבקשים והמבקשות לבטל יחודם ולראות את האשה והאיש שוים גם בכל דבר שבקדושה, בלימוד תורה תפילה וקיום מצוות וכדומה, ברור שלא זו דרכה של תורה, ועל כגון דא נאמר ״חכמת נשים בנתה ביתה ואוולת בידה תהרסנו״, נשים חכמות יודעות לבנות ביתם כנשים בתבונה ולמלא תפקידם כראוי, ואילו אולת בידה תהרסנו, כשמבקשות הם לבטל את יחודם, יעודם ומעלתם. אמת שאין להתעלם מאורח החיים הסובב אותנו שהורגלנו לשויון בכל התחומים ובעיקר בהשכלה ולימוד, ונכון למלא את הנדרש על פי ההלכה ובמסגרות הראויות של חכמת נשים בנתה ביתה, אולם יש להזהר מלערב תחומים ולפרוץ גדרות, יש נשים שאינם ממלאות יעודם ואינם מודעות ליחודם ומעמדם, ומרגישות שלא בצדק כאי נוחות וברגשי נחיתות, על כן נכון להבהיר הדברים בדרכה של תורה בהסברים ובדברי נועם, שתדענה הנשים מעלתם יחודם ותפקידם.

על כן שמחתי לשמוע שהרב אהרון אליהו גלאט שליט״א רחש ליבו דבר טוב להוציא לאור ספר שירכז את הנאמר על הנשים בכל התלמוד ולהבהיר הדברים בדרכה של תורה, וכבר סמכו עליו בזה הרבנים שהמליצו על עבודתו הברוכה ואף ידי תיכון עמו שיזכה לברך על המוגמר להגדיל תורה ולהאדירה כדי שיהיו הכל סוברים תורה בדרך ישראל סבא, ולא יפנו אל רהבים ושטי כזב המבקשים להם חדשות אשר לא שערום אבותינו, וכל כבודה בת מלך פנימה.

והנני לברכו שיזכה שהדברים היוצאים מן הלב יכנסו בלב בנות ישראל הכשרות וימשיך בפעילותו לזכות את הרבים מתוך בריאות גופא ונהורא מעליא וכל מילי דמיטב.

בברכה,
אליהו בקשי דורון
הראשון לציון הרב הראשי לישראל

RABBI BENJAMIN KAMENETSKY
357 BARNARD AVENUE • WOODMERE, N. Y. 11598

בס"ד ט"ו לחודש אני לדודי ודודי לי, שנת תשס"א לפ"ק

אל כבוד ידידי היקר באנשים, גדול בתורה ויר"ש נכונה,
מרביץ תורה לרבים, כליל המדות וגדול המעש, האי גברא
רבא ויקירא מוהר"ר אהרן שליט"א ומשפחת גלאס.
אחדשה"ט בברכה רבה והצלחה.

מה מאוד נהניתי לדפדף את גליונות הספר שבכ"ר מוכן
להוציא "נשיאי התלמוד". אף שאינני יודע אם בין אלפי
הספרים השייכים לפירושי ומקורי התלמוד נמצא ספר
מיוחד לעניינים אלו, מ"מ רואה אני בזה החבור ענין
חשוב מאוד להראות לרבים שמחשיבים את השלשלת דתורת
ישראל מפרט דחלק התורה שבע"פ. וגם בספר זה
ימצאו הקוראים מזון רוחני בשיטות וחשיבות הראשונים מלמדי
דרבותי' והשגי' בקירוב ההדורות.

וכדי שלא להוציא את הניר חלק, אביא בזה מאמר מהגאון
בעל הנחב ספרי צדוק שמסביר את הפסוק בשירת הים (שמות ט"ו כ"א)
"ותען להם מרים .... סוס ורכבו רמה בים" איזו שאלה שאלו
הנשים למרים שענתה להם פסוק זה? והסביר כי באמת שמחת
כלל ישראל על הים היתה שהשי"ת עזר להם בקריעת ים סוף לקבל
התורה בהר סיני, והנשים דאגו המחזור שאלו למרים מדוע אנו
שמחים הלא אנו פטורים מת"ת ואז ענתה להם מרים הפסוק
סוס ורכבו רמה בים וכי מה ראה הקב"ה להטביע את הסוסים
שבמצרים? אלא הטעם שהם סייעו למצרים לרדוף אחרי בנ"י, הם הי'
המסייעים א"כ אנו ג"כ זכאים לשמוח כי לפי הגמ' (ברכות י"ז ע"א)
"אלא נשים במאי זכיין? באקרויי בנייהו לבי כנישתא, ובאתנויי
גברייהו בי רבנן, ונטרין לגברייהו עד דאתו מבי רבנן".
ויהי רצון שהשי"ת ימלא משאלות לבכם ותזכו להמשיך להגדיל דעת הקודש
להחזיר באלה הרבה אורות לבית ישראל ונזכה בזכות הנשים צדקניות
להגאל בגאולה אמתית בב"א.
בברכת כתוח"ט ולאמר לחיים טובים ארוכים ולשנה טובה אח"י וד"ק
לאחב"י ארה"ק בב"א

דש"ה הכותב ומברך בכבוד
בנימין קמנצקי

Rabbi Reuven Feinstein
500 C Grand Street
New York, New York 10002
212-777-7935

שלום ראובן פיינשטיין
ראש הישיבה
ישיבה דסטעטן איילענד
718-356-2101

ג' טבת תשס"ד

ראיתי כמה מאמרים [illegible] המחבר הר' אהרן [illegible] שמסבירין
אותו ביותר. ואם ראיתי חלק מספרו. וראיתי שהוא אומן [illegible] בענייני
בהנהגה, ואף בשאלות שצריכין [illegible] [illegible] [illegible]
שייכין להיות [illegible] [illegible] [illegible] לפיקוח נפש.
בהשקפה [illegible]. [illegible] [illegible] [illegible] [illegible] [illegible] [illegible] האמת
[illegible] [illegible] [illegible]. [illegible] [illegible] [illegible] [illegible] ביותר מספרי
[illegible] [illegible] [illegible] [illegible] [illegible] [illegible] [illegible] [illegible]
אין [illegible] [illegible] [illegible] [illegible] [illegible] [illegible] [illegible] [illegible]
[illegible] [illegible] [illegible] [illegible] [illegible] [illegible] [illegible]. ואף
[illegible] [illegible] [illegible] [illegible] [illegible] [illegible] [illegible] [illegible] [illegible] אלו.
לשום אדם [illegible] [illegible] [illegible] [illegible] [illegible] [illegible] [illegible] [illegible]
[illegible] [illegible] [illegible]. [illegible] [illegible] [illegible] [illegible] [illegible] [illegible]
[illegible] [illegible] [illegible] [illegible] [illegible] [illegible] [illegible] [illegible].
[illegible] [illegible] [illegible] [illegible] [illegible] [illegible], [illegible]. [illegible]
ראובן פיינשטיין [illegible] [illegible]. [illegible] [illegible] [illegible] [illegible]

Rabbi Avraham Zvi Wosner
146 South 9th Street
Brooklyn, NY 11211
Tel: (718) 782-4790

אברהם צבי הלוי וואזנער
דומ"ץ קערעסטיר בערבעסט
וחבר וועד הרבנים דקשעות פת"ם

בס"ד

כבוד ידידנו הרבני החשוב יקר באנשים ומוכתר בנימוסין
גורס באורייתא ודן בעמקה של הלכה מרביץ תורה לעדרים
הרב אהרן גלאט שליט"א

הנני בזה לאחל ברכתי לרגל הוצאת ספרו לאור עולם.
אשר אסף מאוה"ל מכל הש"ס על סדר נשים בתלמוד עם ליקוט
עבודה ממפרשי הראשונים והאחרונים בסדר נאה בדרכה של דרך
התורה. ובדברי מאז אינני משרי המסכימים באותי בזה רק
לאחל למזל שיזכה שיפוצו מעינותיו חוצה ויזכה שלעולם יצלח
ושלא ימוש התורה מפיו ומפי זרעו להגדיל תורה ולהאדירה זכי נזכה
לביאת משיח צדקנו בן דוד במהרה

הכו"ח ד' לסדר הבאים אשה אתה שנת תשס"ב
אברהם צבי הלוי וואזנער

Tel: 548-4765

YOUNG ISRAEL OF RIVERDALE
4502 HENRY HUDSON PARKWAY EAST
RIVERDALE, NEW YORK 10471

Mordechai Willig, Rabbi

חנוכה תשס"ב

הנה תלמידי היקר, רופא אומן מקדש שם שמים,
ד"ר אהרן גלאט נ"י, עושה תורתו קבע, וזה שנים רבות
מגיד שעור בדף היומי במקום מגוריו. ועתה רחש לבו
דבר טוב, ללקט לתרגם ולפרש את האגדות שבש"ס
סדר מועד, הדנות בסיפורי נסים ומעשים. ובזמננו
ענינים אלו חשובים ורגישים מאד, בגלל ההשפעות
מן החוץ שחדרו לתוך בני ישראל הנאמנים. ולכן
ספר זה, שהוא ליקוט של מקורות מחז"ל ומהמפרשים
המפורסמים מהדורות הקודמים בנושא זה, דבר בעתו הוא.
והנני לברך את תלמידי הנ"ל, שימשיך ללמוד וללמד
ולקדש שם שמים, ויזכה לראות, יחד עם רעיתו החשובה מנב"ת,
הרבה נחת מכל יו"ח.

כעתירת המוקירו ומברכו
מרדכי ווילליג

RABBINICAL COUNCIL OF AMERICA · הסתדרות הרבנים דאמריקה

Rabbi Hershel Billet
President

Rabbi Steven M. Dworken
Executive Vice President

ב"ה

ו' שבט תשס"ג

שמחתי מאוד לקרוא בספר החשוב "נשים בתלמוד"
שחבר ידידי הטוב חבר קהלתנו ד"ר אהרן גלאי.
שמח אני להשתתף עם איחוד הקהלות בארה"ב
המכונה אגנסט להמליץ על הספר שבנוי מלא
מקורות בש"ס בענין נשים. חז"ל ראו את האשה
כעקרת הבית ובאספקלריא המיוחדת שלהם הורישו
לנו מבינתם ומחכמתם. ובמיוחד בזמננו שדנים
על מקום האשה בחברה המודרנית חשוב ללמוד
מחז"ל בענין מעמד החשוב של האשה. ספרים
כעין הספר של גברו רבאו כד"ר גלאי וכמו ספרו
של ד"ר אברהם גרוסמן בענין נשים (חסידות ומורדות:
נשים יהודיות באירופה בימי הביניים) מוכיחות לנו
שוב ושוב על גדלותם של חז"ל והראשונים. מפיהם
אנו חיים. בכבוד בהוקרה ובידידות.

רב יצחק צבי בילט
נשיא הסתדרות הרבנים (RCA)

305 Seventh Avenue • New York, NY 10001-6008 • 212.807.7888 • Fax: 212.727.8452 • www.rabbis.org • rabbis@rabbis.org

הרב יואל טוביאס
רב דשכון ו'
בני־ברק

Rabbi JOEL TOBIAS
Rabbi of Shikun Vav
Bene-Beraq - Israel
036748327 .טל

בס"ד

כבוד ש"ב אהובי וידידי, גדול בתורה, ויראתו טהורה גברא רבא ויקירא אדונינו הר"ה אהרן אליהו גלאט שליט"א,

רחש לבי דבר טוב ואומר אני על ספר אשביע היום, ענינים שונים מלוקטים בדברי חז"ל למועדי השנה בגמרא ובמפרשים. ואת הכל עשה יפה בעתו על סדר מהיר בשפה האנגלית.

הראיתי אומר. נוגע שמחה בלבי שאשר בשרי זה, לא רק הוא רופא אומן, והוא מעסיק [illegible] בני אדם בגופות, אינו מזניח ואינו שוכח את תפקיד האדם בעולמו והוא [illegible] לחנוך, שלו ושל אחרים. ובקביעות הוא קובע עתים לתורה. לא רק שהוא לומד בעצמו, אלא זכה גם ללמד לאחרים. והוא מרביץ תורה ברבים, מדי יום ביומו. אשרי חלקו.

ומתוך [illegible] — ספרו זה אשר זכה לחבר — ניכר שטרחו הגון. שהוא מאיר ומעריב על דף. האזין בספרו איפוא מעט, חוזה את העמל הרב שהשקיע המחבר שליט"א, בדברי הגמרא והמפרשים, מהראשונים עד האחרונים. והקב"ה נתן לו לשון לימודים. ובלשון צחה, הוא מסדר את דברי רבותינו, שמפיהם אנו חיים. הלא הם, הריטב"א והמהרש"א, הצל"ח והגר"א, הם יהודע [illegible]. ובשפה קלה ומובנת לכל.

ואחרי אשר גדולי הרבנים כבר סמכו ידיהם עליו ועל מעשיו. אף ידי נתון עמו [illegible] באמונה. שראוים הדברים לעלות לדפוס, ולהפיצם ברבים. ובפרט בזמן הזה, אשר דבר ה' יקר, ויקויים בו [illegible] אשר המחבר בין בספרו.

אהובי ש"ב שליט"א. עלה והצלח בתורה. יפוצו מעינותיך חוצה. ואגב כבר בכוונתך לתרגם הספר ללשון הקודש. יהיו עוד חיבורים נוספים שיהנו מאתו. בקב"ה יעזור שיקוים בך מה שדרשו ז"ל בסוכה [illegible] נפש עמל עמלה לו. הוא עמל במקום זה ותורתו עומדת לו במקום אחר.

בזכות העמל שעושה משפט ללמוד תורה, ולכבוד את התורה [illegible], הקב"ה יזכה אותך [illegible] בשמחה [illegible] ולכל אשר [illegible].

אמן כן יאמר השי"ת.

הכותב לכבוד התורה ולומדיה.

נר ג' דחנוכה תשס"ד.

הרב יואל [illegible]

יואל טוביאס
רב דשכון ו'
בני־ברק

FOREWORD

Rabbi Dr. Aaron Glatt has done a service to all students of Judaism, whatever their background and the degree of their religious education. He has compiled numerous passages of several Talmudic tractates, which describe the role of women in the Talmudic world.

Very often, especially in recent decades, material has appeared which portrays the Talmudic perspective on women in a negative light. Typically, the material used to foster this view is taken out of context, or is misrepresented in other ways. The work before us presents the Talmudic view of women with no agenda except to allow the reader to see for him or her self what the Talmud has to say about femininity and the role of women in religious society.

Rabbi Glatt has systematically quoted passages from the Talmudic tractates of *Berachos* and the entire *Seder Moed,* the first major sections of the Talmudic sequence. He begins each chapter by placing the selected passage in the framework of the general Talmudic discussion. He then provides the explanations necessary to understand the background of the passage quoted. The passages range from brief pithy statements to lengthy anecdotes involving women.

The most useful aspects of Rabbi Glatt's work are his own comments and elaborations upon the quoted text. Often, there are parts of the texts that are simply obscure and need clarification at a very basic level. He provides the clarification necessary by drawing from traditional commentaries, sometimes using his familiarity with far-flung sources to do so. In this manner the reader at least gains an understanding of the simple literal meaning of the text in its context.

This *sefer* then systematically surveys a wide range of traditional commentaries and examines the interpretations that they give to the passage quoted. By doing this the reader is given a range of opinions on the deeper meaning of the text and often, as is the custom of Talmudic commentary, these interpretations differ widely.

The major merit of this work is that it presents the reader with the primary source and additional commentary and makes no attempt to apologize for the views of the Talmud or its commentaries. Rabbi Glatt does not attempt to compare the material which he elucidates with contemporary views, nor does he attempt to explain away what the modern reader might judge negatively. He simply presents the material and allows the reader to come to his or her own conclusions.

The commentaries quoted are culled from the literature of many centuries but the author does not attempt any analysis based upon the historical perspective of these commentators. This, too, is left to the reader to reflect upon.

This work is entitled "Women in the Talmud," and therefore is of interest to anyone who wants an authentic perspective of the Talmud's view of women. But there is a much more general service which Rabbi Dr. Glatt presents to his reader: he gives the opportunity to the reader to become acquainted with Aggadic portions of the Talmud and he familiarizes the reader with commentaries that are perceptive and insightful, many of which are relatively unknown. What we have here is an approach to one aspect of Talmud study, the oft-neglected Aggadic texts, which is thorough, variegated, and truly erudite.

The author is to be especially complimented for including the commentaries of the great Sephardic tradition, especially the Chida and Sefer Ben Yehoyada. This writer remembers struggling with many Aggadot in his yeshiva days without being aware of the expositions of the great Sephardi masters, and has come to personally appreciate their helpfulness and relevance.

What emerges from this study is a view of women which is far from negative. Quite the contrary, the women described in the Talmud are seen as sources of insight, wisdom, and great practical counsel. While they clearly had no direct involvement in the Talmudic "Beis Midrash," they were very much involved in the formation of the society at large and its values, particularly because of the role they played in the marital relationship and in the family generally.

The great geniuses of men like the Maharsha and Rabbi Tzvi Hersh Chajes are here for all to see. It is clear that the commentators quoted were not interested in justifying the views of the Talmud to their reader, but rather were interested in explaining the true meaning of the text by seriously considering every textual nuance. It is always astounding to realize how different commentators can come to very different views of the significance and teachings of a single text.

This work will be of special value to readers who are interested in familiarizing themselves with the Talmud generally, and especially its Aggadic portions. At the same time it will contribute greatly to the growing literature on the role of women in Judaism generally and in the society extant at the time of the Talmud in particular. This is therefore a contribution to the Jewish library which is both interesting, timely, and authentic. Rabbi Dr. Glatt's work is assured a place in the library of all of those who are interested in the Talmud and its relevance to contemporary life. We all look forward eagerly to continued works by this scholar, completing this particular approach throughout the rest of the "Sea of Talmud." But we are also confident that he will continue to contribute in yet other ways to our sacred literature.

Written Rosh Chodesh Kislev, 5763.
Rabbi Dr. Tzvi Hersh Weinreb

PREFACE

WITH GREAT *SHEVACH* AND *HODA'AH* TO HASHEM *YISBARACH*, A preview edition of this *sefer* was dedicated last year in honor of the *bar mitzvah* of our dear son, **Aryeh Chaim** נ"י. With renewed gratitude and tremendous thankfulness to the A-mighty, it gives us tremendous pleasure as well to now rededicate the full *sefer* in honor of our precious daughter, **Chava Raizel** 'תחי, joining the ranks of *Klal Yisrael* as a *bas mitzvah*.

Chazal, in *Maseches Sofrim* (18:5), cite the ancient Yerushalmi custom of bringing a *bar mitzvah* boy to the important people in town to receive their *berachos*. By bringing this *sefer* to the public, it is my fervent hope that readers who benefit from and enjoy these *divrei Torah* will in turn bless our children. May our children, Ephraim Yechiel, Aryeh Chaim, Chava Raizel, and Yechezkel Shraga, along with all of my readers' children, be continuously blessed, and grow into happy and healthy *talmidei chachamim* and *yirei Shamayim*.

This *sefer* was written with one major purpose: to demonstrate the Divine principle: *deracheha darchei noam* — the ways of the Torah are beautiful. This dictum is of such paramount importance that it is even used in deciding halachic issues, i.e. a certain opinion cannot be correct because it conflicts with this standard. In our society today, unfortunately, the discord and debate which have arisen regarding the status of women within Judaism is both disturbing and painful. Women are absolutely equal — albeit *different* and full partners in all endeavors of *Yiddishkeit*. The notion that our tradition has somehow relegated them to an inferior status could not be further from the truth.

Indeed, to classify half of the human race as intrinsically inferior would appear to me to be fervently opposed by the dictum of "*deracheha darchei noam.*" The Torah is Divine, and thus by definition perfect, without possible flaw. For one to suggest that it contains an anti-feminine bias, or even supports such inequity, is essentially to deny its perfection!

The transmission of the Oral Law from generation to generation, parent to child, direct from the mouth of G-d to Moshe Rabbeinu on *Har Sinai*, represents the unbroken chain of our Divine *mesorah*. This acceptance of our tradition is the essence of becoming a *bar* or *bas mitzvah* — the newly mature member of *Klal Yisrael* becomes initiated into religious adulthood. If we believe in our *mesorah*, then how can we condone attacks on our sacred traditions? Tragically and unfortunately, the unwelcome influences of secular society creep into our lives no matter how hard we strive to keep them out. The words of *Chazal* are twisted and misrepresented — sometimes with malevolent intent — by those who should know better, and sometimes by well-meaning individuals whose knowledge of the Torah lacks sophistication. This *sefer* was written to combat such lack of knowledge and unawareness.

Our goal, therefore, is not to answer the many divergent opinions and interpretations regarding the Torah's view on the role of women in Judaism. Rather, it is to provide a scholarly work presenting the words of our *Chazal* and traditional commentators directly and allowing their brilliance and eloquence to inform, educate and inspire the reader. The best way to truly appreciate how a religion and its leaders honestly view this topic is to analyze what is written on the subject. While it is dangerous to use any single narrative as an accurate barometer of a theme, a precise appreciation can be revealed in an analysis of the totality. Therefore, I have set out to convey the attitude of the Gemara and *Chazal* regarding women, as illustrated by the stories and commentaries on women in the Talmud.

Beginning with *Maseches Berachos* and through the twelve tractates of *Seder Moed*, I have recorded almost every story involving a woman. The Gemara itself is first set in italics and translated. I tried to translate the text verbatim, and provide the simple *p'shat*, according to the understanding of the unparalleled *Rashi*. Subsequently, each piece was analyzed using the classic interpretations and commentaries of the *Rishonim* and *Acharonim*, of blessed memory. I have tried to provide a complete and faithful account of their remarks, with occasional observations and additions of my own. I hope and pray that I have accurately portrayed *da'as Torah*. Any errors or misrepresentations are solely due to my own ignorance, and *chas veshalom* are not a reflection on the holy source material.

This *sefer* was written for both men and women, from all backgrounds, circles and *hashkafos*. I especially hope that those with divergent viewpoints will honestly appraise the material without dismissing it out of hand. Those confronted with doubts, or those having reservations regarding the Torah perspective on women can use this text as a way to truly appreciate what *Chazal* have to say on the subject. *Daf Yomi* devotees can refer to this *sefer* as a ready resource for passages dealing with women. Others may want to scrutinize passages regarding specific women or themes, or use it as an aid in preparation for a *d'var Torah*, speech or lecture. The erudite *talmid chacham* can use this work as a starting point for in-depth analysis, while the busy reader with less time or ability to spend on a *sugya* will be able to use this *sefer* to obtain an understanding of a particular passage. In any event, I am most interested in my readers' comments, corrections, constructive criticisms and ideas. Please feel free to e-mail me at aglatt@pol.net or contact me through the publisher. The royalties of this *sefer* are going 100 percent to *tzedakah*. My dear readers can thus accomplish both *limud Torah* and charity at the same time.

ACKNOWLEDGMENTS

MY SON ARI'S *BAR MITZVAH SEDRAH* WAS ואלה שמות, *AND THESE are the names*. There were many names that went into making this *sefer* a reality. I have been most fortunate to have many superb *rebbeim* and *rabbanim*, in person and on tape, from whom to learn Torah. While they are too numerous to be cited, I would be remiss if I did not mention several of the major spiritual influences on my (adult) life.

I am deeply indebted to the *gedolei Yisrael* who gave their approbation/*berachah* to this *sefer*. Their enthusiasm, encouragement and wisdom are something I will always treasure.

My shul rabbis, *HaRabbanim*, **Rabbi Simcha Lefkowitz** *shlita* (who should continue to have a *refuah sheleimah*), Rabbi **Hershel Billet** *shlita*, and **Rabbi Fabian Schonfeld** *shlita*, have been mentors and role models *par excellence*. Their daily influence on me, on their congregations and on their communities at large, as well as their numerous communal *shiurim* and activities demonstrate the tremendous *avodah hakedoshah* the oft-belittled "local" Rav performs. They are true giants. May Hashem give them the strength to continue their superlative *klal* work for many years.

Without the continuing influence and unbelievable Torah knowledge of my rebbeim, **Rabbi Mordechai Willig** *shlita*, **Rabbi Hershel Schachter** *shlita*, **Rabbi Avrohom Wosner** *shlita*, and **Rabbi Yitzchak Knobel** *shlita*, along with my "tape" *rebbeim*, **Rabbi Moshe Meir Weiss**, **Rabbi Yissachar Frand**, **Rabbi Fischel Schechter**, **Rabbi Noach Isaac Oelbaum**, **Rabbi Berel Wein**, and **Rabbi Paysach Krohn** *shlita*, amongst many others, this *sefer* would never have been possible. The tremendous *hakaras hatov* I owe them is incalculable. Any *shiur* I have ever been privileged to give is built upon what they have taught me.

The outstanding yeshivos and camps that I attended during my formative years provided the foundation upon which my *rebbeim* could build. I would again be remiss if I did not specifically mention my six years at **Camp Torah Vodaath**. To this day, I am convinced that their role in spiritually nurturing me was indispensable in my writing this *sefer*.

I am blessed to live in a neighborhood with many *talmidei chachamim*, including *HaRabbanim shlita*, **Rabbi Dovid Spiegel**, **Rabbi Mordechai Kamenetsky**, **Rabbi Chanina Herzberg**, **Rabbi Shlomo Eisen**, **Rabbi Moshe Weinberger**, **Rabbi Dovid Weinberger**, **Rabbi Heshy Glass**, **Rabbi Kalman Topp**, **Rabbi Yaakov Lehrfeld**, and **Rabbi Moshe Katzenstein**, who have always been available for advice and sage counsel. As importantly, Margie and I are privileged to enjoy the closeness of many wonderful and dear friends, both here and in Eretz Yisrael. May Hashem grant them, among all of *Klal Yisrael*, health, safety and peace in these tumultuous times.

"Rabbi Chanina said: Much have I learned from my rabbis, from my friends even more than from my rabbis, but more than all others [I have learned] from my students" (*Taanis* 7a). I have been *zocheh* to give a *daf yomi shiur* for nearly one and a half decades, to an unbelievably dedicated group of *chavrusas* and friends, first at the Young Israel of Kew Gardens Hills and now at the Young Israel of Woodmere. Their zeal in coming early every morning to learn the *daf* was a major spur in preparing the material for this *sefer*. May Hashem grant them and their families *arichus yamim veshanim*. Likewise, my *chaverim* in my *Gemara be'iyun* and *halachah shiurim* and occasional *Chumash* classes force me to constantly spend more hours learning, in order to be able to answer their inquisitive and insightful questions. May *HaKadosh Baruch Hu* grant us all many more stimulating years together to learn His *Torah HaKedoshah*.

It has been a great honor for me to be even minimally associated with the two great *mosdos* involved with this *sefer*. The Orthodox Union, publisher of this work, is familiar to every Jewish person worldwide for its unmatched *kashruth* activities, but that is actually only one part of this celebrated enterprise. I am extremely honored that the OU, and **Rabbi Moshe Krupka**, have shown interest in publishing this work, and that the Executive Vice President, **Rabbi Dr. Tzvi Hersh Weinreb** *shlita*, has written the very generous foreword. May they continue to have *hatzlachah* in fulfilling their goals and special projects on behalf of *Klal Yisrael*, both here and in Eretz Yisrael.

Several editors, including **Rabbi Ben Zion Rand** *shlita*, have helped assure that the quality of the inside matches the outside.

The other שמות that were a major force in the writing of this *sefer* have been those of my family. The *zechus avos* of my saintly grandparents, and my maternal aunts and uncles, *Hashem yinkom damam*, whom I never had the *zechus* to meet, constantly guides me in everything I do. Many unwritten *sefarim* were lost, as well, during the tragic *Sho'ah* epoch of our history. I hope this *sefer* is in some small measure a tribute to my holy predecessors, and all those who perished *al kiddush Hashem.*

Lehavdil bein chayim lechayim, my parents, **Anna and Joseph Glatt** עמו"ש, Holocaust survivors, came to this country under very difficult circumstances with absolutely nothing, yet ultimately persevered and continued in the ways of their parents. They have always lovingly supported, taught and directed me, and demonstrated by stellar example how to participate in all communal activities of worth. They, and my special **Aunt Berta**, have always provided my brother **Avi** (and **Lorraine** and family) and sister **Leora** (and Rabbi **Jay** and family) more than was necessary, sacrificing for us, and clearly showing with their every breath that nothing was more important to them than us. In the foreword to one of his popular *sefarim*, Rabbi Moshe Meir Weiss quotes the *Yesod VeShoresh HaAvodah* that we should have in mind as part of every *mitzvah* that we are also fulfilling the commandment to honor our parents, because performing a *mitzvah* brings honor to one's father and mother. I pray that this *sefer* is a proper testament to the tremendous honor and respect that my parents deserve. *Im yirtzeh Hashem*, may they be *zocheh* to see continued *Yiddish nachas* from all of their children, grandchildren and great-grandchildren, and continue as our role models עמו"ש.

My loving in-laws, **Ethel and Rabbi Marshall Korn** עמו"ש, have equally displayed Torah values to their children, **Margie**, **Karen** (and **Reuben** and family) and **Ronny** (and **Adina** and family), amongst whom I am honored to now be numbered. Their most special and spectacular present to me, their eldest daughter, my wonderful Margie תחי', is truly the impetus behind this *sefer*. Rabbi Yehoshua states (*Shabbos* 152a): What brings *simchas lev* — true happiness of the heart? One's wife. The *Gemara* in *Bava Metzia* (59a) quotes Rav Chelbo: Always be especially careful with the honor of your wife, for blessings are only present in a house of a man because of his wife. Rava added: Treat your wives with respect in order that you should become rich. *Baruch Hashem*, I am the happiest, wealthiest man, as Hashem has blessed me with the perfect *ezer kenegdo* (life partner). This is a gift I can never begin to repay. The best I could do, בע"ה, was to assist in developing four exceptional updated editions, **Ephraim, Ari, Chavi and Chezkie**. It is my greatest pleasure to watch them grow and every day become a little bit more like their incomparable mother. May Hashem grant us, our extended family and friends, my readers, and all of *Klal Yisrael*, *shefa berachah*, peace and health, in our striving to become better Jews. May we speedily see, in our days, the coming of *Moshiach tzidkeinu*.

Aaron Eli Glatt

Women in the Talmud

נשים בתלמוד

Table of Contents

Berachos

Shabbos

Eruvin

Pesachim

Shekalim

Rosh Hashanah

Yoma

Succah

Moed Katan

Chagigah

Index

מסכת ברכות

BERACHOS

BERACHOS

BERACHOS 8B

(See also Pesachim 112b)

THE BED OF AN ARAMEAN

Rava gave his children several instructions ... (The second piece of advice was:) "Do not sit upon an Aramean woman's bed" ... Some explain the statement allegorically. Some interpret it literally: Do not sit upon an Aramean woman's bed, because of the incident involving Rav Pappa. Rav Pappa went to the house of a certain Aramean woman. She offered him a seat on a couch. Rav Pappa refused to sit, however, until she raised the bed. When she did so, it was revealed that a dead child (her own son — Rashi*) had been hidden there. The Rabbis thus cautioned that one should not sit upon the bed of an Aramean woman.*

THIS STORY IS ALLUDED TO IN THE GEMARA IN *PESACHIM* 112B, WHERE a slightly different version is cited by *Rashi* and *Rashbam*. In addition, the Gemara there attributes this advice not to Rava, but to Rebbi (Rabbi Yehudah HaNasi, the great Tanna who redacted the Mishnah circa 200 C.E.). *Rashi* and *Rashbam* there write that this Aramean woman owed Rav Pappa money, and he attempted to collect the outstanding funds. One day, the woman strangled her own son, placed him under the bed, and when Rav Pappa arrived she offered him a seat there, on the pretense that she was going to get the money to repay him. He indeed sat, and when she returned, she "discovered" her dead son. The Aramean woman then libeled Rav Pappa, saying he sat on the bed and killed her child; Rav Pappa was forced to flee the country.

Incidentally, a third somewhat different variant (located on the side of the *daf* in the Vilna *Shas*) is ascribed to Rabbeinu Chushiel by Rav Nissim Gaon. Rav Pappa lent money to a non-Jew (not necessarily a woman), and because of numerous delaying tactics, suspected the borrower was attempting to avoid repaying the debt. The non-Jew took a dead child and hid it under clothing on the couch, and then invited Rav Pappa to the house to collect the loan. Rav Pappa, however, suspected something was amiss, and discovered the corpse before sitting on the bed, thereby exposing the plot against him. The Rabbis then enacted their preventative measure — don't sit on an Aramean bed — to prevent such a libel from ever developing.

Eitz Yosef notes the significant differences between the versions in *Pesachim* and *Berachos*, and is unable to reconcile them — "it needs further study." *Ben Yehoyada* suggests an intriguing solution. Indeed, these are two different stories, separated in time by many years. The *Pesachim* account, with the warning from Rebbi to his sons, occurred first. According to that rendering, Rav Pappa had to flee town, as he had actually sat on the bed, even though of course he did not kill the child. Then, Rebbi's warning (do not sit on an Aramean woman's bed) was to his family — beware of such a situation — but not necessarily an advisement for all Jews and future generations. However, when a similar story transpired in the time of Rava (and he hadn't even sat on the couch!), the Rabbis recognized that this was indicative of a much more hideous and deeper hatred of the Jews by the Arameans. Hence, a more general advisory was issued.

Maharatz Chayes, in the name of *HaGaon Baal Mekom Shmuel*, asserts a similar approach, based upon a very basic question. How could Rav Pappa have sat down on the couch, if in the times of Rebbi such a prohibition had been enacted? *Maharatz Chayes* therefore concludes (in the later *Berachos* version) that Rav Pappa in fact did not originally sit down, yet nevertheless was libeled anyway, leading to the more general dissemination of the *gezeirah* (prohibition).

One last detail requires explanation. How could the Gemara attribute the advice of a Tanna like Rebbi to circumstances that occurred to Rav Pappa, who lived much later? This is not problematic. This is a popular stylistic tool used frequently in the Talmud. Often, a well-known episode that occurred at a later time is cited to help clarify a ruling or opinion of an earlier sage. This is a simple way of delineating the subject matter. It is much easier to simply say the name of the scholar, rather than repeating the entire episode or opinion.

Another interpretation of Rava's instruction was that one should beware of marrying a female convert. *Iyun Yaakov* questions this since the *halachah* fully permits a Jew to so wed. Indeed Yehoshua married Rachav. The Gemara in *Horayos* (13) comments that many men specifically desired to marry converts. Furthermore, and perhaps ironically, Rebbi's own ancestor, Boaz, married the pious convert Ruth! *Rabbi Yaakov Emden* remarks that one cannot bring any proof from the deeds of great Torah personalities. They had the merit to conduct themselves under the focus of the Divine Spirit, and as such had special protection for their actions. (See for example the beginning of the Book of *Hoshea*, and the detailed discussion of those verses in this *sefer*, *Pesachim* 87, regarding *Hashem* commanding Hoshea to wed a harlot.)

Iyun Yaakov provides an alternative approach. While the *halachah* allows a *Yisrael* to marry a convert, a *Kohen* is forbidden to do so. Rava married the daughter of Rav Chisda, who was a *Kohen*. His children therefore had priestly blood in them. As such, Rava perceived that they specifically should be careful not to marry even a righteous convert. Perhaps a similar answer could be applied to Rebbi as well. He too had a special role and place in society as the leader of the Jewish people, and as such possibly deemed it inappropriate for such a marriage to take place in his family.

Berachos 10a

(See also Eruvin 53b-54a, Pesachim 62b, Avodah Zarah 18)

Beruriah's Wit and Wisdom

There were those בריוני *(obnoxious ruffians) who lived in the neighborhood of Rabbi Meir, and they routinely annoyed him. Rabbi Meir prayed that they should die. His wife Beruriah said, "Why do you think it is proper for you to do so? Because the* posuk *in* Tehillim (104:35) *states:* Let the חטאים (sins) cease (from the world)? *Does the word read* חוטאים, sinners? *No, it reads* חטאים — sins. *Let the* sins *be removed, not the sinners. Further proof to this can be adduced from the rest of the verse,* and the wicked will be no more. *If these sinners die, is that a guarantee that there will be no more sinners in the future? Instead, pray to Hashem that they repent, and then* they *will not be evil anymore." Rabbi Meir followed her advice, prayed for them and they did repent. (Note: The* Mitzpeh Eisan *points out that a similar story involving Abba Chilkiah and his wife is related in* Taanis 23b.*)*

Beruriah, daughter of the holy martyr Rabbi Chananya ben Teradyon, wife of the great sage Rabbi Meir, is one of the most acclaimed women in all of the Talmud. The Gemara (*Pesachim* 62b) describes her phenomenal scholarship and halachic knowledge. Indeed, *Ben Yehoyada* makes the remarkable statement that she was famous for her wisdom — like a Tanna. In the *Tosefta* in *Keilim*, several halachic decisions are actually rendered in her favor against Tannaic opinions! Indeed, she appears to have won her argument against her husband, who in Eruvin (54) is described as one of the brightest Tannaim ever. Many additional stories abound about her in the Gemara and other early Midrashic sources. Many of these narratives revolve about her sharp wit and rapier-like tongue. However, there is another side to Beruriah, described in the *Yalkut Shimoni* (964, to *Mishlei* Chapter 31).

The *Yalkut* recounts how two of the children of Beruriah and Rabbi Meir passed away on a Shabbos afternoon. (The Midrash explains that they deserved to die because they left the *Beis Midrash,* House of Study, to engage in eating and drinking. For such great people, who were on a higher level than ordinary students, this was a serious shortcoming and resulted in their premature demise. A similar situation is described in this *sefer,* [*Berachos* 31a] regarding the Navi Shmuel as a child.) Beruriah covered their bodies in their beds, and waited until Shabbos was over.

When Rabbi Meir came home after Shabbos, he asked where the children were. Beruriah responded they were in the *Beis Midrash*. Rabbi Meir recited *Havdalah*, finished his *Melaveh Malkah,* and again asked where the children were. Beruriah responded with a question: "If a person deposits a precious item with you for safekeeping, must you return the object to him when he requests it back?" R' Meir said, "Of course." Beruriah then led her husband to the bedroom and uncovered their two deceased children.

Rabbi Meir cried out over the loss of his sons, his teachers (they were so great he considered them his teachers as well as his students!) but Beruriah comforted him, saying: "You yourself just said that a watchman must return the articles he was asked to safekeep. Hashem gave us a tremendous treasure to safeguard for Him, but now He has requested it back. *Hashem gave, Hashem took; let the Name of Hashem be blessed"* (*Iyov* 1:21). And just as the next verse states that Iyov did not complain against the seemingly harsh decrees of Hashem, Beruriah did not utter a word of anger towards the Creator. The *Yalkut* concludes that it is about such a woman as Beruriah that Shlomo HaMelech wrote in Chapter 31 of *Mishlei*, אשת חיל מי ימצא, *Who can find an accomplished woman?* Rabbi Yitzchak bar Nechemiah adds: Hashem gave the Torah with the twenty-two letters of the *aleph beis*, so too, Shlomo praises the righteous women with the twenty-two letters of the *aleph beis* that begin each verse of the alphabetical acrostic אשת חיל, a song recited till this day by Jewish families when they usher in the Shabbos.

Rashi translates the word בריוני (ruffians) as immoral people or rule breakers. *Yad Yosef* adds that they were ignoramuses, and the *Aruch* translates the word as armed robbers. In *Gittin* (56a) the term is used to describe those Jews who actively chose to rebel against the Roman siege and occupation at the end of the Second Temple period, in defiance of the counsel of the Sages.

The *Tzelach* comments on the most unusual language that Rabbi Meir used — he prayed for *mercy* that the ruffians should die. Rabbi Meir should either have prayed that Hashem should have mercy on *him* or that the ruffians should die. Furthermore, there is a principle that it is not good to be the cause of another person's troubles and punishment, even if it is well deserved. The *Rif* in *Ein Yaakov*, and *Eitz Yosef* answer simply that Rabbi Meir asked Hashem to have mercy on Rabbi Meir himself, and as a result the ruffians will perish.

Tzelach rejoins that this story illustrates Rabbi Meir's greatness. He desired that Hashem have mercy on them and not allow them to use up all of their "credits" in this world. Each person receives reward for any good deeds he or she performs. Hashem usually reserves the full payment of this reward for the future world where the remuneration is far superior. However, the wicked receive their compensation in this world, and are left with nothing for the World to Come. Rabbi Meir did not wish to be the cause for which this punishment would be meted out, and he thus prayed that Hashem not treat these ruffians as totally evil people who would lose their complete share in the World to Come. Better to have mercy on them and kill them now, and save some of their credit.

Menachem Meishiv Nefesh adds that the *Midrash Shocher Tov* tells us that heretics who repent "deserve" death. This is actually for their benefit, so that they should not return to their previous evil ways. Rabbi Meir prayed for Hashem to have this type of mercy on them, that they should repent, and then immediately die cleansed of sin, without danger of regression to their heresy!

Ben Yehoyada provides a different approach. There is a saying: "A righteous man decrees and Hashem fulfills." Rabbi Meir was one of the greatest scholars the Jewish people have ever known (see *Eruvin* 13b where it is stated that Rabbi Meir was considered more intellectually outstanding than his eminent colleagues). As soon as Rabbi Meir requested Hashem's help, the ruffians should have died. Why wasn't his prayer answered immediately (before Beruriah spoke to him)? A person may suffer and ultimately die if his fervent desires are not achieved. Rabbi Meir asked Hashem to deny the ruffians the joy of realizing their desires, and they would subsequently die of their own accord. In this way, Rabbi Meir did not directly precipitate their demise. Indeed, Hashem immediately responded to Rabbi Meir, but the outcome of this response would take some time to be felt. Beruriah rebuked him for not instead trying to save the men.

Why didn't Rabbi Meir adopt Beruriah's course originally? He thought it improper and ineffective to pray for others to do *teshuvah*, based on the famous dictum: "Everything is in the hands of Heaven except fear of G-d." *Maharsha* questions how praying for someone else to do *teshuvah* could even be accomplished, if it is not in the hands of Heaven. *Ahavas Eisan* and *Anaf Yosef* suggest that by people just seeing punishments they would invariably do *teshuvah* on their own!

> *Once, a Tzedoki (a member of a sect of people who adhered to the principles of its founder, Tzadok, who did not believe in the Divine nature of the Oral Law) questioned Beruriah regarding the* posuk (Yeshaya 54:1): The barren one without children sang. *"Because she is*

barren she should sing?" Beruriah responded sharply, "You fool! Read the rest of the verse: The barren one has more children than the woman who had relations, said Hashem. *Obviously, the barren one can't be referring to a truly barren woman, otherwise how could she have any children at all. Instead, the* posuk *alludes to the House of Israel singing praise to Hashem, declaring itself similar to a barren woman, in that it has not begat children who will end up in Gehinnom (Hell) as your (Tzedoki) children will!"*

WHY WAS THE BARREN WOMAN ALSO CALLED A WOMAN WITHOUT children? Isn't that after all what barren means? Why the repetition? *Iyun Yaakov* explains that Hashem is "desirous" of the prayers of the righteous. (We cannot anthropomorphize G-d and think of human "desire" and attribute that emotion to Hashem! Yet, we use such terms to allow us in our limited capacity to begin to understand and characterize the indescribable Hashem!) Thus, Hashem made the Matriarchs unable to give birth easily, requiring them to beseech Hashem for children. The Navi Yeshayah wrote that this barren woman is unlike other righteous women, from whom Hashem *temporarily* withheld the ability to have children. This barren woman is totally incapable of childbirth, hence the double expression, "barren" and "without children." *Maharsha* echoes this sentiment — she never had children and she never will. Thus, we better understand why the *Tzedoki* questioned, "Why are you singing" — her *tefillos* (prayers) will never be answered in the positive, since she can never give birth.

Finally, the *Rif* in *Ein Yaakov* suggests that the two stories about Beruriah's wisdom are interconnected. What is so bad if wicked people are born — maybe they will ultimately repent and eventually reach Heaven? The *Rif* responds that this is what the second narrative alludes to. They were so evil that they would never do *teshuvah*, and therefore they were doomed to Gehinnom!

Berachos 31a-b

Chana and Eli the Kohen Gadol

The Talmud recounts various passages regarding the story of Chana, the barren wife of Elkanah, who prayed for a child. The full text and details of the episode, which occurred on the first day of Rosh Hashanah, can be found in Shmuel Aleph, *Chapters* 1-2. Hashem *hearkened to her prayer on Rosh Hashanah. Indeed, her story is the* Haftorah *of the first day of Rosh Hashanah.*

Chana ascends to the Tabernacle at Shiloh to beseech Hashem *to grant her a child. She prays a long, silent* tefillah *without any sounds emanating from her lips. Eli, the* Kohen Gadol *(high priest), observing that her lips are moving but no prayer is audible, assumes her to be drunk and reprimands her for praying in an inebriated state. Chana responds that the master, Eli, is incorrect — she is not drunk. She is just a bitter and sad childless woman, pouring out her heart to Hashem. Eli wishes her well, and reveals that her* tefillos *have been answered. Indeed, in the coming year, a "man among men," the great Shmuel HaNavi, is born. Chana dedicates Shmuel to "the Master of Legions," Hashem, and brings the 2-year-old boy to live and learn from Eli in the Tabernacle. There, the precocious Shmuel decides a halachic question in the presence of his rebbi, Eli, violating the law of proclaiming a* psak *(ruling) in front of one's teacher. Thus even though he answered correctly, Shmuel is deserving of death. Eli tells Chana not to be distressed — he will pray to Hashem for a new child, one even greater and better than Shmuel! Chana begs Eli* *to stay this judgment, as <u>this</u> is the child she prayed for, and her request is fulfilled.*

WE DERIVE MANY IMPORTANT PRACTICAL *HALACHOS* OF PRAYER from this episode (albeit the *Maharsha* says that this is not their sole source). From Chana's actions we derive the principle of concentrating on *Shemoneh Esrei*, and that one must move the lips and actually pronounce each word (eye scanning is insufficient) quietly, so no one else can hear. *Eitz Yosef* adds that a drunkard shouldn't pray since he cannot have the proper concentration. If a drunk does pray, his *tefillah* is comparable to serving idols! From Eli's behavior, *Tosafos* elucidate the law that one is obligated to reprove a friend committing a rabbinical sin. According to Torah law, only a person who commits a Biblical error is required to be chastised; in criticizing Chana over her rabbinical transgression (improper praying), Eli demonstrates that the law applies here as well.

Why did Eli think Chana was drunk? Apparently, long silent *davening* was unusual. Indeed, the Midrash states that Chana was punished for this excessive *tefillah* — her son Shmuel lived only to the age of 52. We see a similar idea at the time of Sarah's death. Avraham Avinu limited his eulogies and tears to some extent because prolonged praying and wailing could *chas veshalom* imply that *Hashem* acted cavalierly. The *Vilna Gaon* has a fascinating alternative explanation. Eli, as *Kohen Gadol,* utilized the powers of the *Urim V'Tumim* (parts of the *Kohen Gadol's* vestments used as a method of communication from Hashem) to investigate what Chana was doing. The following letters of the *Choshen* lit up: *shin, kaf, hei* and *reish.* It was then Eli's responsibility to decipher the message of the letters. Eli thought that this spelled out שִׁכֹּרָה, *a drunken woman,* but he misunderstood. It really was intended to be read כְּשָׂרָה, *like Sarah,* a reference to the childless Sarah who also poured out her heart to *Hashem* for a son.

Chana vehemently replies to Eli, "No, my master, I am not drunk." The Rabbis comment that she was challenging Eli. "You must not be a master since you are mistaken." Indeed, *Rashi* (in *Shmuel*) comments that Eli had just become the *Kohen Gadol* that very day. Others explain it as a question form. "Aren't you a master? Don't you know I'm not inebriated?" The *Tzelach* adds that she was in fact rebuking Eli, declaring, "You won't be a master (i.e. judge) of the Jews for much longer. Your time is nearly over and my son Shmuel will replace you!"

Why did Chana react so strongly? *Chazal* teach us that it is incumbent upon a person to correct misconceptions about oneself even when they are clearly ridiculous. For example, Moshe Rabbeinu detailed the exact distribution of all funds received for the building of the *Mishkan*, to remove any possible suspicion that he kept money for himself. Our Rabbis decreed that a person should light Chanukah candles at both (opposite) entrances of his courtyard, because a passerby might erroneously conclude that since the side he traversed had no lit menorah, it must be because the owner did not perform the *mitzvah*. Thus, one must strive for innocence in the eyes of Hashem, and the people! Eli clearly accepts her reproof, as he blesses her and wishes her well.

The Gemara states that Chana was the first person to call *Hashem* "Master of Legions." Why did she choose this title? Chana challenged Hashem, as if to say, "It is so easy for You to give me a son. After all, You have so many hosts in Your realm — what is one more or less?" She compared this to a poor person entering a lavish banquet of a rich man, and asking for a morsel of food. Who will notice or care if you give me one portion? Furthermore, she addresses Hashem, as it were, "I could force you to give me a child. I could become a *sotah* — a woman who secludes herself with a man and is accused of acting immorally. Such a woman is promised a reward of bearing children if in fact she did not sin." This brazen conversation with Hashem is favorably commented on by the Talmud, and in fact Hashem acceded to her demand and gave her a son.

How could Chana become a *sotah,* though? It is Biblically prohibited for a married woman to closet herself with a man other than her husband — the prohibition of *yichud* (seclusion)! And furthermore, as part of the process of proving her innocence, the erasure of Hashem's Name is required, yet another transgression if she were to become a *sotah*! *Pnei Yehoshua* explains that she really would not have actually become a *sotah*. She was just saying she could have, so why not give her a child. *Ben Yehoyada* has an interesting twist. Chana told Hashem that He should grant her request in the merit of her not performing these two sins! *Menachem Meishiv Nefesh* takes a different approach. It is normally permissible to erase Hashem's Name in the *sotah* process because of the *shalom bayis* created by restoring the husband-wife relationship. So too with Chana. She and her husband were childless after ten years of marriage, which is potential grounds for divorce. Therefore the erasure of Hashem's Name would be acceptable to prevent this terrible breech of *shalom bayis*!

The *Iyun Yaakov* comments that Chana also asked Hashem, "Why don't You want me to have children? Is it because there are three sins for which women are deemed at greater risk of dying during childbirth if they transgress them? Don't worry — I am very careful with these three commandments." *Ben Yehoyada* even suggests that Chana is telling Hashem, "Go ahead and test me. See if I performed these *mitzvos* as ordained." The *Shelah* notes that this is symbolized in her name, Chana. The initials of Chana are the letters of these three sins — *ches*, for not separating *challah* (a type of *terumah* from dough); *hei*, for not observing *hadlakas haner* (lighting Shabbos candles); and *nun*, for disobeying the laws of *niddah*.

Chana concludes her prayer to Hashem with one final plea. "What is the purpose of giving a woman breasts if not to nurse? Everything that You created is to serve You — please let me serve You by nursing a son." *Iyun Yaakov* says that Elkanah was a very rich man and would undoubtedly have hired a wet nurse to care for the child. Chana said, "No — I will nurse him myself."

Eli tells Chana she will give birth to a "man among men." Commentators differ as to the meaning of this. *Tosafos* say the child will become a great man when he grows up. Others suggest that he will be as great as Moshe and Aharon. Indeed, in *Tehillim*

Shmuel is compared to these two great leaders. Still another interpretation is that Shmuel will grow up and anoint the first two kings of Israel (Saul and David). *Maharsha* mentions that "among men" alludes to the fact that Chana was eventually to have seven children. But there is an even more unusual interpretation. "Man among men" means that he will be an average person, both physically and mentally. *Rashi* states Chana asked for this to ward off the "evil eye." *Maharatz Chayes* quotes a second interpretation in *Rashi*. Chana was concerned that if Shmuel were too smart he might grow up to become an apostate like the infamous Talmudic sage Elisha ben Avuyah, "*acher*," the previously great scholar who unfortunately left the correct path later in life. This idea is reinforced by the *Iyun Yaakov,* who proclaims that the middle ground is most likely to succeed; extremes are quite risky.

After weaning her son at the age of 2, Chana fulfills her promise to dedicate him to Torah by bringing him to the Temple to be raised by Eli. Young Shmuel was very bright (the *Iyun Yaakov* writes that Shmuel could talk at birth!) and resolves a difficult practical Torah inquiry that Eli himself was apparently unable to answer. Eli decrees that Shmuel is deserving of death for answering a Torah question in front of his rebbi without permission. *Maharsha* explains that this refers to a heavenly death, as Shmuel was only 2 years old and thus exempt from the judgment of a human court. Others disagree and state that Shmuel's precociousness made him an exception to the rule that a child can't be judged till his *bar mitzvah*.

Chana implores Eli to spare Shmuel. There is no love like that of a mother for her child. Eli says he will *daven* for a better child, but Chana persists. *Maharsha* notes that Chana wanted the child she prayed for, not one that Eli would pray for. *Ben Yehoyada* asks: Why did Eli want Shmuel to die? Through prophecy Eli saw that Shmuel was destined to die young and he wished to pray for another child who would live longer. Chana, however, wanted *this* child — she had tremendous belief and faith in Hashem that her Shmuel would indeed be able to accomplish much for the Jewish people, and her persistence and strength saved the life of one of the greatest people *Klal Yisrael* has ever had.

BERACHOS 48A

QUEEN SALOME, THE "QUEEN OF ZION"

King Yannai (a Jewish king from the Hasmonean dynasty who lived towards the end of the Second Temple period) and his wife, Queen Salome Alexandra, had concluded a feast, but did not know the proper way to recite the blessing at the end of the meal. Unfortunately, Yannai had previously killed the majority of the rabbis when they disagreed with his desire to be the Kohen Gadol *(high priest) as well as king. The only remaining Torah scholar of note was Shimon ben Shetach, the brother of Queen Salome, who had been hidden by the queen herself at great risk. Queen Salome told Yannai she could bring him a rabbi if Yannai promised to leave him unharmed. The king agreed, Shimon was brought out of hiding and he recited the Grace After Meals.*

WHO WAS QUEEN SALOME? THE TALMUD AND COMMENTARIES refer to her by several names. She is also known as Shel Zion (see *Shabbos* 16b for a rabbinical enactment decreed because of the Queen Shel Zion), Sheilazion (a single long name according to *Menachem Meishiv Nefesh* and *Meiri*) and Shalom Zion. She reigned for ten years after the death of Yannai. The Midrash (*Bamidbar Rabbah* 35) states that during her lifetime the blessing ונתתי גשמיכם בעתם, *rain shall fall in the proper time* (*Vayikra* 26:4), was fulfilled. It rained only on Friday nights, after everyone was home from shul, so as not to disturb people on Shabbos, or during the week, when they were working. Yet, this rain was sufficient to bring bountiful crops of extraordinary size and plenty. (See *Pesachim* 112b for a related benefit of rain occurring only in this time, and how it originally also rained as well on Tuesday evenings.)

The Jerusalem Talmud (*Berachos* 7:2) and the *Bereishis Rabbah* (91:3) have a different version of Shimon's reason for fleeing. Three hundred *nezirim* (people who had completed their nazirite vows and were obligated to bring offerings) arrived in Jerusalem but had very limited funds. Yannai and Shimon agreed to split the cost of the sacrifices. Yannai assumed responsibility for his half and paid for the sacrifices. Shimon, however, found a halachically acceptable opening to nullify the nazirite vows of his half, thereby freeing the *nezirim* (and himself) of their obligation. A slanderer came and provoked Yannai into becoming upset over this legal maneuver, and Shimon was forced to flee for his life. At a later time, at a royal dinner, some of the king's Persian guests asked to converse with the wise sage (Shimon) who had dined with them in the past. Shimon was brought back to the palace by Salome after she had Yannai guarantee his safety.

In addition, there is a censored gemara removed from the standard Vilna Shas printing, but found in old manuscripts and in commentaries to Sanhedrin (107b). It states there that several other scholars escaped king Yannai's decree and ran away to Alexandria, Egypt. Once Shimon returned to "power", he recalled these sages, including, Rabbi Yehoshua ben Perachya and one of his disgraced disciples, back to Israel.

BERACHOS 51B

(See also Shabbos 54b)

YALTA AND THE WINE BARRELS

Rav Nachman and his wife, Yalta, play host to Ulla, one of the great leaders of the generation. Rav Nachman honors Ulla by letting him lead the benching. *At the conclusion of the* benching, *Rav Nachman asks that the* "kos shel berachah" *(the cup on which the* berachah *of* benching *was recited) be sent as a courtesy to Yalta. (The Gemara previously suggested that this was the proper thing to do. The source for this custom is based upon the visit of the three angels to Abraham after his* bris milah, *found at the beginning of* Parshas Vayeira. *The angels asked: "Where is Sarah, your wife?"* Chazal *explain that the reason the angels asked was in order to send her the* "kos shel berachah."*) Ulla responded, however, that this was unnecessary. He stated that a wife indirectly receives a blessing from the* kos shel berachah *— via her husband's partaking of the drink. Since the cup had already been given to Rav Nachman, it would be wasteful to give Yalta a drink as well. Upon hearing this, Yalta became quite angry and went down to the wine cellar where she destroyed* 400 *barrels of wine. Recognizing his mistake, Ulla attempted to send her a new* kos shel berachah, *but Yalta rebuffed him.*

THIS STORY DEMANDS AN EXPLANATION. HOW COULD A HOLY woman like Yalta, who was the daughter of the exilarch (Jewish leader) and wife of the great sage Rav Nachman, act in such a seemingly emotional and irrational fashion? Why was she so upset? And how could she transgress the law of "*bal tashchis,*" the prohibition against wanton destruction of a usable item?

Maharsha explains that Yalta was indeed a great woman. She was appropriately upset that the *kos shel berachah* wasn't sent to her, because of the purest of motives — the desire to participate in this great *mitzvah.* To show clearly that her peeve was not simply at being deprived of imbibing the wine, but that she was instead miffed at being excluded from the *mitzvah* (*kos shel berachah*), she felt she had to act dramatically. Thus, she smashed all the wine in the cellar to show that the wine in the cellar was indeed worthless to her — it was only the *kos shel berachah* that she desired.

The *Pri Megadim* and *Maharatz Chayes* maintain that if there is a purpose in a destruction, i.e. to teach a lesson, then the prohibition of *bal tashchis* does not apply. For example, the custom of breaking a glass at a wedding as a remembrance of the destruction of Jerusalem is not prohibited because of *bal tashchis.* This *minhag* is based upon a Gemara earlier in *Berachos* (31a), where a very expensive crystal glass was shattered to stop excessive lightheadedness.

A fascinating interpretation is suggested by *Ben Yehoyada.* He assures us that her actions were righteous, based upon her name — Yalta. In *gematria* (numerical value), the name Yalta equals 441, "*emes,*" truth. Her actions were indeed truthful and proper. All the wine actually belonged to Yalta — it was a dowry from her father, the exilarch. She was upset at the apparent stinginess of Ulla in not sending her the "*kos shel berachah.*" This is alluded to by the number 400, which has the *gematria* of "*ayin ra*" (bad eye), meaning miserliness. Therefore, as a guarantee that Ulla would not benefit further from any wine in her house, she broke the seals on 400 barrels (not the barrels themselves!), and distributed all the wine to needy poor people to use for *Kiddush* and *Havdalah.* Alternatively, to prevent her ungrateful guest from benefiting any more from her wine, she went down to the cellar to lock the door. As she slammed and bolted it, however, the barrels tumbled, resulting in the destruction of 400 casks. The proof, *Ben Yehoyada* adds, is that Ulla tried to placate Yalta. If she were just a foolish woman, disappointed in not obtaining a beverage, would such a great man have tried to appease her?

מסכת שבת

SHABBOS

SHABBOS

SHABBOS 13A-B

THE DISTRAUGHT WIDOW

A talmid chacham *of great promise died at a very young age, not even reaching half his expected life span, suggesting that he was punished with the Heavenly decree of* kares *(spiritual excision). His distraught and bereaved widow went to the house of study where her husband had learned, and appealed for an explanation. She held up his* tefillin *and cried that her husband was a very learned man, a scholar who had studied Torah and had served* talmidei chachamim *— so why did he die at such a young age? No one in the* Beis Midrash *could provide an answer. Along came one old sage, who some say was Elijah the Prophet, and asked her if her husband had observed the laws of family purity* (niddah). *The widow responded, "Of course," he would not even touch her. Elijah further queried if they were scrupulous in observance of all the relevant laws during the period of her seven clean days. She replied that while they slept in the same bed then, and had casual physical contact (actions that were prohibited but not punishable by* kares*), they never even considered engaging in relations during this time. Elijah responded* *that if so,* Hashem *was justified in condemning her husband; he was instituting his own laws.*

WHAT ACTUALLY WAS THE WIFE'S COMPLAINT, AND WHY DID SHE show off his *tefillin* and stress certain good actions that he performed? How did the scholar die, and why so young? What sin deserving of death did the young scholar actually commit?

The commentaries explain that the widow was a righteous woman who was trying to understand what had transpired. *Iyun Yaakov* writes that she felt that her husband had lived a proper life and had performed *mitzvos* that usually guaranteed a long life. A string of three *mitzvos* is not quickly broken, the Rabbis say, and the merit of his learning Mishnah, reading Scripture and serving of *talmidei chachamim* should have protected him <u>even</u> if he sinned in other matters. Alternatively, his daily donning of *tefillin* and *tzitzis* coupled with the *mezuzah* on their house should have been a triplet of protection. This explains why she displayed his *tefillin* in the study hall, to drive home this point. (The *Maharsha* states that the purpose was to spur the concern of the other scholars over his demise.) The *tzitzis* were buried with him, and the *mezuzah* was still on their door, so the *tefillin* were the only *mitzvah* she could show. Indeed, *Ben Yehoyada* remarks that the observance of this *mitzvah* is usually a *segulah* (augury) for long life!

Iyun Yaakov further adds that his fulfillment of these *mitzvos* was pure and without ulterior motive, as is evidenced by her mention of her husband's service to the rabbis. Some people study for less than ideal motives, to be praised as a smart person, or to acquire honor or material pleasures. If that was her husband's goal, then he would not have ministered to and debased himself for the rabbis. Her husband was solely interested in observing the commandments for the sake of Hashem. Thus her anguish over his seemingly undeserved death. A similar thought is expressed by *Ben Yehoyada*. The husband wore his *tefillin* all day long even though the requirement can be met by wearing them for much less. This non-obligated action further illustrates his intent to serve Hashem selflessly.

And yet, Elijah said he deserved to die. Hashem judges the righteous on a much stricter scale. *Ran* writes that the man died of a snake bite, because he was contemptuous of the Rabbinical decree prohibiting any physical contact with his wife during the seven clean days. (Please see *Eruvin* 63a in this book for a detailed discussion as to why a snake bite is the appropriate punishment for such an act.) This type of death was especially appropriate because of the dictum הפורץ גדר ישכנו נחש, *One who breaks a (Rabbinical) fence deserves to be bitten by a snake. Tosafos* explain that she was actually permissible to her husband on a Torah level, but women have accepted upon themselves additional stringencies in regard to ritual menstrual laws that make them Rabbinically forbidden to their husbands (even touching). While the widow had actually gone to the *mikveh* to remove her Biblical *tumah*, this would not suffice for the Rabbinical component. Furthermore, it is forbidden to go to the *mikveh* while the Rabbinic prohibitions remain in effect. Therefore, *Anaf Yosef* declares, he was creating his own rules — he didn't consider the Rabbis' decree important — and as such he was deserving of *kares*, early death.*

Finally, the Gemara asks, if he was so learned, how could he have made such a costly misjudgment? Two possible answers are given. Either he maintained it was permissible to sleep next to her in the same bed without touching her, or she was in fact wearing a garment so there was no direct physical contact. Either way, he remained in violation of the Rabbinical decree, and ultimately paid dearly for this error.

An alternate reading of Elijah's response to the widow is that Hashem acted correctly in killing him because Hashem does not accept bribes. All his *mitzvos* and good deeds could not protect him from the deserved, albeit strict, judgment.

---

* The gemara in Sanhedrin (106a) states that ("anshei damim umermah lo yechezu yemeihem") "אנשי דמים ומרמה לא יחצו ימיהם" evil men will not live out even half their lives" — as evidenced by Doeg and Achitophel, wicked advisors to King Shaul and King David, respectively, who died prematurely at the age of 34 and 33. (The normal life span of an average man is considered to be 70 years).

Shabbos 16b

(see this book, Berachos 48a, for further discussion of her)

THE QUEEN PURIFIES THE VESSELS

Queen Shel Zion arranged a "party" (a word usually used to indicate a wedding feast) for her son. Unfortunately, just before the feast was to begin, all the metal utensils became tamei *(ritually impure) in such a way that they would require a seven-day process to purify them. Since there was insufficient time to make them* tahor *(ritually clean), Shel Zion instead devised a brilliant plan. If such vessels become damaged to the point that they are no longer usable, they lose their impure status. Thus, Queen Shel Zion minimally (but halachically sufficiently) damaged the metal vessels, thereby rendering them no longer* tamei. *Subsequently, she could send them to a craftsman who would repair the damage prior to the party, and thus allow the utensils to be absolutely acceptable for usage. Her husband, King Yannai, and her son, both of whom were* Kohanim, *were thus able to eat at the meal without concern that they would become* tamei *from these vessels.*

As a result of her ingenious act, the Rabbis became very concerned that such behavior would theoretically lead to a laxity in observance of the purity laws. Now, anytime that someone had a problem with *tumah,* it could be potentially bypassed. The laws of purity might be forgotten! Alternatively, not all the people would be as scrupulous as Shel Zion. Many people would only symbolically break the vessel, thereby not removing the *tumah*. (Today, unfortunately, we see similar errors in observance. Some people only observe certain customs in spirit, but not the letter of the law, and as a result do not truly perform the precept. For example, the pinning of a torn ribbon onto a mourner's garment, instead of performing actual rending of the garment, to fulfill the *mitzvah* of *kriah* (tearing), as a symbol of mourning.) To prevent these problems, the Rabbis instituted a Rabbinical decree. Upon fixing a broken metal vessel, the *tumah* that was initially present is "recreated," even though it is technically pure from a Torah point of view.

The *Boneh* in the *sefer Ein Yaakov* explains the incident metaphorically. We Jewish people have become so full of *tumah*, that suffering alone (i.e. the breaking of the vessel) would not be sufficient to purify us. We therefore need the ritual sprinkling from the *Parah Adumah* (Red Cow) — i.e. the kindness of Hashem — to purify us.

Shabbos 23b

Reward for Candle-Lighting

One who is "accustomed" to light (Shabbos and Chanukah) candles will certainly have sons who are Torah scholars.

R' Huna regularly passed by the doorway of R' Avin, the carpenter, and saw that many candles (Shabbos and Chanukah) were regularly lit there. R' Huna said that two great men will certainly come from that house, and indeed, R' Avin had two great and righteous sons (Rav Idi and Rav Chiya). Similarly, Rav Chisda used to pass by the doorway of Rav Shizvi's father (some say it was Rav Shizvi's father-in-law) and saw many candles lit, and he remarked that a great scholar will come from this house. Indeed this was true, as Rav Shizvi came from there.

Rav Yosef's wife would delay lighting the Shabbos candles till the very last halachically acceptable time. Based on various pesukim *(verses) in the Torah, her husband told her it is preferable to light earlier. She therefore thought she should kindle the lights much earlier on Friday afternoon. But an old sage (many say Elijah the Prophet) came to her and remarked, "Don't light too early or too late; light at the proper time."*

I*YUN YAAKOV* EXPLAINS THAT HAVING LOTS OF LIGHT IN THE HOUSE AT night is conducive to and will result in extra Torah learning, thus the reward of scholarly sons for observing the *mitzvos* of candle-lighting is particularly appropriate. *Meiri* states this as the principle of "*middah keneged middah*" (measure for measure) —

one is treated in the very same fashion as one acts. The *Rif* in *Ein Yaakov* further expounds that during the period before the Chanukah miracle, the *Yevanim* (Assyrian-Greeks) prohibited the Jews to learn Torah, so it is especially appropriate that the performance of the *mitzvah* of Chanukah candle-lighting, symbolizing the victory over that persecution, should result in Torah scholars being born.

Why is the reward that the children will be scholars — why not the person who performs the *mitzvah*? The *Levush* answers that the man may already be a *talmid chacham*, and thus the reward is for his children. Others say that since a woman lights the Shabbos candles, and she is not herself obligated to study Torah, the reward is therefore more appropriate for her children.*

Why did the Talmud use the term "accustomed" (*ragil*) to regularly light, instead of the more frequently used term "careful" to light? *Maharsha* writes that the *mitzvah* of Shabbos candle-lighting is on the wife. Thus the husband must "accustom" his wife to light properly, instead of being careful about its performance himself. *Ben Yehoyada* adds that this is why Rav Yosef gently told his wife to light earlier by using references to Scriptural verses rather than telling her directly. A husband must not cause excessive fear or terror in the house. Even when correcting an improper practice, he should do so gently and calmly.

Rabbi Shimon Schwab comments that women light Shabbos candles as they are a *mitzvah* upon the house, whereas men light Chanukah candles since they are more for the external world. Women set the tone and atmosphere of the family environment. It is their special domain and sphere of influence. After all, it is by far the mother who influences the rearing of the children, and is more directly involved day-to-day in their upbringing.

---

* I would suggest that we see a similar idea by the reward Hashem gave to Shifrah and Pooah, the Jewish midwives described in the first chapter of Parashas Shemos, they willingly put their lives on the line to save the Jewish babies that Pharaoh wanted killed. Their reward was not for themselves — but they were promised children who would be kings and priests.

Why did the first story result in two great sons being born, while the second episode only led to the birth of a single scholar? *Tosafos* remark that in the case of Rabbi Avin, both the father and mother participated in the *mitzvos*, thus their combined merit resulted in two great sons. In Rabbi Shizvi's case, however, only the mother was involved, and thus only a single meritorious son was born. *Meiri* and *Maharsha* have a different twist. In the first case, both Shabbos and Chanukah candles were lit, while in the second only one of the two *mitzvos* was performed. Incidentally, according to the version that it was Rabbi Shizvi's in-laws, we see that a son-in-law is considered just like a flesh and blood child.

Ben Yehoyada, quoting the *Arizal,* comments that a woman gets more pleasure from a *talmid chacham* son than does a man. This is based upon verses describing the man's joy as just *simchah* (gladness), whereas the woman's joy is depicted as both *simchah* and *gilah* (rejoicing).

The blessing of having two great sons, *ravrevi*, was actually a blessing to have sons with qualities of the scholars of both Israel and Bavel. *Ravrevi* is a shorthand form of *rav* and *rabbi,* illustrating the titles used for a *talmid chacham* in Israel (*rabbi*) and Bavel (*rav*). Their two styles of learning were distinct. In Bavel, the rabbis were noted for their sharpness; in Israel, the scholars were especially polite and pleasant. The true blessing is that both of these qualities should be present in each son.

Finally, why did the Prophet Elijah come tell to Rav Yosef's wife that she should not light too early? Why didn't Rav Yosef tell her himself? *Sfas Emes* notes that the Talmud said only that she <u>thought</u> to light earlier — she did not actually say she would, thus her husband did not realize, but Elijah knew. It is also possible that the Talmud wished to let us know that she was worthy of meeting Elijah, something only the greatest and holiest people are worthy of.

Incidentally, the *Sfas Emes* (quoting the *Magen Avraham* in the name of the *Maharshal*) says that the story was not regarding Shabbos candles, but concerned Chanukah lights. Rav Yosef was blind, and his wife lit the candles for him. Earlier on this page, the Talmud relates that women are equally obligated in the *mitzvah* of Chanukah, since they too participated in the miracle. *Rashi* explains that women were particularly persecuted by evil decrees enacted at that time, since, prior to marriage, all women were required to be violated by an Assyrian-Greek (*Yevanim*) leader. Also, it was through the daughter of Mattisyahu (Yehudis) that the military victory was achieved. Yehudis, at great risk, bravely and successfully took upon herself the task of killing the Assyrian-Greek general. When she displayed the general's amputated head to the *Yevanim* army. It demoralized his troops and they fled in disarray. A similar idea is expressed in the Gemara in *Pesachim* (108b) and *Sotah* (11b) — righteous women suffered along with the men, and indeed were often the cause of the final redemption. (See this book on those Gemaras for further details.)

Shabbos 25b

WHO IS A RICH MAN?

The Talmud asks: What is the definition of a rich man? Among the answers is that of Rabbi Akiva: A rich man is one who has a wife with beautiful deeds.

BEN *YEHOYADA, MAHARSHA, RABBI YAAKOV EMDEN* AND OTHERS ALL state that Rabbi Akiva gave this answer because it was his own personal experience. Rabbi Akiva's wife, Rachel, the daughter of the wealthy Kalba Savua, was such a woman. Her father was so opposed to her marriage to the then ignorant shepherd Akiva, that he expelled her from his home. She and Akiva were impoverished, but he felt rich because he was married to this righteous woman. *Maharatz Chayes* explains that it was solely due to Rachel that Rabbi Akiva achieved success, i.e. riches, in Torah learning. Rabbi Akiva declared to his students, "Everything I (and you) have is hers." All the respect, honor and Torah learning I have obtained is solely due to her support, encouragement and selfless sacrifice. (See *Kesubos* 63 for a full discussion of Rachel and Rabbi Akiva.) She was satisfied with very little, yet truly happy with her lot in life. This is true wealth!

An alternative explanation is provided by *Iyun Yaakov.* Beautiful deeds are a reference to generosity. A good wife is not stingy; she is always willing to provide the needy with charity. It is this *tzedakah* that is the source of wealth coming to the house. Hashem tests us with money. If we handle it well, i.e. are successful managers as demonstrated by "smart investments" in charitable causes, then Hashem will entrust us with lots more of His funds to "invest." A similar thought is expressed by *Ben Yehoyada.* Blessing and wealth enter a house only through the wife's actions. She improves the financial bottom line not by income from her labors, but as a result of her actions.

SHABBOS 32B-33A

PAMPERED WIVES

The prophet Amos derisively protests to the פרות הבשן, cows of Bashan (Amos 4:1), *living in the mountains of Shomron, that they will be severely punished with many harsh plagues and catastrophes for oppressing, damaging and stealing from the impoverished multitude. Rava comments that the women of the city of Mechoza are comparable to these cows; they eat but do not work.*

BASHAN WAS AN EXTREMELY FERTILE PASTURE LAND, AND THE COWS grazing there grew very fat and beautiful. All of the major commentaries on the Book of *Amos* (*Rashi, Radak, Ibn Ezra, Abarbanel* and others) state that Amos uses the simile of well-fed cows to depict the pampered wives of wealthy Jewish noblemen. Amos writes that they tell their husbands to bring them beverages; all they are concerned about is their own material desires. Rava remarks that the women of the opulent city Mechoza are the same.

Rashi defines the egregious sin of these women. They cheat and steal from their own husbands, since they do not perform any work yet constantly consume. Alternatively, *Rashi* remarks that they have become so obsessed with corporeal pleasures, like eating, drinking and partying, that their husbands can no longer support them through honest endeavors. Instead, the men are forced to steal from poor and needy people to sustain the evil habits of their wives. *Metzudas David* derives an important principle from this. Causing an evil deed to occur, even if you didn't perform the vile act yourself, is as bad as directly committing the transgression.

These wicked wives are described as "fat cows" who have committed robbery, even though they never left their homes!

Ben Yehoyada has difficulty with *Rashi's* answer. If the women were so rich, then why would they necessarily *have* to do work in the house? After all, they had many servants. Further, their husbands obviously saw what was going on. By their lack of protest, they clearly demonstrated approval, so why were only the women castigated by the prophet? *Ben Yehoyada* explains that the work Rava refers to was giving food and sustenance to the needy. The Mechoza wives were stingy, and wanted to retain all their material goods only for themselves; they were delinquent in the performance of this "job" of *tzedakah. Middah keneged middah* (measure for measure), they were punished in a very appropriate fashion — with the curse of hunger and poverty.

Woman was created by Hashem to be an "*ezer kenegdo.*" *Ezer* means that one of the myriad functions of a wife is that she is a great asset to her husband in his performance of Hashem's directives. *Kenegdo* means that the wife is supposed to *oppose* her husband when he tries to do something wrong. Unfortunately, a woman can also be *kenegdo*, against him, acting to divert her husband from the proper path — against the purpose for which he was created — if she troubles him unnecessarily by demanding worldly pleasures and material desires. Contrast these women with Rivkah Imeinu. The Sages explain that when she instructed her son Yaakov to bring Yitzchak two goats in order to receive his blessing, she assured Yaakov that the goats belonged to her. There was no element of theft involved; her marriage contract entitled Rivkah to these goats. Yaakov should not fret that Rivkah was possibly taking Yitzchak's possessions without permission!

SHABBOS 33B

RABBI SHIMON'S WIFE

Rabbi Shimon bar Yochai spoke out strongly against the wicked government in charge of the Jewish people, and he was sentenced to death. Along with his son Rabbi Elazar, Rabbi Shimon left his house and hid in the Beis Midrash *to escape his pursuers. Every day, his faithful wife risked her life by bringing them bread and water. However, the government pressed further in their attempt to locate them. Rabbi Shimon told his son he was concerned that their enemies might apprehend his mother and torture her, and she might reveal their hideout. Thus, Rabbi Shimon and his son miraculously escaped to a secluded cave. They remained undiscovered for twelve years, when the evil decree against them was rescinded because the emperor died. They actually did not return to society, however, for an additional year.*

IT IS CLEAR FROM THE CONTEXT THAT RABBI SHIMON WAS EXTREMELY concerned for his wife's safety, and did not wish for her to be at any undue risk. He reasoned that women in general are more susceptible to physical torture than are men, and thus it would be best if he escaped to a different location to remove her from danger. His wife was certainly a woman of valor, willing to sacrifice her own life to aid her husband's flight.

Shabbos 53b

TWO UNUSUAL TALES

A women died, leaving behind her husband and a nursing baby. Impoverished, the husband had no funds to hire a wet-nurse. Hashem performed a miracle for him. The man developed breasts and was able to suckle the child himself. Rav Yosef remarked how great a person this poor husband was, that Hashem should perform such an outstanding miracle for him. On the other hand, Abaye stated that the man was actually gorua *(inferior), since Hashem was obliged to change the rules of creation for him.*

The Gemara relates another story. A one-armed woman died, yet her husband did not realize she had only one arm until the day of her death. Rav declares that this woman must have been extremely modest, if her own husband was unaware that she had only one arm. Rabbi Chiya states that it is not so unusual; after all, women are modest by nature. What is unusual, however, was the husband's modesty, that he never noticed this physical defect in his wife.

The commentators grapple with Abaye's description of the impoverished husband as inferior. Does Hashem effect such a wondrous deed for an inferior man? *Rabbi Yaakov Emden* tersely remarks that the husband may have been inferior, but the child must have been unique and deserving, and the miracle was in the baby's merit. *Ben Yehoyada* opines that since only the baby but nobody else benefited from this miracle, and since it required that the father's body become physically deformed, he is thus termed inferior. *Maharsha* and the *Geon Yaakov* take a different approach. Indeed, the husband must have been quite special, but this miracle obviously had to come at the expense of his merit. Hashem therefore deducted from his "Heavenly account" the appropriate worth of this miracle, leaving his overall balance-sheet inferior! *Maharsha* adds that the miraculous phenomenon was not actually a case of *nolad* — a brand new occurrence, as we have a rule that there is nothing totally new under the sun. Since women breast-feed, it is only an extension of this normal act that was transpiring.

In light of this, why does Rav Yosef remark that the husband is obviously a great man? *Ben Yehoyada* explains that it is the miraculous way that the baby was helped that clearly shows the husband's greatness. If Hashem wished to simply help him, he could easily have provided the money to hire a wet-nurse in a non-obviously miraculous fashion. By dramatically changing the normal order, Hashem was declaring the saintliness of the husband. And just what was his merit? *Ben Yehoyada,* quoting from the *Sefer Gilgulei Neshamos*, as found in the *Seder HaDoros,* states that the man was a *gilgul* — "shared the soul" — of a famous woman in history, the mother of the Roman emperor Antoninus who, according to some scholars was also known as Mareus Antonius (Mark Anthony). Rebbi, the great Rabbi Yehudah HaNasi, was born at a time when the Romans prohibited circumcision. Nevertheless, his parents defied the evil edict and circumcised the 8-day-old child. The authorities discovered this and summoned baby Rebbi to court as "evidence." Rebbi's mother switched Rebbi with a kind gentile neighbor's uncircumcised son. The gentile mother cared for and nursed baby Rebbi, and in this merit her son, Antoninus, grew up and became emperor. Indeed, Antoninus and Rebbi were life-long friends. This gentile mother's soul became the *gilgul* of our impoverished husband! *Middah keneged middah*, his baby was now saved via a miracle involving breast-feeding.

This was not the first time such a miracle happened. The Midrash in *Bereishis Rabbah* writes that Mordechai nursed his orphaned relative Esther, the future queen and savior of the Jewish people in the miracle of Purim!

How does Abaye's opinion that this miracle was proof of an inferior man jibe with the unopposed view that Mordechai was a great and righteous man? *Ben Yehoyada* remarks that Mordechai was a rich man, so lack of money was not the reason that Hashem made the miracle. Mordechai did not want the world to know of Esther's existence. He knew prophetically that years later Esther's hidden identity would be of paramount importance in lulling Haman into a false sense of security that his plan to destroy the Jews would be successful. Thus Esther's sustenance as a baby needed to be kept secret, and thus the miracle of Mordechai nursing her was essential to the overall success of the Purim miracle. *Rabbi Elazar Moshe HaLevi Horowitz* adds to this idea. Mordechai nursed Esther without enlargement of his mammary tissue. Hashem just allowed milk to flow from his male breasts. But in our Gemara, Hashem unnaturally enlarged the breasts, disfiguring the man and shaming him, thereby causing the husband to be referred to as inferior.

We see from the Gemara's second story — that of the one-armed wife — the importance of modesty in a woman. Both sages agreed that she was righteous and modest, however the opinion of Rabbi Chiya is that this is expected and normal! What was unusual was that a man should have such modesty. Avraham Avinu, upon entering Egypt for the first time and being afraid that he would be killed so that the Egyptians could steal his beautiful wife Sarah, remarked הנה נא ידעתי כי אשה יפת מראה את, *See, now I know that you are a woman of beautiful appearance. Rashi,* quoting the Midrash, writes that until now, Avraham's modesty prevented him from looking at his wife in a wanton fashion. So too, here. The husband was unique among men in his approach to modesty. So much so, *Rabbi Yaakov Emden* records, that he even was allowed to marry her without investigating her physical appearance. Normally, a man is prohibited from marrying a woman without seeing her, lest he subsequently finds that she is not pleasing to his eye. However, this modest man was an exception to the rule.

Why did Rav not give the answer of Rabbi Chiya? After all, Rav also agrees that women are naturally more modest. *Ben Yehoyada* explains that her modesty was also extraordinary. She was such a chaste and righteous woman that she had no enemies in the entire world! Not even one person disliked her and went to inform her husband about her missing limb.

Ultimately, on the day she died, how did the husband finally discover her infirmity? *Iyun Yaakov* suggests that possibly some of the people who came to comfort the bereaved husband remarked that the loss wasn't really so terrible, because she had only one arm! *Ben Yehoyada* strongly objects to this explanation, and provides a practical alternative. When the undertaker removed her prosthetic arm during the *taharah* process, he asked the husband if the prosthesis should be buried with his wife or returned. Only thus was the husband made aware of the physical limitation of his wife.

Shabbos 63a-b

(see also Bava Kamma 83b)

THE EVIL DOG

Reish Lakish states that a person who raises an evil dog in his house prevents goodness from entering the house. ... A pregnant woman went into a neighbor's house to use the oven, and was startled by the neighbor's dog barking. The neighbor told her not to be alarmed — the dog's sharp teeth and claws had been removed. The woman replied, "You can take your goodness and throw it on the thorns, as I have already miscarried."

R*ASHI* EXPLAINS THAT THE GOODNESS THE PREGNANT WOMAN WAS referring to was the neighbor's kind remarks about the defanged/declawed dog not being dangerous. *Ben Yehoyada* writes that the pregnant woman was referring to the neighbor's act of kindness in sharing her oven with the pregnant woman. Either way, the kindness was wasted, as the woman spontaneously miscarried because of the evil dog in the house. *Meiri* understands this episode as teaching an important lesson. A person must always be very careful that, even indirectly, he is not preventing goodness from occurring. One must constantly be observant and recognize even potential obstacles to *chessed* and remove them before their influence can be harmful. Evil can take many different guises, and may not be easily discernible, therefore, we must always be vigilant.

This story appears as well in the Gemara in *Bava Kamma* (83b). The Talmud there discusses the loss to the world of this unborn child.

SHABBOS 80B

(See also Moed Katan 9b)

MORE ISN'T NECESSARILY BETTER

Rav Bibi had a daughter whom he anointed with lime, limb by limb (not all at once), in order to remove excess hair and to beautify her complexion. He was so successful in making her attractive that he received from a prospective suitor 400 zuzim *(a very large amount). Upon seeing this, a gentile neighbor who also had a daughter applied lime to her, but he anointed her entire body simultaneously, and the daughter died. The gentile neighbor declared, "Rav Bibi killed my daughter." Rav Nachman stated: In Rav Bibi's house, beer (which causes excessive and dark hair growth —* Rashi*) is frequently drunk, thus there is a need for smearing girls with lime. However, in our houses, where beer is not drunk, lime application is unnecessary.*

R*ASHI* ADDS THAT IN ADDITION TO RECEIVING THE 400 *ZUZIM*, RAV Bibi's daughter now had worthy suitors, which undoubtedly was the real goal of Rav Bibi. Indeed, elsewhere, Rav Bibi is referred to in the Gemara as a great man.

Why didn't the daughter of the gentile neighbor have a good outcome? *Rabbeinu Chananel* explains that putting on too much lime at once is dangerous because the heat generated by the body will remain internalized and lead to hyperthermia (excessive body temperature). Presumably the lime would block the normal channels for heat to escape from the body. Blocking only small percentages of this heat transference (by applying lime one limb at a time) results in no heat buildup; however, total body anointment can be fatal.

Why did the gentile refer to Rav Bibi by his title "Rav"? Indeed, the similar story told in the Gemara in *Moed Katan* deletes the word Rav and simply says — "Bibi killed my daughter." Alternatively, the *Rashash* attributes the remark here not to the gentile, but to a commonly expressed thought — "*People* said that Rav Bibi killed the man's daughter"; i.e. because of Rav Bibi, the gentile erred, and that resulted in his daughter's death.

However, *Ben Yehoyada* has an interesting explanation that maintains our printed version of the remarks attributed to the gentile. The non-Jew thought to himself, why did Rav Bibi only anoint one limb at a time? It must be that he is a poor rabbi and could not afford to purchase sufficient lime to apply simultaneously to her entire body. Since I have enough lime, reasoned the gentile, I will proceed quickly with my daughter's treatment. Thus, indirectly, the fact that Rav Bibi was a rabbi was important and actually connected with the girl's death, and hence the usage of the title "Rav" by the gentile. Indeed, this explanation fits in very well with the previous Talmudic statement that only poor girls used lime as a depilatory/beautification agent. The wealthier women used less toxic oils and lotions.

Shabbos 81b

(see also Pesachim 110-111 and Chullin 105b)

The Ship's Sorceress

Rav Chisda and Rabbah bar Rav Huna were voyaging together on a boat when a prestigious gentile woman asked to travel with them. The rabbis refused, and the woman uttered an incantation that brought the boat to a standstill. The rabbis countered with their own words, and the voyage continued. The woman remarked, "What can I do? My powers are ineffective against rabbis like you, who are scrupulously careful about practices that lead one to be susceptible to witchcraft."

B*en Yehoyada* writes that Rav Chisda and Rabbah rented the entire boat, and thus the woman could not ask the captain for permission to come on board, but had to ask the rabbis. Why did they not permit her to travel with them? *Iyun Yaakov* suggests three possible reasons. Previously, the Gemara stated the opinion of Rav that under certain conditions a person should not go on a boat with others because of the potential danger that a particular voyager may be destined for punishment. If the ship capsizes, thereby killing the evil person, other passengers may drown. Here too, the rabbis were concerned that she was an evil person deserving of death and they were afraid to travel on the same boat with her. Possibly that is why they rented the entire ship! (*Ben Yehoyada* adds that the sailors were not a concern as they were in general good swimmers, and these types of boats only traveled in relatively shallow rivers. Thus only a passenger, but not the crew, would be potentially punished by Hashem with the sinking of the ship.)

Second, the rabbis recognized the woman as a wicked sorceress (as evidenced by her response to their refusal), and didn't want to be placed at risk by her powers. In those times, sorcery and magic were indeed real threats to people via a certain "*koach hatumah*" (impure force) that Hashem placed in the world, and the rabbis wished to avoid possible danger. Alternatively, *Iyun Yaakov* suggests, it is possible that they were especially stringent with the *halachah* of *yichud* — the prohibition of a man being alone in a secluded place with a woman other than his wife or immediate family, and thus they could not bring the gentile woman with them.

What did the rabbis say to restart the boat after her spell immobilized it? *Rashi* remarks that it was a holy Name of Hashem, but in a parallel Gemara in *Chullin* (105b) *Rashi* prefers the idea that they actually used an incantation themselves to reverse her spell. *Iyun Yaakov* derives from here that although normally it is prohibited to perform sorcery, one is permitted to practice magic to negate magic.

Menachem Meishiv Nefesh records the view of several *gedolim* taking a different approach. The text of our Gemara uses the term "*milsa*" — literally "word" (*mem, lamed, tav, aleph*) — to describe the rabbis' response. If you remove the last letter (*aleph*), you have the initials of the phrase מכשפה לא תחיה, *You shall not permit a sorceress to live* (*Shemos* 22:17). The rabbis actually recited this phrase, which is a sacred method of warding off the dangers of magic. *Menachem Meishiv Nefesh* concludes that an old text of the Talmud was found with exactly this spelling of the word "*milsa*" (*mem, lamed, tav*), including an abbreviation mark!

Why is the *posuk* written for a sorceress — after all, the prohibition applies to male sorcerers as well? The Talmud in *Sanhedrin* states that most magicians were female, thus the Torah uses the feminine to reflect that phenomenon. The *Yalkut Yehudah* adds that this explains the unique construction of the *posuk*. Most prohibitions are phrased in the positive — *you shall kill the transgressor* — yet here the text reads *you shall not permit a sorceress to live.* The *Yalkut* explains that the negative is a stricter level, as if to say that under no circumstances may the transgressor be permitted to live. Since most magicians were women, and men would naturally tend to have mercy on them, the Torah felt it necessary to state their punishment in the stronger negative tone. (For further discussion of this *posuk* and subject, see this book, *Pesachim* 110.)

Shabbos 113b

RUTH IN THE FIELDS

(The Gemara discusses various verses from the Book of Ruth.) Naomi tells Ruth ורחצת וסכת ושמת שמלתיך, Bathe and anoint yourself, and don your finery (Ruth 3:3). *Rabbi Elazar says Naomi told her to put on Shabbos clothes. A verse in* Mishlei (9:9) *states:* תן לחכם ויחכם עוד, Give to a wise man and he will be yet wiser. *Rabbi Elazar says that this refers to Ruth the Moabite (and also to the prophet Samuel). How so? Naomi told Ruth to wash and anoint herself, and get dressed and then go to the storage area, whereas the verse relates that Ruth first went to the silo, and only afterwards did she do what Naomi instructed.*

ותלך ותבא ותלקט בשדה, She (Ruth) went and she came and she gleaned in the field (Ruth 2:3). *Rabbi Elazar states that she went to many areas till she found a place where she could glean fallen stalks of grain.*

Boaz asked who she was. The Gemara interjects — was it Boaz's nature to ask after the young maidens? Rabbi Elazar responded, Boaz detected wisdom in Ruth. Two stalks she collected, but three leftover gleanings she did not take, because that is what the halachah *permits poor people to collect. The* Baraisa *states that Ruth collected the gleanings in a very modest fashion. If the stalks were standing, she stood. If she had to stoop to pick them up, she did so from a sitting position so as not to reveal her legs. Furthermore, Rabbi Elazar notes that when Boaz observed how nicely Ruth treated Naomi, he resolved that such a person was an appropriate choice for him to marry.*

RASHI EXPLAINS THAT RUTH OBVIOUSLY MUST HAVE DRESSED IN special clothes, otherwise why would the *posuk* even mention that she dressed before going out to the field? And the most special garments are obviously Shabbos attire. *Benayahu* (included as part of the *sefer Ben Yehoyada*) adds that this is derived from the Hebrew word ושמת שמלותיך עליך, *and you should put the clothes on yourself*. The word עליך literally means *above yourself.* Shabbos clothes are described as being "hard," as they are worn less frequently and therefore do not have a soft "broken-in" feeling. In the order of the *aleph beis,* each letter of the word קשה (hard), comes exactly one letter ahead of, or "*above,*" the letters of the word Ruth (רות). Thus the apparently unnecessary word עליך is written to teach us that it refers to Shabbos garments.

What was so wise about how Ruth acted regarding the gleanings? After all, the *halachah* is that only two stalks left behind are permitted to the poor people. If three stalks are forgotten, the owner is allowed to reclaim them. *Maharsha* states that this rule is actually the subject of a dispute between Beis Shammai and Beis Hillel. Only the latter is of the opinion that three are prohibited. At that time, the law was not yet decided. Beis Shammai based their ruling on the Torah's use of *three* words — for the convert, orphan and widow — thus implying that three stalks are permitted. Ruth was an orphan, widow and convert, and thus could have legitimately considered herself entitled to the extra stalk. Instead, she chose to follow the opinion of Beis Hillel, even though this hurt her financially.

Shabbos 116a-b

(see also Eruvin 63a)

AIMA SHALOM

Aima Shalom was the wife of Rabbi Eliezer and the sister of Rabban Gamliel. There lived a certain "philosopha" (translated by the Rabbis as either an apostate Jew, philosopher, astrologer or intellectual) in her neighborhood who held himself to be a scrupulously honest judge, but whom Rashi *tells us covertly took bribes. Aima Shalom and her brother Rabban Gamliel devised a plan to expose him. Aima secretly went to the fraudulent judge and bribed him with a golden candelabra. On the morrow, she appeared with her brother in court and demanded that Rabban Gamliel give her half of their father's inheritance. The corrupt judge decreed this to be fair, and ordered that the estate be split. Thereupon Rabban Gamliel told him that Jewish law does not recognize a daughter's right to inherit if there are sons. The judge replied that those laws were no longer in effect since the Jews were exiled; instead, the new law states that sons and daughters inherit equally. During a recess, Rabban Gamliel offered the judge an expensive donkey as a bribe if he would overturn his preliminary decision. When court resumed, the philosopha proclaimed that he had delved further into the book and at the end it says that indeed Moshe's law remains intact — daughters do not inherit if there is a son. Aima Shalom promptly announced, "Let your light shine like a candelabra" (intending to remind him, and the listening public, of her bribe). Rabban Gamliel then proclaimed, "My donkey came and kicked over your candelabra," alerting the entire gathered audience to the true nature of the hypocritical judge.*

M*AHARSHA* COMMENTS THAT THEY DID NOT ACTUALLY GIVE THE judge the valuable bribes. The giving of bribes is expressly forbidden by the Torah, and it is impossible to even think that these great *tzaddikim*, Rabban Gamliel and his sister, would transgress such a commandment, even to do a good deed — such as exposing this hypocite. They only promised him these gifts if he decided in their favor.

Ben Yehoyada adds that the gifts are representative of the roles men and women play. A woman is supposed to be the light of the house, shining forth brightly and removing darkness and depression. A man, however, is intended to work outside the house, like a donkey, carrying packages, making a living and supporting the family.

Shabbos 151b

The Loss of Rabbi Chanina's Daughter

(The Gemara is in the midst of a discussion regarding how, at times, crying and tears in older men may potentially result in blindness.) The daughter of Rabbi Chanina passed away, yet Rabbi Chanina did not cry about this great tragedy. His wife asked, "Did you just take a chicken out of the house? How can you not be moved to tears at the death of your daughter?" He replied: "Is it not sufficient that I have suffered the great loss of the death of my daughter? Should I also lose my vision?"

B*en Yehoyada* comments that Rabbi Chanina's wife was a very wise and learned woman. She saw her husband seemingly unaffected by the loss of their daughter, and reasoned that he is not easily moved to tears by the death of a person. The Gemara elsewhere states that one of the reasons that a parent may lose a child at a young age is because the parent did not appropriately mourn the passing of a great person. *Middah keneged middah*, if you are unmoved by someone else's tragic loss, *Hashem* will not take your feelings into consideration when deciding about the life or death of your family member. If Rabbi Chanina did not cry for his daughter, certainly he did not cry over the loss of an unrelated person, and therefore, on a spiritual level, Rabbi Chanina's wife felt her husband somewhat responsible for the death of their daughter! Thus the Gemara has to explain that only now — because of his old age — did he not cry, because he was concerned about losing his eyesight. Similarly, the *Ahavas Eisan* remarks that crying is one of eight actions that decreases a man's fertility. Rabbi Chanina may have also held himself back from crying to preserve his ability to procreate — which was especially important now that he had lost one of his children. (Perhaps "vision" is a hidden allusion to the future progeny of a person.) If he cried excessively, this would compound the tragedy by preventing him from trying to somehow replace his daughter with another child.

Rabbi Yaakov Emden states that Rabbi Chanina was very old and was thus appropriately concerned about losing his eyesight should he cry. Furthermore, *Rabbi Emden* deduces from this story that there is no *mitzvah* to cry over a loss of a family member, i.e. crying and wailing are not necessarily components of the *mitzvah* of mourning. Even though our forefather Abraham cried for three days over the loss of his wife Sarah, crying is permitted, but not *mandated*, by the Torah in such a situation.

Shabbos 154a

(see also Berachos 16a; Yevamos 45b; Kesubos 23a; Bava Metzia 73b; Bava Basra 149a)

RAV MARI BAR RACHEL

Rav permitted Rav Mari bar Rachel (i.e. declared his lineage to be halachically legitimate) and appointed him as a minister ("police" officer — Rashi*) in Bavel.*

THE RISHONIM DISCUSS WHETHER THE RABBI WHO RULED ON RAV Mari's legitimacy was Rav or Rava. *Rashi* and *Tosafos* discuss the correct version of the text in the Gemara immediately preceding the line above. The controversy revolves around who exactly this Rav Mari was. *Rashi* and *Tosafos* here and elsewhere (*Yevamos* 45b and *Bava Metzia* 73b) comment that Shmuel had a daughter, Rachel, who was captured and assaulted by a band of marauding gentiles. She ultimately became pregnant. Prior to her giving birth, Issur — the father — converted (he became known in the Talmud as Issur Giyura, *Issur the convert*), and then married Rachel. Then she bore this son, Mari. Since his conception was "unholy" (i.e. his father was still a gentile at the time), even though his birth was in holiness, Rav Mari is referred to throughout *Shas* as the son of Rachel, to spare him embarrassment regarding his less than ideal lineage. (See *Yevamos* 45a for further discussion of this.) According to this version, our Gemara should read "Rav," a contemporary of Shmuel, instead of Rava, who lived much later. However, *Tosafos HaRosh* disagrees, and writes that the proper reading is Rava, a contemporary of Rav Mari. The version found in the *Rif* in *Yevamos* is Rav Ashi.

Kesubos 23a has an interesting prologue to the story. Shmuel's father, known throughout *Shas* as Avuha DeShmuel, expounded a lenient ruling regarding "captured women" and their legal status, regarding whether they were considered to have been violated in captivity. Shmuel disagreed with the lenient ruling, and his father exclaimed — would you be so harsh if they were your daughters? When a great person like Avuha DeShmuel utters a statement, it has impact, based upon the verse in *Koheles* (10:5): *Like an erroneous [ruling] from before the ruler.* Shortly thereafter, Shmuel's daughters were captured by a legion of marauders, whose members included Issur.

Shabbos 156b

Maternal Protection: A Future Changed

An astrologer told Rabbi Akiva that his daughter would die on the day of her wedding. Rabbi Akiva was very troubled by this and constantly agonized over it. On her wedding day, she removed a golden hairpin and stuck it in the wall for safekeeping, till she would need it the next day. The following morning, as she removed the pin from the wall, a snake pierced between the eyes was pulled out along with it! Rabbi Akiva, realizing she must have performed a meritorious act that saved her life, asked her what she did. His daughter replied that on the day of the wedding, a pauper knocked on their door. Everyone else was too busy with the wedding preparations to notice, so she gave the poor man her portion of food from the wedding. Rabbi Akiva proclaimed, "You performed a mitzvah, *and* צדקה תציל ממות, charity rescues from death."

The mother of Rabbi Nachman bar Yitzchak was told by an astrologer that her son would turn out to be a thief. As a result, she was always very careful to keep his head covered. She told her son that he should always cover his head, have fear of Heaven and plead with Hashem that he should overcome his evil inclination — but she did not tell him why. One day, while sitting under someone else's date palm tree, his head cover fell off. In that instant, his evil inclination overpowered him, and he bit off a cluster of dates.

BOTH STORIES INDICATE THAT OUR RABBIS UNDERSTOOD THERE WAS some significance to the astrologers' remarks, yet recognized that nothing is truly predestined. We have the ability to overcome any circumstances that arise. In the times of the Gemara and earlier, astrology had real potency, unlike the quackery it is today. There were certain *kochos* (powers) that Hashem allowed astrologers to have, as we see from the stories regarding Pharaoh's astrologers/advisers, who were able to accurately predict that a Jewish savior would arise. They also knew that the savior would be done in by water, hence their suggestion of the wicked plan to throw all male babies into the Nile. Of course, since their powers were not their own but were only available through *Hashem*, He limited their abilities. The astrologers did not realize that the demise of the savior Moshe would be as a result of Moshe hitting (instead of speaking to) the rock to bring forth water, and this was the water they foresaw. Likewise, the astrologers were capable of duplicating some of the miracles Moshe wrought (as the agent of Hashem) to convince Pharaoh that he should let the Jewish people leave Mitzrayim. Again, Hashem limited their power, and they ultimately recognized that Hashem was the source of their potency.

Maharsha asks why Hashem picked a snake to be the potential killer of Rabbi Akiva's daughter — after all, the Creator has many servants to choose from if he wishes to kill somebody. *Maharsha* answers that the snake brought death into the world, but it is powerless to do anything unless Hashem directs it to, based upon a person's merit.

Why was the snake pierced between the eyes? *Ben Yehoyada* explains this through the principle of *middah keneged middah*. She had a "good (generous) eye," so the eyes of the snake were destroyed. Her philanthropy was complete — she gave her entire portion, not half; she gave the *tzedakah* before it was even requested; and she spoke nicely to the poor person. Indeed, the Hebrew words עין (eye) and עני (poor person) have the same letters! Quoting the *Chida, Ben Yehoyada* adds that

Rabbi Akiva's daughter inserted the צ of צדקה into the decree of מות (death) to make the new word מצות, *good deeds,* and this saved her life.

Why was Rabbi Akiva so worried? *Iyun Yaakov* remarks that when a person has a terrible dream, the suffering he undergoes worrying about the dream (if it will come true) actually serves to fulfill the "prophecy" of the dream and thereby nullify its evil portent. So too, Rabbi Akiva hoped that his constant agony would take the place of the projected death of his daughter. The *Rif* in *Ein Yaakov* adds that certainly Rabbi Akiva prayed all the time that the decree should not be realized (that explains how he let her get married). Indeed she would have been saved from the snake through Rabbi Akiva's prayer. However, it was through her merit that the snake was actually killed; otherwise it would have been thwarted in its attempt to kill her, but it still would have lived to possibly hurt someone else!

What special action did Rabbi Nachman's mother take to protect her son? *Maharsha* states that he wore an extra special head cover, as is evidenced by the language of the Gemara. *Ben Yehoyada* writes that he wore it continuously, never being without it for even less than the time it takes to walk four cubits, the normal minimal requirement. The *Maharatz Chayes* quotes the *Magen Avraham* that very young children are not obligated to cover their heads. In any event, we clearly see the love of Rabbi Nachman's mother for her son, and the great lengths to which she went to spare him the ignominy of stealing. Indeed, the word "yarmulke" means ירא מלכא, *fear of the King.*

מסכת עירובין

ERUVIN

ERUVIN

ERUVIN 22A

MATERNAL INSTINCT

Rava proclaimed: One who acts towards his children in the same neglectful fashion that a raven acts towards its offspring, will be successful in Torah studies. This is exemplified by the story of Rav Adda bar Masna, who was going to the local yeshiva to study Torah. His wife called to him as he left and asked, "With what shall I feed your little babies" (i.e. there was no food in the house — Rav Adda was so engrossed in his Torah learning that he did not support his family). Rav Adda responded, "Are there no vegetables left in the field?"

RASHI EXPLAINS THAT A RAVEN IS UNIQUE AMONG BIRDS, IN THAT IT alone does not supply food to its young. Instead, the baby birds are sustained directly by Hashem, Who places the worms in their mouths Himself, as it were (*Tehillim* 147:9). The Schottenstein Edition of Talmud Bavli (*Eruvin* 22a) explains that only one who totally divests *himself* from all worldly pursuits, and who relies solely on Providence for his support, is capable of reaching the loftiest heights of Torah scholarship. Obviously, this level of spirituality is seldom reached by even the most accomplished rabbis. Yet, in the abstract, this is the objective we must all try to achieve: the understanding that everything we have is really ours only because of the benevolence of Hashem. Yes, we must make efforts to sustain ourselves, but the ultimate success of our endeavors is determined solely by Hashem and not our own skills and intellect.

We also see here a clear distinction between the roles and attitudes of men and women. The Torah clearly tells us that a child must honor and respect both its mother and father. But the two verses that address these commandments, כבד את אביך ואת אמך, *Honor your father and mother* (*Shemos* 20:12), and איש אמו ואביו תיראו, *A man shall fear his mother and father* (*Vayikra* 19:3), clearly reflect a different focus. In the case of honor it is the father who is mentioned first; in the case of fear, the Torah states the mother first and then the father. Why this dichotomy? The Torah understands human psychology and the normal tendencies of a person. The "stern" father figure has less need for a commandment to have his children fear him, whereas the "gentler" mother may not routinely command that same awe. Thus, though the Torah stresses the requirement to fear both parents, it gives precedence to the maternal aspect. Conversely, it is far more natural to give honor to the "kinder" mother figure than it would be to the "harsher" father. Thus here too, while obligating the children to honor both, special precedence is provided to the father by listing him first in the *posuk*.

So too, in their respective attitudes towards child rearing, are there potential intrinsic differences between men and women. The sound of "Just wait till your father comes home" still brings a chill to many a grown person. And in the animal kingdom, it is usually the female that looks after the well-being of the children, often at her own expense (see this *sefer, Eruvin* 100b and the *Maharsha* there). Rashi in Sanhedrin (103a) clearly describes differences between a father's blessing for his children (more towards spiritual goals), versus the maternal blessings concerning health and nourishment. Our Gemara poignantly illustrates this as well.

Rav Adda was single-minded in his pursuit of Torah, and as such was willing to subject even his wife and children to great physical hardship in pursuit of this goal. However, Rav Adda's wife was as determined in her pursuit of the welfare of her children, as was her ancestor Chana (see this *sefer, Berachos* 31). Chana was willing to give up the potential of having an even greater Torah scholar son in order to save the life of her child. It is especially noteworthy to point out that Rav Adda's wife's sole concern was the happiness and health of her children. The Talmud does not record that she asked for a nicer house, jewelry or even food for herself. She was perfectly content to sacrifice all of *her* own materialistic desires and wants for the sake of the Torah learning of her husband — her request was only for her children!

ERUVIN 25A

AND JUSTICE FOR ALL

(The Gemara is in the midst of a discussion regarding the laws and requirements for establishing ownership of an abandoned yard.) A woman attempted to establish ownership of an ownerless property by erecting partitions on top of an already existing wall. A man subsequently came along and dug up part of the ground in the yard, and claimed ownership despite the woman's previous action. They went before Rav Nachman to adjudicate their dilemma, and Rav Nachman pronounced the man the rightful owner. The woman was naturally upset, and protested loudly that she was there first. Rav Nachman said, "What can I do — you did not establish ownership in an acceptable fashion." (The technical reasons for this are discussed in the Gemara.)

THIS SECTION ILLUSTRATES A SUPREMELY IMPORTANT POINT IN OUR G-D-given judicial system. There is no playing of favorites. Hashem is not a sympathetic jury to be convinced of the tragedy of a case while ignoring the legal principles and facts involved. It would be very easy to support the claim of this poor woman, who seems to have at least some basis for her distress. It was only because of her lack of knowledge of the laws of establishing property rights that she lost the field. How easy, and even "proper" would it have been for Rav Nachman to give her the property! But that is not the system of the Torah. Judges are commanded to establish ownership based solely on well-defined halachic precepts, and not by emotional reaction. Our laws do not allow individual claims to be evaluated based upon sex, wealth, physical prowess or any other factors, except that which the *halachah* determines to be appropriate.

Eruvin 53b

(This story is found also in Derech Eretz Rabbah [Chapter 6] and in Midrash Eichah [1:19], where some additional details are provided.)

Rabbi Yehoshua's Lessons

Rabbi Yehoshua ben Chananyah said that he never was defeated in a verbal encounter except for three cases, involving a woman, a young girl and a young boy. What was the case with the woman? Rabbi Yehoshua once stayed at a certain inn, where the hostess, a widow, served him a dish of ground beans. He cleared his plate without leaving any for the waitress, as was the expected custom. The same thing occurred on the second day. On the third day, the hostess served him the same dish but she intentionally oversalted it. Rabbi Yehoshua tried to eat the entire serving, but could not, and ate only the bread she served him. She asked why he did not eat the dish, and he replied he was not hungry, as he had already eaten earlier. She responded, "Then why did you eat all the bread? Why did you not leave over part of the previous day's meals, as the Rabbis stated is the proper thing to do?"

What was the case involving the young girl? Rabbi Yehoshua was walking on a road that ran through a private field. The little girl asked him, "Isn't this a private path?" He replied, "No it is a well-used public route." The girl retorted, "It is a well-trodden public road only because thieves like you have usurped it from its rightful owners!"

The Gemara relates the third story involving the young boy, whereupon Rabbi Yehoshua remarks how wise are all the Jewish people!

RABBI YEHOSHUA IS WELL-KNOWN THROUGHOUT THE GEMARA AS A very sharp-witted person, and frequent debater of apostates and government officials who tried to oppress the Jewish people. Upon Rabbi Yehoshua's death, the Rabbis (in *Sotah* 49b) proclaimed that now there is no one capable of defending us against the heretics. Indeed, this makes the verbal victories of his three protagonists here that much more remarkable.

Ben Yehoyada remarks that these stories did not actually occur, but were listed to illustrate and teach proper behavior. *Maharsha* points out that the widow in the first case demonstrated the proper way to give *mussar* (criticism). Instead of directly telling him that his actions were inappropriate the first time, she let it pass, and even overlooked his mistake a second time. When she finally felt it necessary to correct him, she did so in an indirect, non-embarrassing fashion. The *Vilna Gaon* comments that she even phrased her remarks in a positive fashion. He says the comment she made was, "Maybe you are now leaving the appropriate amount behind for the entire three days!"

What was the reason for their custom of leaving over food? Obviously, it was intended to feed the server. But *Maharsha* adds that it served a very practical purpose as well. It provided the opportunity for the hostess to taste the food and make sure it was good. If nothing was left for the waitress, the hostess would not know if everything turned out well.

Why didn't Rabbi Yehoshua leave any over, if this was the proper practice? *Maharsha* explains it is possible that Rabbi Yehoshua did not know this custom. Alternatively, it is not truly a requirement, but just good advice, and thus it could be ignored. *Benayahu* (by the *Ben Yehoyada*) suggests that indeed he did leave a portion of the *meat* meal for the waitress. She taught him that the rule applies even to other dishes as well. Alternatively,

Benayahu comments that Rabbi Yehoshua wanted to show her how good her food was, so he "cleaned his entire plate" to show his appreciation.

The second story teaches us another important principle. If the owners had indeed given an easement to the public to use the path, then Rabbi Yehoshua would have been perfectly within his rights to walk on it. But the little girl taught Rabbi Yehoshua that even though many people had made it their practice to use the path, that did not make it public property. Even though the public habitually does something wrong, that does not in any way change the nature of the sin/error. The latter transgressors are just as liable as the original wrongdoers.

> *This* daf *also contains several semantic sections. The Gemara informs us that the famous maidservant of Rebbi (Rabbeinu HaKadosh; Rabbi Yehudah HaNasi) was a linguist of particular renown. Her distinction in this area is the subject of other similar Talmudic passages (see* Rosh Hashanah 26b; Moed Katan 17a; Kesubos 104a).

THE ACTUAL GEMARA IS NOT QUOTED IN DETAIL HERE AS IT INVOLVES technical language usage rather than stories about women, which is the theme of this *sefer*. The Rabbis were not ashamed, however, to note that they relied upon a female servant to elucidate difficult linguistic questions.

Eruvin 53b-54a

(see also Berachos 10a and Pesachim 62b)

BERURIAH AND RABBI YOSE

Rabbi Yose the Galilean was walking on a path, and he met Beruriah. He asked her, "By which road can we travel to the city of Lod?" She replied, "Foolish Galilean, didn't the Rabbis write (Pirkei Avos 1:5) *that one should not have excessive conversation with [the] woman! You should have spoken more succinctly and simply stated, 'With which to Lod?'"*

Once Beruriah found a certain student engaged in learning, but doing so silently. Beruriah kicked him and said, "Isn't it written (Shmuel II 23:5) arranged in all, and secure? *If your learning encompasses all of the 248 organs of the body, then your learning will be secure and not easily forgotten. Otherwise, you run the risk of not remembering it well."*

Beruriah, daughter of the holy martyr Rabbi Chananya ben Teradyon, wife of the great sage Rabbi Meir, is one of the most acclaimed women in all of the Babylonian Talmud. The Gemara in *Pesachim* (62b) describes her phenomenal scholarship and halachic knowledge. Indeed, *Ben Yehoyada* makes the remarkable statement that she was famous for her wisdom — like a Tanna!

On a simple cursory level, the conversation between Rabbi Yose and Beruriah appears trite and unworthy of discussion. However, *Ben Yehoyada* explains that their pithy remarks actually involved a detailed discussion of the Mishnah in *Avos* quoted by

Beruriah. Rabbi Yose thought that the purpose of the Mishnah was to prevent lightheaded conversation between men and women in a setting that was inappropriate and that could lead to immoral behavior. But a serious discussion with a woman scholar would not be included in this prohibition, and thus there was no need to speak to Beruriah in the briefest language possible. Beruriah corrected him and pointed out that the Mishnah uses the definitive article הָאשה — "the" woman — to teach us that even a female sage is included in the ban. In his *Benayahu* commentary, *Ben Yehoyada* gives a different twist on this explanation. Beruriah admonishes Rabbi Yose, "Do you think I need a long-winded question to understand your query? *Pirkei Avos* teaches us that with a smart woman — הָאשה — one can be brief; it is with simple folks that one needs to be more loquacious." *Maharsha* adds that it was at a fork in the road that the incident occurred, and that Rabbi Yose should have pointed and just said, "With which to Lod?" and his question would have been easily understood.

Beruriah also spoke derisively to Rabbi Yose for an additional reason, according to *Ben Yehoyada*. It was improper to use the word נלך, *we travel*, implying that they would travel together. Even if Rabbi Yose was using the formal "royal we," and actually meant only himself, Beruriah held that it was incorrect to speak this way with a woman. How careful must a person be in his actions and conversations with a person of the opposite sex.

In the second story, Beruriah was teaching the Torah scholar an important lesson in *halachah*. One should preferably learn out loud, in an energetic fashion (just visit any yeshiva *beis midrash* to see Beruriah's advice vigorously carried out with zeal!). This will be of tremendous assistance in successfully retaining one's learning.

Eruvin 63a

(see also Shabbos 116a-b)

The Snake — Hashem's Messenger

Rabbi Eliezer had a student (Yehudah ben Guria) who rendered a halachic decision in the presence of Rabbi Eliezer. Rabbi Eliezer said to his wife, Aima Shalom, "I would be surprised if that student lives out the year." Indeed, the student did not live out the year. Aima Shalom asked her husband, "Are you a prophet?" He answered, "I am not a prophet, nor the son of a prophet, but I learned from my teachers that anyone who renders a halachic decision in the presence of his rebbi is liable to death," i.e. death from Heaven (Rashi). *Rabbi Chiya bar Abba said in the name of Rabbi Yochanan: Anyone who renders a halachic decision in the presence of his rebbi is worthy of being bitten by a snake.*

The Gemara explains that the prohibition of rendering a halachic decision in front of one's rebbi is derived from the case of the two eldest children of Aharon HaKohen, Nadav and Avihu, who died at the hand of Hashem via a Heavenly fire that entered their nostrils and burned them from the inside. *Ben Yehoyada* questions this explanation, however. Several different reasons for the premature demise of Nadav and Avihu are in fact brought down: They died for bringing an unnecessary fire on the altar; or for not getting married (they mistakenly thought no girl could be good enough for the sons/nephews of the great leaders Aharon and Moshe!); or because they had imbibed wine prior to performing the holy service in the *Mishkan. Ben Yehoyada* therefore postulates that under normal circumstances, their merits would have protected them from the punishment for these transgressions. However, since they spoke up and rendered a halachic decision in front of their teachers Moshe and Aharon, this protective benefit was removed and they were left to suffer the consequences of their act without Divine forbearance. *Menachem Meishiv Nefesh* adds that this is why they were burned through both nostrils, representing the lack of respect they showed both Moshe and Aharon.

What does the symbolism of dying via a snake bite embody? What is the connection between a snake bite and burning via Divine fire? *Menachem Meishiv Nefesh* and *Iyun Yaakov* offer similar explanations. The Gemara in *Sanhedrin* relates that from the time of the destruction of the Temple (actually forty years prior to its devastation), Jewish *batei din* (courts of law) did not impose capital punishment. However, the Heavenly Tribunal still exacts punishments, albeit in an indirect fashion. For example, if a person is liable to death by שריפה, *burning,* Hashem will cause such a person to die in a fire or via a snake bite. (Metaphorically, the venomous poison "burns" the victim.) Thus, the renderer of a halachic decision in front of his rebbi receives the requisite שריפה penalty when he is bitten by a snake. *Menachem Meshiv Nefesh* further expounds from the *Midrash Rabbah* that arrogance is also punished by שריפה. This is especially suitable, for the flames are constantly "contesting one another" to see which one can leap higher, just like the arrogant person who speaks up in front of his teacher.

Ben Yehoyada remarks that the snake sinned with its mouth, enticing Chava through words. The student speaking up rebelliously in front of his master likewise transgresses with speech, and it is especially proper that he should be killed with a bite of the snake's mouth! Furthermore, the snake trespassed into a forbidden domain; so too the errant student has entered the forbidden realm of speaking up in front of his master. *Maharsha* concludes his discussion in a similar vein. Adam and Chava attempted to defend their actions by telling Hashem that the snake told them to sin. Hashem replied, "To whom should you have listened — to the Teacher (Hashem) Who forbade eating from the Tree, or to the student (the snake)?" Here too, the student should not have spoken up in front of the rebbi, as he should not be listened to.

Further explanations abound regarding the snake comparison. *Ben Yehoyada* quotes *Chazal* who express the sentiment that a rabbi must act like an avenging snake and strongly attack personal affronts to the rabbinate and Torah. In this case, Hashem Himself sends a real snake to address this affront to the rabbinate. Indeed, the snake is a frequently used messenger of Hashem to accomplish Divine acts in a seeming "natural" fashion.

Iyun Yaakov comments very insightfully on the wording of our Gemara. It states that the student is *worthy* of being bitten by a snake — but not that he will necessarily indeed be so smitten! Why not? *Iyun Yaakov* writes that there are two situations where jealousy is nonexistent: A father is never jealous of a child's accomplishments, and a rebbe is always happy when his student surpasses him in learning. The greatest joy for a teacher is when the pupil reaches the stage whereby he is capable of answering the questions posed to the master. Even if this is done in a disrespectful manner, as in rendering a halachic decision in his presence, the teacher will be willing to let the insult slide, and not demand that a punishment be carried out. Undoubtedly, therefore, the student will only be worthy of the punishment but not actually receive it! (However, see this *sefer* regarding young Shmuel and his teacher Eli, *Berachos* 31a and b.)

Finally, regarding the expression, "I am not a prophet nor the son of a prophet," *Rashash* says that this is a paraphrase of the words of the Navi Amos (7:14) and is a popular idiomatic usage. *Ben Yehoyada* suggests that the word "prophet" means true prophecy, and the words "son of a prophet" are meant to represent either the students of a "prophet" or a lower form of prophecy, the Divine Spirit. Rabbi Eliezer was simply stating that he had no special Heavenly powers to predict the future. However, Hashem has created the world to function under strict rules and guidelines. The Oral and Written Law is a blueprint and "instruction manual" under which the natural world operates. To the initiated Torah scholar, this is as predictable as day and night!

Eruvin 63b

PRIVACY BETWEEN MAN AND WIFE

(The Gemara is in the midst of a discussion regarding the reason why the great leader Yehoshua (Joshua) was considered unworthy of having children.) Rav Abba bar Pappa said that Yehoshua was punished because he caused the Jewish people to abstain from engaging in marital relations for one night. (The Gemara derives this from an elucidation of verses from Joshua *[5:13, 8:13] and* Bamidbar *[28:3].)*

Rav Bruna said in the name of Rav, "A person who sleeps in the same room in which a husband and wife are staying, about such a person the prophet (Michah 2:9) *states:* The wives of My nation you have chased from the house of enjoyment." *Rav Yosef added, "This is true even if the wife was a* niddah *(ritually impure) at that time." Rava disagreed, remarking, on the contrary, "In that case the person should receive a blessing, as he helped protect the couple from possibly sinning." However, the Gemara concludes that Rava is incorrect, no protection is necessary; until now, who was guarding them while the wife was a* niddah?

THIS GEMARA CLEARLY ILLUSTRATES THE IMPORTANCE THAT *CHAZAL* attach to the intimacy and privacy between a husband and wife. Yehoshua was severely punished simply because he delayed the return of the Jewish soldiers from battle by one day (only!), causing them to be away from their wives for one extra night. *Middah keneged middah*, since he possibly prevented the conception of Jewish children, Hashem did not permit him to have progeny. (There is a discussion among the commentaries whether this punishment was regarding male children only, or did it encompass having no descendants at all.) Similarly, the great children of the Judge Eli HaKohen, Chophni and Pinchas, are classified as adulterers. Not *chas veshalom* that they actually cohabited with married women, but because they delayed the bringing in the Tabernacle of the childbirth offerings of women, and thus delayed their departure home to their husbands by one extra day. For doing so, the Torah put them in the category of adulterers! We see the significance and respect with which the Torah and *Chazal* regard the intimacies of marriage.

This concept is further stressed by *Rabbeinu Yehonasan*. In the Gemara, Rav Yosef stated that even when the marital act is prohibited because of ritual purity laws, a person who intrudes upon the privacy of a man and wife is considered as having "chased (the wife) from the house of enjoyment." The verse in *Michah* is obviously not simply referring to physical pleasure. *Rabbeinu Yehonasan* (quoted by the *Maharsha*) explains that this is a reference to the private intimate conversations between a husband and wife. It is a great honor for them to spend exclusive time together. Having another person in the room, even when there is absolutely no impropriety, disconcerts the married couple and prevents them from communicating. *Meiri* adds that anything /anybody that causes a separation between husband and wife is not good; even minimal segregation should be avoided.

Eruvin 65a

Eternal Sleep

The daughter (some texts read daughters) of Rav Chisda said to her father, "Doesn't the master (her father) require a little sleep?" (Rav Chisda was so deeply engrossed in his learning that he apparently had not slept much.) Rav Chisda replied that soon there will be days that are long and short, and there will be plenty of time to rest then.

R*ashi* explains that the long days refer to the days of the grave, after a person dies. Then there will be plenty of time to sleep. But why are they also called "short" days? Because they are bereft from learning Torah and performing *mitzvos.* This concept is encapsulated in the common expression and blessing: "May you have אריכות ימים ושנים, *long days and years.*" If you are blessed with numerous years, what additional benefit is yielded with a blessing of multitudinous days? *Chazal* explain that the *quality* of one's days is the essential determinant — what a person does and accomplishes with his time. Some people have a long life span, but they squander this grace and *truly* exist only a short time. Others may have materially shorter durations on this world, but have actually left their mark as if they existed for centuries.

In the Gemara (*Eruvin* 22a), we find Rav Adda so engrossed in his learning that he neglects the physical needs of himself and his family. It is possible that these stories reflect the different roles that the Torah has ordained for men and women. Men are obligated in the study of Torah, whereas women are not, since it is a time-dependent positive commandment, and women are exempt from such laws. The *posuk* in *Bamidbar* (19:14) states: *A man, if he dies in his tent ... Chazal* homiletically expound this verse to connote that a man must *figuratively* die striving (i.e. work extremely hard) in his Torah analysis (his "tent"). Men are required to learn Torah even when it is physically uncomfortable and even somewhat dangerous, and thus the relative neglect of the physical necessities by the aforementioned rabbis. Women are not so commanded, and inherently are more concerned with the daily activities and requirements of living.

Eruvin 96a-b

Tefillin and Time-Dependent Mitzvos: Michal and Yonah's Wife

(The Gemara is in the midst of a discussion regarding the commandment to wear tefillin. *Among the subjects discussed is whether it is a time-dependent obligation from which women are exempt.) A* Baraisa *states: Michal the daughter of Kushi would put on* tefillin, *and the Rabbis did not protest. The wife of the prophet Yonah would routinely travel to Jerusalem and the* Beis HaMikdash *for the* Shalosh Regalim *(holidays of Pesach, Shavuos and Succos) pilgrimage, and the Rabbis did not protest. Since the Rabbis did not protest (and thereby gave tacit approval to the performance of these precepts), we see that these two* mitzvos (Shalosh Regalim *and* tefillin) *are not time-dependent commandments, and thus women should be required to perform them. The Gemara rejects this assumption however. Certainly, everyone must agree that the* Shalosh Regalim *pilgrimage is time dependent — it occurs only at specific times of the year. The* Baraisa *must therefore follow the opinion of Rabbi Yose, that women may perform* mitzvos *that are time dependent even though not obligated to do so. If so, women, normally exempted from the time-dependent obligation of* tefillin, *could wear them electively if they so choose.*

RASHI EXPLAINS (BASED ON *MOED KATAN* 16B) THAT MICHAL WAS the daughter of Shaul, the first king of Israel, and subsequently the wife of King David. Why does the Gemara refer to her father as "*Kushi*"? A *kushi* is a dark-skinned individual. Just as a *kushi* stands out and is physically recognizable among fair-skinned people, King Shaul, because of his exceptional character and physical status, was literally and figuratively head and shoulders above his subjects.

Why was Michal so zealous regarding *tefillin* rather than other commandments? *Ben Yehoyada* answers by quoting a *Midrash Shocher Tov*. The Jewish people told Hashem that they really would love to learn all day and night, but were merely incapable of doing so. Hashem replied: Because you desired to learn all the time, I will give you the *mitzvah* of *tefillin*. While you wear *tefillin*, I will consider it as if you are learning Torah. Women are not obligated in learning Torah, as this is a time-dependent commandment. Michal wanted to take the *mitzvah* of *tefillin* and use it as her substitute for learning Torah. Why weren't other women also interested in doing this? Michal had her own special considerations — she was unable to have children (some say male children) because she once rebuked her husband King David inappropriately. When the Holy Ark was being brought to Jerusalem, King David publicly danced joyously with tremendous abandon in honor of the Torah. Michal reproached him for acting in this less than regal fashion. For this criticism, she became barren. *Tefillin* are a special *segulah* (aide) to begetting children. She hoped that in her zeal to perform a commandment for which she was not even obligated, Hashem would grant her desire for children. Indeed, according to some commentators she eventually bore a child, but only on the day she died!

The Gemara seems to conclude that while women are not obligated to do so, they may wear *tefillin* if they so choose. Rabbi Yosef Caro, in his definitive *Shulchan Aruch* (*Orach Chaim* 38:3) states that women are exempt from wearing *tefillin*. The *Rama* (quoting an earlier *Rishon*, the *Kol Bo*) adds that women who wish to be stringent and wear *tefillin* anyway should be <u>precluded</u> from doing so. Indeed, it has always been the custom of Jewish women over the years <u>not</u> to wear *tefillin* (see also *Beis Yosef, Pri Megadim, Magen Avraham, Aruch HaShulchan* and *Mishnah*

Berurah there). *Mishnah Berurah* quotes *Tosafos* that women are unable to maintain the necessary state of physical cleanliness required while wearing *tefillin* because of their female physiology. Indeed the *halachah* states that a man with intestinal or other illness which renders him incapable of sustaining cleanliness is likewise not permitted to wear *tefillin*. *Geon Yaakov* remarks that Michal was such an exceptional individual of elevated spiritual status that in her case (*only*), the Rabbis did not protest her wearing *tefillin*. Indeed, the *Rashba* states that not only did they not protest Michal's actions, but she actually donned *tefillin* with their wholehearted approval! Rabbi Aharon Feldman points out (*Tradition*, volume 33:2) that the Talmud Yerushalmi and *Pesikta* disagree and state that *Chazal* in fact did protest against Michal, and the *poskim* cited above all follow this opinion. The *Maharam* adds that women should not don *tefillin* today because they are unable to keep "a holy body," which includes physical as well as mental purity (i.e. clean thoughts). *Aruch HaShulchan* comments that this is not to suggest that a man is more capable of doing so than a woman. On the contrary, man has at least the same difficulty in keeping his body holy. However, a man, who is obligated in the *mitzvah* of putting on *tefillin*, simply doesn't have a choice in the matter. He must wear *tefillin* and risk violating the precept of a holy body. (And that is why in general men take off their *tefillin* as soon as *davening* is over. They do not want to tarry beyond the minimum necessary to perform the *mitzvah*, and face the severe consequences of transgressing with improper thoughts or actions.) Whereas a woman, who does not have the obligation to wear *tefillin*, should certainly not put herself at risk of violating the "holy body" directive.

Ben Yehoyada explains why Yonah's wife pointedly chose the specific *mitzvah* of traveling to Jerusalem, as opposed to any other. She recognized that her husband was somewhat deficient in his observance of getting close to Hashem. After all, Yonah had tried to run away from Hashem rather than go to Nineveh, as is related in the famous story from the Book of *Yonah*. Yonah had been instructed to inform the people of Nineveh that unless they repented, the city would be overturned and destroyed. Fearing that they would truly repent, and that this would then serve as a terrible reflection against the Jewish people (who unfortunately did not always repent upon a prophet's directive), Yonah tried to flee from speaking the word of G-d. Yonah boarded a vessel that was sailing for Tarshish. Shortly out of port, however, a severe storm engulfed Yonah and the crew. Ultimately realizing that you can't run away from the ubiquitous King, Yonah asked to be thrown overboard to save everyone else. Immediately, the storm subsided; Yonah was swallowed and miraculously saved by a large "fish," and thereafter went to Nineveh to carry out his prophetic task. His wife now wished to correct Yonah's apparent "transgression." By voluntarily performing the pilgrimage to Jerusalem and the Temple, she clearly demonstrated their desire to be closer to the Creator.

Maharatz Chayes asks: What about Yonah? Didn't he go too? According to the Talmud Yerushalmi, Yonah was from the tribes of Zevulun and Asher (either his father was from Zevulun and his mother from Asher, or vice versa), located in the Northern Kingdom (Israel). The wicked Israeli kings, from Yeravam ben Nevat and continuing afterwards, did not let the Jewish people in Israel leave the Northern Kingdom to make the pilgrimage to Jerusalem (in the Judean Kingdom). This was because only kings from the lineage of David were permitted to sit down in the Temple Courtyard. Were the Judean and Israeli kings to be there together, it would be quite clear to all that the seated Davidic monarch was the true king, and the standing Israeli potentate merely an imposter. Thus the Israeli kings established heavily armed brigades and roadblocks at key crossroads to forcibly prevent their citizens from embarking on the *Shalosh Regalim* pilgrimage. Yonah was thus exempt from this commandment because of the inherent danger involved, for one is obligated to sacrifice one's life only to prevent transgressing the three cardinal mitzvos — sexual immorality, murder and idol worship. Certainly therefore, he was not obligated to give up his life to observe the *Shalosh Regalim* pilgrimage. Yet, Yonah was not afraid to do so, and he was rewarded. When he entered the Temple, and witnessed the spectacular water-drawing ceremonies of the Succos festival, the Divine Spirit rested upon him and he became a prophet. Yonah's wife was likewise willing to sacrifice her life for this *mitzvah*, even though she was not even obligated to embark on the pilgrimage under normal conditions. While in general the Rabbis may have thought such behavior improper, because of the greatness of Yonah's wife's, they did not object to it here.

ERUVIN 100B

RELATIONS; CHAVA AND CHILDBIRTH REVISITED

Rami bar Chama said in the name of Rav Assi: A man is not permitted to force his wife to perform a mitzvah *(*Rashi: *the* mitzvah *of marital relations). And Rabbi Yehoshua ben Levi adds that if a person forces his wife to engage in marital relations against her wishes, he will have children who are not of good character. (These statements are based upon derivations from* Mishlei 19:2.*)*

*Rav Shmuel bar Nachmani said in the name of Rabbi Yochanan (*Mesoras HaShas *changes this to Rabbi Yonasan): Every woman who petitions her husband to have marital relations will have children [of such high caliber] that even in the generation of Moshe Rabbeinu, such progeny were not seen! This is derived from* Devarim (1:13, 15). *Hashem told Moshe to find wise and understanding men of good repute, but Moshe was able to locate only wise men with good reputations — but not anyone described also as understanding (*Rashi: *— men with excellent deductive skills). Yet, we find regarding our Matriarch Leah* (Bereishis 30:16), *that she was able to conceive and give birth to Yissachar because she actively petitioned Yaakov to have relations with her, when it was not her scheduled evening. Because she was so desirous of performing this* mitzvah *with Yaakov, her progeny (Yissachar) merited exceptional wisdom and understanding, as noted in Divrei HaYamim I* (12:33), *where the tribe of Yissachar is praised for its deep understanding and astronomical profundity in calculating the variations in the Hebrew calendar.*

The Gemara asks: Is it indeed meritorious to petition one's husband for relations? Don't we find that the opposite is recommended? Rav Yitzchak bar Avdimi remarked: Chava was cursed with ten curses for her involvement in the sin of partaking from the Tree of Knowledge (עץ הדעת). *Hashem told her* (Bereishis 3:16): I will greatly increase your suffering and your childbearing; in pain you shall bear children, yet your craving shall be for your husband and he shall rule over you. *Rav Yitzchak derived seven curses from this verse:* (1) *menstruation;* (2) *hymenal bleeding;* (3) *travails of child rearing;* (4) *pregnancy;* (5) *childbirth;* (6) *yearning for one's husband (*Rashi: *desire for marital relations) just before he leaves for a trip;* (7) *not expressing those desires verbally — as opposed to the man who may do so (hence, "he shall rule over you"). Rav Yitzchak concludes: And this trait of not verbalizing such desires is considered especially virtuous for a woman. Thus, the suggestion is that women not be brazen in their desire for relations. How do we harmonize this with the actions of Leah and the previous statement of the Gemara? The Gemara explains that it is meritorious for a woman to initiate marital relations, but she should do so via hints and indirect actions, rather than explicit verbalization.*

The Gemara (Rav Dimi) completes the listing of the ten curses: (8) *a women is required to keep her hair covered like a mourner;* (9) *she is permitted to have only one husband at a time;* (10) *she is somewhat restricted in her activities.*

R*ABBI YAAKOV EMDEN* STRESSES THAT TO FORCIBLY HAVE MARITAL relations with one's wife (i.e. against her wishes) is strongly condemned and prohibited. This is even if the husband claims to be doing so for the purpose of fulfilling the *mitzvah* of procreation, and/or fulfilling his marital obligation on the evening that his wife returns from the *mikveh* after her ritual immersion.

Why are the curses seemingly written out of order? Shouldn't the travails of child-rearing come after the hardships of pregnancy and delivery? The *Rif* in the *Ein Yaakov*, and other commentators provide a fascinating insight. When did the sin of eating from the Tree of Knowledge occur? According to one opinion, this happened on the very first Friday of Creation, after the birth of Kayin and Hevel. The Midrash tells us that Chava gave birth to five children that day — Kayin, Hevel and three daughters. All were born without Chava suffering any labor pains or distress, and all were actually begotten as full-grown adults! Only later that very day, after the sin, was the curse of childbirth assigned. Thus, the Gemara's order actually is quite appropriate. Chava undoubtedly first experienced the travails of child-rearing — certainly during the episode where Kayin kills Hevel if not at other times! — and only 130 years later, with the birth of Sheis did she undergo the pains of pregnancy, labor and delivery.

Eitz Yosef quotes the other opinion in the Midrash, which states that Chava's children were all born after the sin. According to this version, the order actually is incorrect, and should be revised (i.e. pregnancy, delivery and only then, child-raising). *Menachem Meshiv Nefesh* takes an alternative approach. Pregnancy is most difficult when a woman has several little children to care for. Thus, the order of our Gemara conveys the increasing potential for hardship, but is not necessarily in chronological order. *Ben Yehoyada* exposits along a similar vein. The potential troubles of child-rearing last for much longer (for some they never end!) than pregnancy or childbirth, and that is why it is listed first. *Maharsha* adds that men also suffer the hardships of child-rearing, but women certainly have always taken an inordinate share of this task.

Ben Yehoyada also describes why the sixth curse, desiring one's husband before he departs on a journey, is indeed a burden. In all likelihood, there were be many people present at the husband's send-off. This will increase the emotion and love that the wife will experience, and increase her desire for her husband. However, it will not be an opportune time to fulfill those yearnings, and as a result she is considered afflicted. Regarding the seventh curse, that a women has to be more circumspect than a man in telling her spouse that she is desirous of relations, *Ben Yehoyada* interprets this from a different viewpoint. Since it is meritorious to have relations, the curse is that the husband may misinterpret and/or not realize what his wife is actually suggesting, and this potential misunderstanding is the tragedy.

Ben Yehoyada further states that the final three curses are not as severe as the initial seven, and that is why there is no specific reference to them in the *posuk*. Many women actually prefer to cover their hair at times, so that this requirement for a married woman is not that much of a burden. Various hats and other hair adornments are used by women to beautify themselves, and thus covering the hair is not a complete negative. Likewise, the inability to have more than one husband simultaneously is not truly a restriction. Most women — and *Ben Yehoyada* adds most men — clearly prefer to have only one spouse. In Ashkenazi communities, and today in almost all segments of the Jewish and non-Jewish world, monogamy is the norm and polygamy is prohibited.

Finally, the tenth curse, restriction on her activities, is also not such a tribulation. *Rashi* quotes the verse (*Tehillim* 45:14), *Every honorable princess dwelling within.* A woman's modesty, majesty and elevated status in Judaism sometimes preclude her presence at certain activities of society. *Ben Yehoyada* explains that this is not an absolute curse, as women often prefer other women's company anyway.

מסכת פסחים

PESACHIM

PESACHIM

PESACHIM 48B

WOMEN'S STRINGENCIES

Rav Yosef said: Our women have the custom not to bake more than one kapiza *(a measure of flour equivalent to three-quarters of a* kav *— 2.16 liters) at a time for Pesach to avoid the possibility of* chametz.

Abaye asked Rav Yosef: Why do you think this is a good idea? Is it because it is commendable to prohibit kneading a larger dough in order to prevent the possibility of chametz? *But it is a stringency that will lead to a leniency; for* challah *(a priestly tithe similar to* terumah*) need not be given from a dough that size. Thus you are causing the avoidance of this* mitzvah. *Rav Yosef answers that these women fulfilled the* mitzvah *of* challah *by placing the proper amount of baked goods in a basket. The basket united them and it was as if they belonged to a single large dough which required that* challah *be taken from it.*

THE GEMARA RELATES THIS STORY TO TEACH US PARTICULARS ABOUT the laws of Pesach, *chametz* and *challah*. However, I believe there is an additional message as well. It is the women of Rav Yosef's city who took it upon themselves to fulfill all the possible stringencies. *Chazal* repeatedly remind us that it was through the actions of righteous women that we were redeemed from Egypt. This did not happen only at the time of the Exodus (*Yetzias Mitzraim*), but throughout our history — the Jewish woman has been steadfast in her faith and adhered to the Torah and its *mitvos*. What more fitting way to remind us of this than with another narrative of an example dealing with Pesach, the time of the original emancipation from Egypt.

Pesachim 49b

Wives of Ignorant Men

Rabbi Chiya taught that the hatred amei haaretz *have towards Torah scholars is even greater than the hatred the nations of the world have towards the Jewish people — and the wives of these* amei haaretz *hate the Rabbis even more than their husbands do.*

The Gemara is in the midst of a discussion regarding the *amei haaretz* (those who are not only devoid of Torah scholarship, but who actually purposefully provoke Hashem).

This book cannot begin to adequately treat the subject of the *amei haaretz* and their differences with the Rabbis. Certainly, the Gemara is not speaking about an unlearned decent Jew. Such a person has the status of "a baby who was captured and raised by non-Jews"; he is not responsible for his lack of Jewish knowledge. The Gemara is concerned about someone who should know better and yet goes out of his way to deliberately provoke Hashem. Such Jews throughout our tortured history have sometimes been more spiteful and dangerous to us than even the most vicious gentile anti-Semites.

We will concentrate on the statement that the wives of these *amei haaretz* hate the scholars more than their husbands do. Why? The *Meiri* explains that the wives are more jealous of the Rabbis than their husbands. The *Chidushei Geonim* (in the *sefer Ein Yaakov*) elaborates. The wives of the *amei haaretz* realize that a woman shares half of everything with her husband. All his deeds and rewards are partially hers too. Thus, as she recognizes the absolute worthlessness of her husband's anti-Torah lifestyle, and sees that she is therefore a half-owner of essentially nothing of value, this makes her jealousy even stronger, and her hate for the Torah scholars even greater than her husband's.

The *Chidushei Geonim* writes further that the tendency is for the wives in a neighborhood to congregate together and be socially active. Yet the Torah scholars' wives are prohibited from lending their vessels and participating in many activities together with the wives of the *amei haaretz*, because of the laws of ritual purity. Indeed, they must keep their distance, and this leads to a greater level of hatred amongst the women than among the men.

Finally, the *amei haaretz* husbands treat their wives with less respect than the Rabbis treat their wives. For the Torah commands and *obligates* a husband to respect and honor his wife even more than he does himself. The wives of the *amei haaretz* sense this difference of treatment, and it further spurs their jealousy and animosity. *Iyun Yaakov* adds that this loathing is only present in the wives if it is found in the husbands. But if the husbands do not show disdain towards the Rabbis, their wives also will not.

I thought it interesting that part of the excessive enmity which they feel is due to taking their husbands' side, which is in itself normally a very positive attribute. Hashem created women as an עזר כנגדו, literally "a (help)mate opposite him" (*Bereishis* 2:21). This is an apparent contradiction! Is the wife an equal partner or is she an opposing force? I have heard rebbeim homiletically explain the verse as follows: A husband and wife are at times supposed to be a unit acting in complete accord, but at other times, they must be diametrically opposite. When a spouse is doing a positive act, the partner must be totally on his/her side, acting together in total harmony. However, if one spouse is off the mark, the other spouse must be quick to respectfully disagree, and set the errant partner on the right path. Siding with a spouse who is wrong is no virtue.

Pesachim 50b

(see also Shabbos 32b-33a)

The Reward of "Laziness"

The Rabbis learned in a Baraisa: ... There are those that are indolent and rewarded. An example is someone who does not work all week, and also abstains from labor on erev *Shabbos (Friday afternoon). Rava said: The women of the town of Mechoza, even though the reason they do not toil* erev *Shabbos is because they are delicate — and not because they are following the advice of the Rabbis to honor Shabbos by abstaining at that time, since they also did not work during the rest of the week as well — nevertheless, they are considered in the category of "the lazy who are rewarded."*

R*ASHI* AND OTHER COMMENTATORS EXPLAIN THAT WHILE THE INDOLENT person is fulfilling the *mitzvah* of abstaining from work "not for its own sake," yet this is still meritorious, because it will hopefully eventually lead to the performance of the precept for the proper reason.

The women of Mechoza are often described in the Gemara as being very delicate, materially insubstantial and dainty. They performed little real work all week long, and as such, their abstaining from working Friday afternoons was not any deviation from their normal habit.

Many of the commentators ask: What did Rava contribute to our understanding of the subject by providing his example. After all, the *Baraisa* clearly stated this already? *Ben Yehoyada* remarks that there is an additional insight in the words of Rava.

One might have thought that since the women of Mechoza had cleaning help and other assistance during the week, they might not be considered in the category of the lazy worker, because they essentially had no work. Rava teaches us that this, too, is called indolent, for indolence brings harm along with it. *Ben Yehoyada* also adds, however, that this does not suggest that a husband should just sit around and expect his wife to bring in money with her hard work. On the contrary, such a man will not enjoy the fruits of her labor. A man who does not have concern for his wife's honor and puts her to work at shameful lowly labor will not merit the blessings that normally accrue to a Jewish house because of the Jewish wife!

Tzelach offers a different approach. The women of Mechoza couldn't work because of their infirm nature. One might have opined that such women should not be considered as abstaining from labor; they should be deemed a step below even the person who performs the *mitzvah* for an improper reason. Therefore, Rava adds that at least these women, too, are considered as fulfilling the precept "not for its own sake" and are meritorious.

Pesachim 56a

Daughters of the King

Rabbi Yitzchak said that in the academy of Rabbi Ami they said: This is analogous to the daughter of the king who smelled a dish seasoned with certain spices. If she were to say that she desired of this dish, she would be degrading herself. Yet, if she says nothing, she will be in pain (from not tasting the food). Her servants, realizing her predicament, therefore brought her the food in secret.

The Gemara is in the midst of a discussion regarding the proper way to say the first paragraph of the *Shema.*

The Jewish people are often compared in the Gemara to a king's daughter. I believe we can learn from this how we should act. The proper attitude we should maintain is not to debase ourselves and demand every pleasure that we see or desire; instead, we must trust in Hashem. If we truly need something, *He* will make sure it is provided to us in a dignified and timely fashion.

I have heard in the name of many different *gedolei Yisrael* (great Torah sages) that a person should always limit his pleasure to some extent, even for permissible items, to train oneself in the constant battle against the evil inclination. Some *gedolim* would always leave some leftover food on their plate to symbolize this idea. Others would not eat certain desserts or delicacies; yet others would put pebbles in their shoes. All of this was done "for the sake of Heaven" — to constantly be aware of and vigilant against the pursuit of physical pleasures.

Pesachim 57a-b

(see also Kereisos 28a)

"Off with His Hand" — A Royal Decree

The Temple Courtyard cried out: Depart from here, Yissachar, the man from the village of Barkai, who honors himself but desecrates the Holy sacrifices, as he wrapped silk around his hands during the sacrificial service. What happened to Yissachar? The Gemara states that once the king and queen were sitting, and the king said that kid meat is superior, whereas the queen said that lamb's meat is tastier. They said; Who should decide the matter? Let the Kohen Gadol *be the judge, because he offers sacrifices daily. Yissachar [the* Kohen Gadol*] came and gestured derisively with his hand saying: If the kid were superior, then it (instead of a sheep) should be brought as the daily* tamid *sacrifice. The king said: Since he did not have awe of the majesty of the kingship, cut off his right hand! Yissachar bribed the appropriate royal officers and he had them sever his weaker left hand instead. However, the king subsequently heard about this and had Yissachar's right hand chopped off as well. Rav Yosef said: Blessed is the Merciful One Who exacted retribution from Yissachar in this world!*

It is prohibited to have any separation (*chatzizah*) between the hands and whatever must be touched or had during the performance of the priestly duties.

This story is a classic example of *middah keneged middah*. Yissachar was repaid in the manner by which he showed his disrepect for the Almighty; and he himself was the immediate determinant of part of his punishment. *Benayahu* notes that the Gemara adds the seemingly unnecessary words that the king and queen were sitting around when they began this conversation to stress this Divine retribution. This wasn't a practical discussion based upon the food they were eating; it was a spontaneous conversation, directed by Hashem as a mechanism for punishing Yissachar.

Rashi explains that the king and queen were of the Hasmonean dynasty. *Menachem Meshiv Nefesh* comments that *Rashi* is not relating trivial historical detail. The later Hasmonean monarchs belonged to the sect known as the Tzedokim, who did not believe in *Halachah LeMoshe MiSinai*, laws transmitted by Moshe which he heard at Sinai, such as the law of *chatzizah*.

Ben Yehoyada explains that the conversation between the king and queen was really a high level debate on their status. The king, a Hasmonean descendant, believed in the importance of the Hasmoneans' dynasty. This is expressed in his preference for the goat, whose astrological sign (Capricorn) is found in the month of Teves, during the end of Chanukah, the holiday of the great Hasmonean victory. On the other hand, the queen was arguing that Pesach — which occurs during the zodiac sign of the sheep — was more important than Chanukah. The king argued that Chanukah is eight days long (and Pesach only seven), and that the complete *Hallel* prayer is said daily during the entire Chanukah but only on the first day of Pesach. Yissachar solved the dilemma by pointing out that we bring a sheep-offering daily — signifying the daily mentioning in our prayers of the miracle of Pesach, yet no similar *tefillah* is said daily about the miracle of Chanukah. However, since the *Kohen Gadol* made his remarks in a rebellious and impertinent fashion, *Rashi* in Gemara *Kereisos* states that he deserved the death penalty as one who rebelled against a king.

PESACHIM 62B

(see also Berachos 10a and Eruvin 53b-54a)

THE UNPARALLELED BERURIAH

Rav Simlai came before Rabbi Yochanan and asked him to teach him Sefer Yuchsin. *Rabbi Yochanan asked Rav Simlai where he came from, and where he now lived. Rav Simlai replied that he was originally from Lod and now resided in Nehardea. Rabbi Yochanan said that it is not proper to teach residents of either Lod or Nehardea the* Sefer Yuchsin. *However, Rav Simlai pressed him and Rabbi Yochanan relented. Then, Rav Simlai requested that Rabbi Yochanan teach him the entire work in just three months. Rabbi Yochanan picked up a clod of earth and threw it at him, and remarked: If it took Beruriah — the wife of Rabbi Meir and the daughter of Rabbi Chananya ben Teradyon — who learned* 300 *teachings in a day from* 300 *different Rabbis more than three years to complete the study of* Sefer Yuchsin, *how could you possibly expect to finish it in three months?*

YUCHSIN MEANS LINEAGE. HOWEVER, ACCORDING TO *RASHI, SEFER Yuchsin* was a collection of Tannaitic statements on *Divrei HaYamim* (*Chronicles*). *Maharsha* writes that *Rashi* was reluctant to explain *Sefer Yuchsin* as a book of genealogical records, because the Gemara in the fourth Chapter of *Kiddushin* states that it is prohibited to reveal the ignoble lineages of people (those not able to marry *Kohanim, Leviim,* and *Yisraelim*) except once in seven years. *Rashi* (commenting on that Gemara) states that the Sages were literally afraid for their lives because of the strong-armed tactics of those of impure lineage, and thus they were forced to stop publicly announcing the lineage blemishes. Instead, once every seven years they would orally transmit this data to the next generation of Rabbis and students. Thus *Sefer Yuchsin* here must refer to something else — a commentary on *Chronicles.*

As we have already seen several times, Beruriah was a woman famous for her Torah erudition and knowledge. *Ben Yehoyada* elsewhere describes her as [like] having the status of a Tanna; indeed, our Gemara compares her very favorably to the great Rav Simlai. In his commentary *Benayahu*, the Ben Ish Chai adds that her name itself demonstrates her caliber: ברור י-ה, *the clear one of Hashem.* Her greatness is further evident from the praise the Gemara relates about her. Not only did she learn a tremendous amount of Torah (300 teachings in a single day), but she learned this from 300 different teachers — itself an unbelievable feat. It is difficult enough to become accustomed to the style and methodology of a single rebbi; how much more so to be able to successfully acquire knowledge from 300 different educators! Indeed it is almost too much to believe, and maybe this is why the Gemara also mentions Beruriah's distinguished family — her great husband and righteous father. With their own considerable merit added to her own strengths, she was able to succeed where others might not. It is also important to remember that the Rashbam notes that the Gemara frequently uses the number 300 as an exaggeration. (E.g. — 300 *Kohanim* were required to lift the *Paroches* [Curtain] in the *Beis HaMikdash* to place it in the *mikveh* if it became impure.) This in no way detracts from Beruriah's luster. On the contrary, that the Talmud deemed it necessary to use such glowing language to describe her intellect further adds to her standing.

Why was Rabbi Yochanan concerned with Rav Simlai's background and current dwelling place? *Rashi* suggests that he was merely trying to push him off or he did not want to discuss the matter with people from Lod or Nehardea because they were not of noted lineage. *Iyun Yaakov* points out that the Talmud Yerushalmi has a slightly different version of our story. Rav Simlai desired to learn *Aggadeta* — stories of the Talmud with deep and often mystical meaning. Rabbi Yochanan responded that it is not permissable to teach this to Babylonians or Southerners, because they are arrogant. An arrogant person cannot truly comprehend Torah; one must be humble to successfully study it.

Ben Yehoyada further questions the strange interaction between Rav Simlai and Rabbi Yochanan. Why did Rabbi Yochanan agree to teach him, and then recant in a seemingly bizarre fashion by throwing a קלא, *a clump of earth,* at Rav Simlai, when the three-month time constraint was mentioned? *Ben Yehoyada's* approach is similar to that of the previously mentioned Yerushalmi. Asking to be taught the *Sefer Yuchsin* in such a short period, when even the sagacious Beruriah required much longer to master the material, appeared to Rabbi Yochanan as the height of arrogance. He responded by retracting his offer to teach him, and throwing the clod of dirt. The gematria of קלא is 131, which is the numerical value of ענוה, *humility.* Furthermore, dirt is the symbol of humility, as [we] say (in אלקי נצור): ונפשי כעפר לכל תהיה, *And let my soul be as dust to all.*

Below on the same page, the Gemara relates that eventually the *Sefer Yuchsin* was נגנז, usually translated as hidden away, but here *Rashi* explains it as forgotten. *Tzelach* comments that *Rashi* purposefully used the variant interpretation. At that time in Jewish history, the oral tradition was not permitted to be written. That was to come only at a later period. Therefore, there was actually nothing material that could have been hidden away, and *Rashi* very correctly explains the word נגנז as forgotten.

PESACHIM 66B

(see also Pesachim 117b; Megillah 14b)

DEVORAH, JUDGE OF ISRAEL

> *Rav Yehudah said in the name of Rav. Anyone who acts in an arrogant fashion — if he is a wise man, his wisdom will leave him; if he is a prophet, his prophecy will desert him. ... The latter can be seen from an incident regarding Devorah the Prophetess. The* posuk (Shoftim 5:7) *quotes Devorah:* They [Israel] ceased to dwell in the open [unfortified] cities until I, Devorah, arose; until I, a mother, arose in Israel. *Several* pesukim *later, however,* (posuk 12), *Devorah pleads to Hashem:* Awake, awake, Devorah; awake, awake and speak your song.

THE PREVIOUS LEADERS OF THE JEWISH PEOPLE HAD BEEN UNABLE to free the nation from the oppressive yolk of their enemies, and the people were constantly subject to great peril and the intimidation of war, until the arrival on the scene of Devorah, their savior. Because of her apparent haughtiness, Devorah lost the Divine Spirit and was forced to implore Hashem to return prophecy to her.

The verses comes from the "Song of Devorah" that comprises the *Haftorah* of the *Parshah* of *Beshalach.* This song is the companion to the famous אז ישיר — "Az yashir" — in *Beshalach,* joyously expressed by Moshe and the Jewish people after their miraculous crossing of the split Red Sea. Obviously, if *Chazal* gave this Divinely inspired Song of Devorah such a prominent place in our liturgy, we can only begin to appreciate the greatness of its author. The Gemara in *Megillah* (14b) writes that Devorah was one of only seven women prophetesses; she was an independently wealthy woman who spent her life teaching Torah publicly and expertly guiding the Jewish people. The *posuk* here refers to Devorah as the mother of the Jews. *Meam Loez* says that the comparison to a mother is most apt. Just as a mother constantly worries about her children and steers them on the right path, so too, Devorah was a true mother for *Klal Yisrael*. *Metzudas David* comments that she was like a mother, always correcting and chastising her children, the people of Israel. *Abarbanel* equates her mercy and pity for her nation to that of a mother for her children. So why does the Gemara choose Devorah of all people as its archetype of (momentary) arrogance deserving (momentary) loss of prophecy?

Maharsha notes that we find "awake, awake" elsewhere in the Holy Scriptures used in its literal sense of arise. Here, however, it is used in the sense of departure — as a sign that the Holy Presence has withdrawn from the prophetess. Devorah's momentary conceit caused this to occur here. She did not mention her partner, the Jewish general Barak, in her illustrious victory song over the evil general Sisera and his troops. (As an interesting aside, the *Radak* on *Shoftim* 4:4 writes that Barak was none other than Devorah's husband — making this slight even more egregious!) Very uncharacteristically, she seemingly took all the credit for herself. Upon realization of her error, she immediately corrected this oversight, and Barak is prominently portrayed in the remainder of the elegy. The *Midrash Lekach Tov* (*Shemos* 15:20) comments that it actually was quite appropriate for Devorah to be mentioned first in the Song, as it was only due to Devorah's persistence, encouragement and active involvement in Barak's military triumph that this redemption occurred. *Meam Loez* adds that indeed it was her *tefillos* that secured the victory over Sisera; Barak's military prowess was not the essential determinant.

Indeed, the *Zohar* (*Bereishis* 3:19b) writes that two women — Devorah and Chana — praised Hashem in an incomparable fashion, as no man had ever done. (See *Berachos* 31a-b, for additional characterization of Chana.) Furthermore, the Gemara later in our tractate (*Pesachim* 117a) relates that according to the opinion of Rabbi Elazar the Moda'i, Devorah and Barak were the authors of the *Hallel* prayer recited throughout Jewish history at the times of greatest joy and happiness. How then is it appropriate that Devorah is portrayed with even the slightest negative connotation by our Gemara? Obviously, we see that Hashem judges the most righteous *tzaddikim* different from ordinary Jews. This is the concept of בחוט השערה, *judgment as fine as a thread of a hair*. Devorah's actions cannot be inspected like those of the ordinary human being. They need to be viewed in the context of her lofty accomplishments and the deeds she has performed. We can then try to understand why the gemara in *Megillah* (14b) describes her and another Jewish prophetess, Chuldah, as having unappealing names (*Rashi* — מאוסות). Devorah means a bee; Chuldah means a weasel. They allude to something improper; in the case of Devorah, a momentary lapse of superciliousness.

What is so terrible about arrogance that Hashem showed his dissatisfaction with Devorah so quickly and sharply? *Eitz Yosef* suggests that anybody who is haughty is essentially not telling the truth. He is clothing himself in falsehood. And Hashem cannot stand, as it were, to be together with such a person, and thus He must immediately depart. Indeed the Gemara in *Berachos* 6b states that a person who *davens* regularly in the same place will be eulogized as a righteous and humble person. Why humble? The *Tzelach* there explains that every time you *daven* in a place you elevate that spot in sanctity. The next time you pray there, you are more likely to be answered because of that additional holiness. Therefore, a person who regularly returns to pray in that exact spot demonstrates to Hashem that he feels he needs every extra merit possible; on his own, he would be too insignificant to be answered! This is the mark of true humility and the opposite of the arrogant man who says: I can *daven* anywhere and have *my tefillos* accepted.

Our skills and virtues pale in comparison to those of the Almighty — they are, in fact, just small gifts from the Creator. So how can we be excessively proud about possessing such traits? Thus, arrogance represents שקר, *falsehood*, and שקר is incompatible with אמת, *truth*, another name for Hashem.

Of all the possible examples that Hashem could have chosen to illustrate the above, why did He select Devorah? Why not Shmuel HaNavi, who through his own hubris mistakenly thought that Eliav, the oldest son of Yishai, was destined to be anointed the next king of Israel, instead of his less acclaimed younger brother David? Several approaches are suggested by the *Ben Yehoyada*. As opposed to Shmuel, whose arrogance in presupposing that he knew G-d's will was only private, Devorah's Song was very public. Therefore, her loss of prophecy was a clear sign to all observers that such behavior did not sit well with the Almighty. Furthermore, Devorah's indiscretion was immediately punished by the total loss of prophecy; this would be an unequivocable example to all of the severity of haughtiness. Finally, Devorah not only put others down (the previous leaders as well as Barak) but she seemingly raised herself at their expense. This was not the case with Shmuel.

In conclusion, in trying to better comprehend this Gemara, let us consider the following. The value and beauty of a near-perfect diamond is marred much more by a very slight blemish than is a larger defect on a plainer, more flawed stone. The owner will expend significantly greater time, effort and attention to polishing and shining this jewel than the worthless bauble. Chastisement is one way that Hashem cleans and polishes our *neshamos*, the diamond within us.

Pesachim 89a

(See also Nedarim 36a and Gittin 25a)

Zealous Daughters

Similarly, it was taught in a Baraisa*: Once it occurred that a man encouraged his children to hasten to Yerushalayim — the first one to arrive would be rewarded with the merit of accepting the* korban pesach *on the others' behalf. Subsequently, the daughters arrived before the sons. The daughters were zealous and the sons lazy.*

The Mishnah speaks of a man who told his children that whichever one of them reached Yerushalayim first, he would be the one to merit the *korban pesach* on behalf of the others. The Gemara stated that the father did this in order to encourage and stimulate his children to be more zealous in their performance of the *mitzvah*.

Rashi points out that since all the children were actually able to partake in the *pesach* sacrifice, clearly the father's intent was just to encourage the sluggards, but not to restrict them, from participating in his sacrifice.

The Gemara is never bashful or concerned about describing differences between men and women, even when modern society may not consider such descriptions "politically correct." Where a woman is different from a man or vice versa, the Gemara does not "pull its punches" in detailing the contrasts. Nowhere in the Torah does it say that men and women are equal; they are not. Each person and gender has a special role and responsibility to fulfill as part of our service to Hashem. It is up to each of us to see that we do our task properly, and not be distracted (or Heaven forbid tempted) by the American secular world's generic job description for everything. The Divine Torah, and not passing popular fancy, dictate to us the different roles that a man and a woman have.

Pesachim 106b

Rav Assi's Wife—Eating Before Havdalah

Rav Huna said that a person who ate is still permitted to recite Havdalah*; however, Rav Assi is of the opinion that once a person eats he is forbidden to say* Havdalah *that night. Rav Yirmiyah bar Abba came to the home of Rav Assi. He felt faint and ate something (prior to* Havdalah*). They then gave him a cup of wine to recite the* Havdalah*, and he did. Rav Assi's wife said: But you, my husband, do not do that (you forbid a person to recite* Havdalah *after eating). Rav Assi replied: Leave Rav Yirmiyah alone. He is following the opinion of his rebbi.*

This issue is taken up by the Gemara. One is not *allowed* to eat after the conclusion of Shabbos prior to saying *Havdalah*; but if one did in fact eat, can he still recite the blessing?

We see that Rav Assi's wife was quite familiar with the teachings and halachic decisions of her husband. After all, this was not a routine occurrence, and it was only because Rav Yirmiyah felt faint that he ate before *Havdalah*. She therefore must have been well versed in these, and presumably other, halachic matters.

We can also learn that it is important not to embarrass a guest who may follow a different halachic opinion than the host. Both Rav Assi and his wife apparently were careful not to reprove Rav Yirmiyah publicly, and let him act in a manner contrary to their position, rather than embarrass him.

Tosafos ask: Why wasn't Rav Yirmiyah protected from eating before saying *Havdalah*? After all, even the animals of the great *tzaddikim* are protected from eating food prohibited to their masters. How much more so, therefore, does Hashem safeguard the righteous regarding even inadvertent gustatory transgressions. *Tosafos* point out that here, the food itself was not prohibited. It was the timing of the eating that was in error. Shielding from such a sin is not guaranteed.

Rashbam states that Rav Yirmiyah was following the opinion of his rebbi, the great teacher Rav, as recorded in the Gemara above in the name of Rav Huna. *Tosafos* claim that Rav was also Rav Assi's rebbi, and thus Rav Assi must have held the viewpoint that Rav also considered it impermissible to eat and then recite *Havdalah*. Thus Rav Yirmiyah's rebbi must have been Rav Huna himself. *Tosafos* in *Kiddushin* 46a, however, suggest that there were two different Rav Yirmiyahs: one, a *talmid chaver* (disciple almost on the level of the master) who was the colleague of Rav Huna, and another Rav Yirmiyah who was indeed Rav Huna's *talmid*.

Pesachim 108a-b

(see also Sotah 11b)

A Woman's Obligation to Rejoice on Pesach

Rabbi Yehoshua ben Levi said: Women are obligated to drink the four cups of wine (required on the first night of Pesach at the Seder *according to Rabbinical law) because they too were involved in the miracle of the Exodus (from Egypt).*

Tosafos, Meiri, Ran, Mordechai and the *Korban Nesanel,* based upon the Gemara Yerushalmi, all explain that women, too, were slaves in Egypt, and therefore they also are obligated to rejoice and commemorate the Exodus. *Rashi, Rashbam* and other commentators add that it was in the merit of those righteous woman that we were ultimately all redeemed. This is based upon a Gemara in *Sotah* 11b (see there for the details and explanations). The same is said of Chanukah and Purim, when courageous saintly women also saved the Jewish people. (See this *sefer, Shabbos* 23b [end], for a brief discussion of the story of Yehudis on Chanukah. The famous story of how Queen Esther saved the Jewish people is related in the Book of *Esther* which is read twice every Purim.)

Tosafos add that if it weren't for the Rabbinical command to include women, they would not have been required to drink the four cups. It is a time-dependent *mitzvah,* and the rule is that women are exempt from such obligations. However, the Rabbis specifically deemed it desirous to include women in this particular time-dependent precept (even though it will potentially engender hardship in fulfilling their other responsibilities), because of their central role in this Yom Tov.

Pesachim 110a-b

(See also Shabbos 81b, Pesachim 111 and Chullin 105b)

Our Gemara is in the midst of a particularly deep discussion concerning sorcery and demons. This is a very enigmatic subject for us, especially given our technologically sophisticated society and cultural perspective. In brief, two basic approaches are taken by the major Talmudic commentators. (1) These Gemaras are purely allegorical, with deep mystical meaning for those few able to plumb their true depth. (2) Alternatively, at one time true magical powers and abilities existed, bestowed on this world by Hashem. *Rashi*, (*Sanhedrin* 91a) and (*Bereishis* 25:6) comments that the "presents" Avraham Avinu gave to his children from Hagar/Keturah were the knowledge and mastery of these mystical powers of sorcery and magic. Over the centuries, these abilities have been lost, or attenuated, to the point that they no longer are in our realm of existence to any recognizable extent. Thus, up until the times of the Mishnah or thereabouts (circa 200 C.E.) these forces were present and practical consideration was required in dealing with them. This included the knowledge of various incantations and practices meant to prevent or allay damage caused by these forces. Thereafter, and certainly by the conclusion of the Talmudic period (circa 500 C.E.) the practical applications of these Gemaras was greatly lessened if not totally unnecessary.

The following selections should be read with the above introduction in mind. The interested reader is referred to the superb overview on this subject, found in the Schottenstein Edition of the Talmud Bavli, beginning on *Pesachim* page 109b note 8.

WITCHCRAFT AND SORCERY

Ameimar said: The chief sorceress told me: One who encounters women engaged in sorcery (and is concerned about harm they might do to him) should state the following incantation: "Let hot excrement in torn (punctured) baskets be placed in your mouths, you sorceresses. Let your hair be plucked out, let your bread crumbs, spices, and fresh saffron fly away. While I had my favor and your favor I did not come among you. Now, however, that I have come among you, it is apparent that this favor has cooled."

There once was a man who divorced his wife. Subsequently, she married a store owner. Every day her ex-husband would drink wine there and his former wife attempted to work witchcraft upon him, but she was unsuccessful, because he was careful not to drink "pairs." Once, however, he drank a lot and lost track of how many cups he had drunk. After sixteen glasses, his thinking became unclear, and he was not careful in his count, and left the store having drunk an even number of cups. Upon leaving, he met an Arab who remarked, "A dead man walks here." The ex-husband grasped a palm tree. The palm tree shriveled up and he burst.

BEFORE I EXPLAIN THE DEEPER MEANING OF THIS UNUSUAL GEMARA, let us understand the basic *pshat* (explanation) of the words:

Your hair — with which you perform magic (*Rashi* and *Rambam*).

Bread crumbs — with which you perform magic (*Rashi*). The *Rashbam* also mentions this but then, on the basis of a verse in *Yechezkel* (13:20), suggests that it may refer to an instrument of witchcraft.

My favor — when Heaven had mercy on me and when I took care (*Rashi* and *Rambam*).

Has cooled — It no longer exists.

Store owner — Her ex-husband was accustomed to drink there (*Rabbeinu Chananel*).

"Pairs" — two cups or multiples of two cups

A palm tree — because he was ill and worried, he used it for support.

The palm tree shriveled up and he burst; the *Rashbam* has a version that the tree cried out and burst. He understands this to mean that the palm shriveled from the force of witchcraft.

There is a controversy whether the Torah prohibition against sorcery applies to non-Jews. According to the opinion in *Sanhedrin* 91a that even gentiles are included in the prohibition, how could Avraham have given his children these powers? *Tosafos* ask further: How is it permitted to use *pesukim* to heal oneself ? It is forbidden to do so. Both *Tosafos* and the *Maharal* (*Gur Aryeh*) give the same answer. Prevention is different (see Gemara *Shevuos* 15). Avraham gave his progeny the abilities to understand and ward off harm from the forces of magic. Unfortunately, his descendants used those powers for evil and improper practices. So too, one is permitted to state *pesukim* to prevent harm from happening. Alternatively, *Tosafos* suggest that the prohibition doesn't apply to a person in mortal danger (see *Tosafosm, Shevuos* 15b).

The Torah forbids witchcraft upon pain of death: *You shall not permt a sorceress to live* (*Shemos* 22:17). The female form מכשפה is used. *Rashi, Ibn Ezra, Baal HaTurim* and others remark (based upon the Gemara *Sanhedrin* 91a) that sorcery was more frequently practiced by women than by men. Thus even though the prohibition applies to both genders, the female form is used. So too, in the Gemara, most examples of witchcraft involve women.

Finally, I heard a *shiur* from HaRav Yissachar Frand *shlita,* in which he gave a fascinating etymological derivation for the incantation "*abra cadabra.*" Transliterated in Aramaic, the language of the Gemara, *abra cadabra* becomes אברא כדברא. Translated, that means "I created as I spoke," possibly a lame allusion by the magician to the fact that Hashem created the world from nothingness by simply speaking!

Pesachim 111a-b

(See also Pesachim 110a-b and Chullin 105b)

DEMONS AND SORCERY

A niddah *(a menstruating woman) passing between two men — if she is in the beginning of her period, she may cause the death of one of the men; if she is at the end of her period, she will precipitate a quarrel among the men. What is the antidote for prevention of this witchcraft? Recite certain* pesukim *(referring to sorcery) that begin and end with the word* אל*. Two women sitting at a crossroad, one on each side of the path, with their faces directly opposite each other — surely are performing witchcraft. What is the remedy (for a passerby for protection)? Preferably, take an alternate road. If there is no other route, if there is a companion traveling with you, hold hands as you pass by the women. If that is not possible (there is no other person walking with you), say the following incantation: "Agras, Azlas, Asiya, and Belusya have already been slain with a crossbow."*

One who encounters a woman at the time that she ascends from her required immersion, if he first engages in marital relations, a spirit of immorality will rest upon him. If she first engages in relations, the immorality will rest on her. What should these people do to prevent such harm (once their paths have inadvertently crossed)? Recite certain pesukim *...*

A female demon told her son: Fly away from a service-tree, for that tree killed your father and it will kill you as well (if you are not careful).

THE GEMARA CONTINUES RELATING VARIOUS POTENTIAL DANGERS associated with demons, in a discussion begun on the previous *daf.* See the commentary to this topic there.

Tosafos explain that concern exists only regarding women who are actively trying to cause damage through witchcraft. *Ben Yehoyada* adds that there are certain demons who can only cause their harm under very specific settings, as in the case described in the Gemara. However, *Ben Yehoyada,* who was known for his deep knowledge of matters pertaining to the supernatural and Kabbalistic realms, clearly writes that these forces have essentially lost their sway today and we are not as concerned with them as we once were.

See *Rashbam, Tosafos* and others for details regarding which *pesukim* are to be recited.

I heard in a *shiur* from HaRav Mordechai Gifter *zt"l* that this story in the Gemara has particular meaning in our time. In the Book of *Lamentations* (*Eichah* 1:8), Yirmiyahu HaNavi refers to Jerusalem "becoming a *niddah.*" HaRav Gifter explained that this is actually a blessing from Hashem to the Jewish people. We are today at the end of the "*niddah* period" of the Jewish people — i.e. the days of the long exile are coming to an end, and the Moshiach will, please G-d, quickly in our time, soon be here. The State of Israel is surrounded by many bellicose nations ("men") who want to harm us. However, Hashem causes them to "quarrel amongst themselves," like the men between whom the woman in the terminal days of her menstruation passes. In quarreling they are distracted from their destructive desires against Israel.

PESACHIM 112B

(See also Berachos 8b)

THE DEMON AGRAS

Rabbeinu HaKadosh (Rabbi Yehudah HaNasi, "Rebbi," the redactor/editor of the Mishnah) gave instructions to his children about four things ... (the second of which was): Do not sit upon the bed of an Aramean woman. Some explain this statement to mean: Do not go to sleep without reciting the Shema. *Some say it means: Do not marry a female convert to Judaism. Others take it literally: Do not sit upon an Aramean woman's bed, because of the incident involving Rav Pappa ...*

Rabbi Yose ben Rabbi Yehudah gave instruction to Rebbi about three things ... (the first of which was): Do not go out alone at night ... as it is stated in a Baraisa: *Do not go out alone at night, especially on Tuesday and Friday evenings, because of the demon Agras bas Machlas (see above,* Pesachim 111a-b*). She and 180,000 destroying angels go out then, and each one itself has the power to cause damage. Originally, these destroyers were prevalent all the time, but on one occasion, Agras met Rabbi Chanina ben Dosa and told him, "If it weren't decreed in Heaven to beware of Chanina and his Torah, I would put you in danger." He replied to her, "If I am so important in Heaven, I hereby ordain that you shall no longer pass in the inhabited parts of the world." She begged Rabbi Chanina for at least a little room for leeway, and he gave her Friday and Tuesday evenings. Furthermore, she once met Abaye and told him, "If it weren't decreed in Heaven to beware of Nachmani*

*(*Rashbam — *Abaye was an orphan raised in the house of Rabbah bar Nachmani, and he was thus also referred to as Nachmani) and his Torah, I would put you in danger." He replied to her, "If I am so important in Heaven, I hereby decree that, forever, you shall no longer pass in the inhabited parts of the world."*

R*ASHI* AND *RASHBAM* EXPLAIN WHAT TRANSPIRED BETWEEN RAV Pappa and the Aramean woman that caused Rebbi to caution his children regarding an Aramean bed. (See this *sefer, Berachos* 8b, for variants of, and commentary on, the story.)

Rabbi Chanina ben Dosa is famous as a man of great piety and righteousness — even the heavens declare: The entire world is sustained because of Chanina My son, and Chanina My son is satisfied with just carobs (*Tannis* 24b). (See *Tannis* 24b till the end of the third *perek* for more stories illustrating Rabbi Chanina's greatness.) It is therefore not surprising that Rabbi Chanina and Abaye (see *Rosh Hashanah* 18a) were able to defeat and limit a powerful demon like Agras. The restriction to Tuesday and Friday evenings was a wonderful boon for the Jewish people. The *Midrash Rabbah* and the Gemara (*Taanis* 23a) comment that when the Jewish people follow the will of Hashem, the rains come in an opportune time, when everybody is safe in their homes (Tuesday and Friday nights) so that the downpour will not disturb them. Thus, since most people were secure in their homes during this period, even if Agras held sway at these times, she could do only minimal damage. Jews rarely traveled during these particular nights. There was no Torah reading Wednesday morning which would require people to come to town from the nearby villages on Tuesday evening, and people could not travel far Friday night due to Shabbos.

Who was Agras? *Maharsha* suggests that her mother's name, Machlas, is specifically mentioned to clue us in as to her origin. Machlas is mentioned in the Torah as the daughter of Yishmael who eventually married Esau. Of Esau's first two Canaanite wives it is written: ותהיין מרת רוח, *and they were a provocation of the spirit (Bereishis* 26:35). However, taken literally, the *posuk* can be translated: and they had (bore) evil spirits — they gave birth to demons. A similar idea is brought down regarding Adam HaRishon, the first man. After his sin, Adam did not have conjugal relations with Chava for 130 years. During this time, however, he sired (created) demons. The *Maharsha* suggests that Agras was possibly such a creature created from the liaison of Machlas and Esau. However, the *posuk* only speaks of Esau's first two wives and not Machlas. One must conclude that according to the *Maharsha*, the *posuk* includes her as well.

מסכת שקלים

SHEKALIM

SHEKALIM

SHEKALIM 6B

(See also Nedarim 49b)

WOMEN'S STRINGENCIES

(**Note:** Gemara *Shekalim* is actually only extant in the Talmud Yerushalmi, the Jerusalem Talmud; it is not actually part of the Talmud Bavli. However, by convention, the *daf yomi* learning cycle incorporates this tractate alone from the Yerushalmi, otherwise it would be the only tractate in all of *Seder Moed* not learned with Gemara. Therefore, we have incorporated it in this *sefer* as well.)

> *Rabbi Yonah said: One is able to fulfill the commandment (i.e. the Rabbinical precept to drink four cups of wine on Pesach night at the* Seder*) with "cooked" wine. Rabbi Yonah is consistent in this lenient position — since when Rabbi Yonah would drink the four* Seder *cups of wine, he would get a headache that lasted till the next holiday (Shavuos). A certain woman (from the Aramean officers or leaders —* Korban HaEidah*) noticed Rabbi Yonah's shining complexion, and called to him, "Old man! Old man! One of three things must have caused your redness. Either you are a drinker, a lender with interest, or you are involved in swine husbandry." Rabbi Yonah retorted, "Let*

the spirit of that woman swell up! Not even one of those reasons is correct. My face is so ruddy because of my learning, as the posuk (Koheles 8:1) *states:* A man's wisdom illuminates his face."

The Gemara in *Nedarim* (49b and Berachos 55a) relates a very similar story which transpired with Rabbi Yehudah (bar Ilai). An aristocratic woman asked Rabbi Yehudah how was it possible for a teacher and scholar to be a drunkard like him (because he was so rosy-faced). He insisted that she must believe him that the only wine he imbibed was that of the *Kiddush*, *Havdalah*, and the four cups on Pesach. And the latter was so painful to him that he had to bind his head until Shavuos as a result of the agonizing headache he suffered from drinking that night! Subsequently, the Gemara there relates how a certain Tzedoki observed Rabbi Yehudah's flushed glow, and likewise remarked, "Your face has the appearance of a lender with interest or a person involved in swine husbandry." Rabbi Yehudah replied that according to Jewish law, both of these professions are forbidden. His face was only shining because of his regular usage of the many bathrooms on the way to the house of study. (i.e. Rabbi Yehuda attributes his ruddines to regularly examining himself to see if he required to use the bathroom.)

Both of these narratives are also written in the Talmud Yerushalmi (Shabbos, Chapter 8, *Halachah* 1), and a combined version is found as well in the *Midrash Rabbah* (*Koheles*, Chapter 8:1,4).

We have previously discussed (*Berachos* 8b and *Pesachim* 112b) the hatred Aramean women had for the Rabbis, so it is not surprising that this noblewoman spoke disparagingly to Rabbi Yonah. Likewise, the Tzedokim had an intrinsic abhorrence for all that the Rabbis stood for.

Excessive alcohol intake certainly can precipitate a lustrous ruddy complexion. How does lending with interest and pig-raising cause a rosy appearance? Both the *Korban HaEidah* and the *Taklin Chaditin* explain that these are very easy professions. One does not have to work overly hard to garner a significant financial profit at these tasks. Both items (money and the swine) work day and night on behalf of their owner, without undue effort or exertion by the owner. Hence, they account for the ruddy health of the owner. Rabbi Yonah answered that Torah study has the same outcome. Torah is like a fine wine that gladdens the heart. Intensive learning broadens the mind and increases mental capacity, thereby permitting even deeper understanding and happiness. Thus Torah can also induce the identical corporeal benefits and pleasures that wine and wealth bring about.

Taklin Chaditin also points out that Rabbi Yonah (and Rabbi Yehudah) allowed one to fulfill the obligation of the four cups with cooked wine even though cooked wine was not permitted to be used for sacrificial libations. Cooked wine was less strong than regular wine and less intoxicating, and thus was preferred by Rabbi Yonah as his benedictal beverage. This important leniency helps form the basis for permitting sweetened and pasteurized wines/grape juice to be used today for *Kiddush* and at the Pesach *Seder* (see *Bava Basra* 97a, *Tosafos* ad loc., s.v. *e'layma*).

Why was the response of Rabbi Yonah different than the reply of Rabbi Yehudah regarding the explanation of their facial illumination? Both answers were indeed correct, but why not give the same response to the Aramean woman and the Tzedoki? *Ben Yehoyada* writes (in *Nedarim*) that it would have been improper for a man to discuss such private personal details (i.e. his bathroom hygiene and habits) with a woman. Similarly, the Tzedoki would not have believed that Torah study could possibly have resulted in such physical benefit, whereas the Aramean woman indeed accepted this rejoinder. Thus each Rabbi gave an explanation appropriate to the questioner, teaching us the proper way a person should always respond. Sometimes the best answer for one individual will be unacceptable for another. We thus learn an important idea and practical life attitude from a seemingly quaint anecdote.

(Author's note: I did find a difficulty with this last answer of the Ben Yehoyada however. The gemara in berachos [55a] also relates the identical story of Rabbi Yehuda and his regular bathroom usage — but there the questioner was a "matroniasa" — a noblewoman. Apparently, it was not improper to discuss his personal hygiene with the noblewoman; or possibly, the Ben Yehoyada had a different text in the gemara.).

מסכת ראש השנה

ROSH HASHANAH

Rosh Hashanah

Rosh Hashanah 17b

(see also Yevamos 46a)

BELORIA THE CONVERT

Beloria the convert asked Rabban Gamliel: It states in your *Torah* (Devarim 10:17): Hashem does not show favoritism, *yet it also states* (Bamidbar 6:26): Hashem will show favor to you *(the Jewish people). How do you reconcile these apparently contradictory verses? Rabbi Yose the* Kohen *jumped in and answered with a parable. To what is this comparable? To a person who has a claim against his friend for a* maneh *(a denomination of money). In front of the king, they agreed on a time of repayment. And furthermore, the debtor swears by the king's life that he will repay at that time. When the time to repay comes, however, he does not have the funds to reimburse the creditor. The debtor comes to appease the king (for taking the king's name in vain —* She'iltos 66*), and the king replies to him: For causing my embarrassment, you are forgiven. Now go and apologize to the creditor for not repaying him. Here too, Rabbi Yose the* Kohen *tells Beloria: Hashem,* so to say, *plays favorites — but only in regard to sins between man and G-d. He does not look the other way though in matters of transgression between man and his fellow man.*

BELORIA'S CONVERSION IS BRIEFLY DISCUSSED IN THE GEMARA IN *Yevamos* 46a. She is called a convert there even before she actually becomes a Jewess. Here too, it is probable that this event occurred in her pre-Jewish days, as she refers to the Torah as "your" Torah, not "our" Torah.

Tosafos note that there really is no contradiction between the verses. The first verse alludes to Hashem as a judge Who will not be swayed or fooled by riches, greatness, respectability or age in one of the litigants. The second *posuk,* though, refers to Hashem Himself electing to turn a pleasant countenance to you. *Maharatz Chayes* builds on this theme. In the first verse (stating that Hashem will not display favoritism), Hashem's role is the equivalent of a judge between two litigants. He thus cannot demonstrate favor for one over the other. This is the scenario of a transgression between man and man. However, in the second *posuk* dealing with sins between man and G-d, Hashem appears as if He is the equivalent of one of the litigants. And a litigant can always willingly renounce his rights and demands, defer what is his due, if he chooses to do so. Thus, here, Hashem has seemingly elected to voluntarily look the other way, because it is only His honor that is at stake.

Iyun Yaakov comments that Hashem will not even consider forgiving a person till the sinner has rectified the error with his fellow man first. Only then will Hashem become involved and forgive the transgressor. This is indeed the *halachah* regarding performing *teshuvah* for sins between man and man. Before one can approach the Almighty on Yom Kippur and ask forgiveness, one must first appease the injured person.

Rabban Gamliel was originally asked the question — why did Rabbi Yose respond in his place? *Ben Yehoyada* opines that since he was a *Kohen,* who recites the first verse daily as part of the priestly blessing, he felt it appropriate to speak up and provide the answer. The proof of this is from the Gemara itself. Why is his priestly lineage mentioned? Normally the Gemara does not routinely provide us with such data. It therefore must be to illustrate this point.

Rosh Hashanah 19a

(see also Taanis 18a)

THE MATRONISA'S WISE ADVICE

Rav Tovi bar Masnah quotes a section from the Tannaic work Megillas Taanis *as part of a proof. (*Megillas Taanis *was written by the Tanna Chananyah ben Chizkiyah. It describes many minor holidays that the Sages established during the Second Temple era to commemorate miracles and great events that occurred to the Jewish people).*

On the twenty-eighth day of the month of Adar, good news was brought to the Jews. (An evil decree was lifted.) They would not have to stop learning Torah. The secular (Roman) government had originally decreed that Jews were forbidden to engage in Bible study, were not permitted to circumcise their children, and were required to desecrate the Shabbos. What did Yehudah ben Shamua and his colleagues do (about this harsh law)? They went and sought counsel from a certain non-Jewish matronisa *(noblewoman), who was frequently visited by many senior officials of the Roman government. This* matronisa *told Rabbi Yehudah and the Rabbis to go out and demonstrate in the nighttime. They followed her advice, and protested and cried out against the evil decrees. They said:* אי שמים*, For Heaven's sake. Aren't we your brothers? Aren't we the sons of the same father (Yitzchak —* Maharsha*)? Aren't we the sons of the same mother (Rivkah —* Maharsha*)? Why are we singled out from all the other nations under Roman rule to have such harsh decrees promulgated against us? The demonstration was successful — the Romans abolished those anti-Jewish* *laws, and the Rabbis established the twenty-eighth of Adar as a (minor) holiday.*

LITTLE IS KNOWN ABOUT THIS ROMAN NOBLEWOMAN (NOT EVEN HER name!), except that she clearly was from the righteous gentiles of the world. *Ben Yehoyada* provides a more complete picture of her *chessed* (kindness). She told Rabbi Yehudah and the Jewish leaders to protest at night near her house — not at the seat of the secular government, or in the neighborhood of the officials, but in her home area. Why? She was accustomed to having many of the secular leaders at her house, and that very night there was to be a large gathering of them as well. A demonstration would certainly attract their attention, and would be the subject of heated discussion amongst the leaders. During the debate, she could nonchalantly state her opinion that the Jews were not a threat, and that the decrees were unfair and should be abolished. Her opinion was highly valued and would probably be listened to, and the problem would be solved. However, if she had gone directly to the government and voiced her thoughts, then she would have been seen as just another "paid lobbyist" advocating her (bought!) opinion, and possibly she would have been ignored, with calamitous outcome for the Jews. This way, her advice appeared spontaneous and from the heart, and it was accepted.

Why did she suggest a nighttime demonstration? *Ben Yehoyada* exposits that she (and the Romans!) knew that many miracles were specifically wrought for the Jews over their tormentors at night. Yaakov defeated the angel of Eisav at night. Avraham defeated the four kings then. Sarah was saved from the lecherous advances of Pharaoh and Avimelech at night. The tenth plague (the killing of the Egyptian firstborns) was at midnight. Sancheirev's siege of Yerushalayim was foiled at night, and the miracle of Purim transpired when the wicked King Achashveirosh was unable to sleep at night. She thus wished to subtly remind her gentile colleagues of this history, hoping they themselves would relent out of self-preservation to avoid possible defeat. *Eitz Yosef* suggests that the Jews were publicly proclaiming their lack of animosity towards their Roman brothers. Crying at night is especially heart-rending, and she correctly assessed that even the cruel Romans would be moved by such a plea. *Maharsha* provides a practical consideration. In the pre-microphone epoch, their voices would carry better and be more clearly heard in the still of night than during the hustle and bustle of a busy day.

Finally, why was the preamble "For Heaven's sake" cried out? *Ben Yehoyada* notes that the word שמים (Heavens) is comprised of the Hebrew words אש (fire) and מים (water). When Hashem created the Heavens, He combined these two protagonists and forced them to co-exist in peace and tranquility. So too, by their cry of אי שמים, "For Heaven's sake," they were alluding to the constant antagonism that Eisav displays towards Yaakov. Why can't we also live together in harmony like the fire and water of the Heavens! *Tosafos* in *Taanis* (18a) comments that the words "For Heaven's sake" were directed to Hashem in שמים. They were shouting and crying to Hashem: Why should the gentile nations say, "Where is your G-d?" Hashem, save us.

ROSH HASHANAH 25A

WOMEN AND ROSH CHODESH: A SPECIAL HOLIDAY

The Rabbis taught in a Baraisa*: One time on the twenty-ninth day of the month, the skies were covered with clouds. It appeared to the people that the New Moon was visible; they thought that Rosh Chodesh should be declared, and they wanted the court to sanctify the new month. Rabban Gamliel said to them: I have a tradition from the house of my father's father. The New Moon cannot occur prior to twenty-nine and a half days, two-thirds of an hour, plus seventy-three* chalakim *(a* chelek *— singular of* chalakim *— is one-eighteenth of a minute). That day, it happened that the mother of Ben Zaza died, and Rabban Gamliel eulogized her with a lengthy panegyric. He did so not because she merited such a distinguished eulogy, but in order to clearly establish publicly and make everyone aware that the* Beis Din *had not sanctified the new month.*

R*ASHI* EXPLAINS THAT IT IS FORBIDDEN TO DELIVER A EULOGY ON A holiday. Thus, by publicly giving a long and great homage on this day, Rabban Gamliel vividly demonstrated that the day could not be Rosh Chodesh.

As nothing happens accidentally, why did Hashem cause the eulogy to be for a woman, and not a man? Why was specifically the death of a woman the mechanism for publicizing this *halachah*?

This may be an allusion to the famous episode of the sin of the Golden Calf, cited by *Tosafos* on *Rosh Hashanah* 23a from the

Gemara in *Megillah* 22b. *Tosafos* remark that the celebration of Rosh Chodesh and making it as a holiday by not working on that day is observed by women especially, and not as much by men. Rosh Chodesh was especially designated for the women since they refused to participate in the horrendous transgression of making and serving the Golden Calf. When they were asked to donate their gold and precious metals for completion of its construction, the women refused while the men gave theirs freely. As a reward, women were given Rosh Chodesh. Thus, Hashem desired the demonstration of Rabban Gamliel's ruling to come about through a woman.

Rosh Hashanah 26b

(see also Eruvin 53b; Megillah 18a; Moed Katan 17a; Kesubos 104a)

Rebbi's Maidservant

The Gemara is in the midst of a series of linguistic forays that are based upon the understanding of certain pesukim. *The maidservant of the great Rebbi, Rabbi Yehudah HaNasi, explains four such complex translations to the Rabbis. As their derivation is technical and dry, we will not detail the actual Gemara here.*

The famous maidservant of Rebbi was obviously an accomplished linguist and is described in the Gemara (*Eruvin* 53b) as being quite clever and verbally adept [literally: she spoke in the language of wisdom]. The Rabbis clearly respected her, going so far as to accept her placing a person under a Rabbinical ban for three years (*Moed Katan* 17a). Her devotion and admiration of Rebbi are also legendary, as described in *Kesubos* 104a.

Rosh Hashanah 31b

Ameimar's Beis Din

There was a certain woman who was summoned to court to appear before the Beis Din *of Ameimar in the city of Nehardea. Subsequently, Ameimar moved to the city of Mechoza. Although she was now required to do so, this woman was not willing to follow him to that town. Ameimar therefore wrote a document excommunicating her for refusing to submit to the* Beis Din's *summons. Rav Ashi questioned Ameimar, "We have learned (in the Mishnah earlier on the* daf*) that even if the head of the court travels elsewhere, the witnesses (coming to testify about the New Moon) are not obligated to follow him. Instead, they only have to go to the regularly scheduled place of the* Beis Din. *Why, then, do you compel this woman to follow you to Mechoza?" Ameimar answered Rav Ashi, "This rule is specifically only for New Moon testimony. If we were to create too many difficulties for them, we would create a stumbling block for the future (they will be reluctant to come next time if we put them through too much). However, in regard to financial claims, the rule is:* the borrower is a servant to the lender (Mishlei 22:7). *This woman must therefore submit herself and appear in the court wherever it convenes."*

R*ASHI* COMMENTS THAT EVEN THOUGH WE NORMALLY PREFER THAT the head of the court preside over the New Moon declaration, we are willing to forgo this so as not to unnecessarily inconvenience and burden the witnesses. They are doing us a favor by coming to testify, and we want to make their task as easy as possible. This is, in fact, a general court principle, and is the rule in our relationships with our fellow man. Yet, the Rabbis deemed that in regard to monetary loans, the opposite effect would occur if the same rule were applied blindly. The Sages wished to encourage lending to poor people. If we were to allow the borrower to decide to refuse to appear at the court of the lender's choice and location, this would inhibit charitable actions. For this reason, *Chazal*, following the *posuk* in *Mishlei*, decreed that the debtor must follow the lender.

מסכת יומא

YOMA

YOMA

YOMA 18A

(See also Gittin 56a and Yevamos 61a)

MARTA — WIFE OF THE KOHEN GADOL — WHAT IS TRUE WEALTH?

(The Gemara is in the midst of a discussion regarding the fact that during the Second Temple period, many of the Kohanim Gedolim *were not worthy of their position, and in reality often procured the job only via bribery and other illicit methods. This was not the case during the First Temple period, when the* Kohen Gadol *was invariably the greatest of the* Kohanim.*)*

And Rav Assi (Rav Yosef — according to the version of this story in the Ein Yaakov*) said (as a proof that the High Priesthood was often obtained illegally in the Second Temple period): Marta the daughter of Baitus gave three* kavim *(a large volume) of gold* dinarim *to King Yannai in order that Yannai appoint her husband, Yehoshua ben Gamla, as the* Kohen Gadol.

This story is also appended by the Bach (addendum aleph*) to the standard text of the Gemara in Yoma 9a.*

RASHI TELLS US THAT MARTA WAS A WEALTHY WIDOW WHEN SHE married Yehoshua. Subsequently she bribed King Yannai with this considerable present so she could become the wife of the *Kohen Gadol.*

Normally, the *Kohen Gadol* is prohibited to marry a widow. However, the Gemara in *Yevamos* 61a states that prior to Yehoshua becoming the *Kohen Gadol,* Marta was already married (albeit incompletely) to Yehoshua. Though they had only undergone the first stage of marriage known as *kiddushin,* they were halachically considered married, and the law is that a regular *Kohen* is permitted to marry a widow. Thus, she was allowed to remain married to the *Kohen Gadol* even though she was a widow.

Tosafos point out that this King Yannai should not be confused with a different King Yannai discussed previously in this *sefer* in *Berachos* 48a. That King Yannai was of Hasmonean (a priestly family) descent and simultaneously served as a *Kohen Gadol* for eighty years (against the wishes of the Rabbis). That Yannai would certainly not have voluntarily given over the High Priesthood to Yehoshua.

Yehoshua ben Gamla became the *Kohen Gadol* as a result of his wife's bribe. This fits in well with the Gemara in *Yevamos* that states he was not truly deserving of being selected, but was only appointed to the position. Yet, we find elsewhere in *Yoma,* as well as in other places in the Gemara, that Yehoshua was a very well respected personage, a truly great man. Yehoshua is recorded as donating beautiful golden boxes to the *Beis HaMikdash* to replace wooden containers previously used in the Yom Kippur lottery to decide which goat would be sacrificed in the Holy area, and which would be sent out of the Temple to Azazel. Furthermore, the Gemara in *Bava Basra* (21a) documents that the name of Yehoshua ben Gamla should always be remembered favorably, for if not for him, the Torah would possibly have been forgotten! He was the innovator of the first communal Yeshiva program. Until his time, fathers were the sole teachers of their children. But Yehoshua saw that there were many orphans (and others) who were not receiving appropriate education. As a result, he established the first system of public classes for all students. Thus, how could a man of his stature and holiness have accepted the High Priesthood if it was acquired improperly? The *Ritva* in *Ein Yaakov* gives several possible solutions. Initially, Yehoshua indeed was not worthy of the position, just like many of his predecessors and contemporaries. However, he grew into the position, and matured into a great sage. Alternatively, the *Ritva* suggests that there were two different men named Yehoshua ben Gamla. The one mentioned in *Bava Basra,* and later in *Yoma,* is not the same Yehoshua mentioned on our *daf.* Finally, the *Ritva* posits an answer that both the *Maharsha* and the *Tosafos Yeshanim* also consider. Yehoshua ben Gamla was in reality a great man with the credentials to be the *Kohen Gadol.* However, in his generation, there were several people even more deserving of the honor and title. Since he therefore did not meet the stringent requirement of becoming the *Kohen Gadol* — being the great<u>est</u> of the current *Kohanim* — the Gemara views his ascension to the High Priesthood in a somewhat negative fashion.

Yad Yosef in the *Ein Yaakov* takes a diametrically opposite approach. Yehoshua indeed knew that he was the most deserving person for the job, and if anyone else had received the High Priesthood it would have been a travesty. Plus, the chosen person, if not worthy, would not have lived out the year, as occurred with the majority of the unsuitable *Kohanim Gedolim* of the Second Temple period. Thus, Yehoshua asked his wife to bribe Yannai so that *he* would be selected. In this fashion, justice would be served, and an incompetent, possibly heretic *Kohen* would not be chosen! Similarly, *Ben Yehoyada* agrees that Yehoshua is the same righteous individual described elsewhere in *Shas.* How could he have gone along with this charade? *Ben Yehoyada* responds that, in fact, he didn't! Yehoshua was totally unaware that his wife bribed Yannai! She desired to become the wife of the *Kohen Gadol*, a prestigious social position, and she payed Yannai off for this privilege. But Yehoshua himself never participated in the deception, and he was not even cognizant of its existence.

Who was Marta bas Baitus? She is mentioned in the Gemara in *Yevamos* described above, but she is more famously known from a Gemara in *Gittin* (56a) studied by Jews all over the world on Tishah B'Av — the story of Kamtza and Bar Kamtza, and the destruction of the *Beis HaMikdash*. Marta was a very wealthy woman, accustomed to the finest delicacies and an aristocratic way of life. When the terrible famine resulting from the siege of Yerushalayim engulfed the city in the days immediately prior to its destruction, Marta ordered her servants to obtain fine flour for her. Alas, none was to be found; she was willing to settle for even coarser and less expensive food, but still her attendants could not obtain even this. She finally had to go out herself to search for food. Not being used to such mundane activities, the Gemara relates that she died a very ignoble death. Either she stepped in some excrement (she was of such a delicate nature that she could not survive this additional insult and affront to her life) or she died after eating a certain fruit that the great Rabbi Tzadok had discarded after sucking out its nutrition. Rabbi Tzadok fasted for the forty years leading up to the *Churban* (the destruction), surviving only by daily sucking out the juice and nutrition from a date. The remaining dried up shell was somehow dangerous to one's health, and it was this fruit that killed Marta.

Finally, there is also a Gemara Yerushalmi (*Kesubos* 38b; *Halachah* 5:11) that records Marta in a less than enviable manner. Upon the death of her first husband, the childless Marta was waiting to undergo the Levirate marriage. That is a procedure whereby her dead husband's brother would either marry her or perform the *Chalitzah* ceremony — a process akin to divorce — required of a (childless) widow if she does not marry her brother-in-law. The *Beis Din* meanwhile established certain financial entitlements for her from the estate of her late husband, but she was unhappy with the settlement, and spoke harshly against the Rabbis. The Sages remarked that she would undoubtedly receive her proper "reward," which she eventually did at the time of the *Churban*. Money can purchase a lot of trinkets and worldly items, but ultimately it is of little true value when measured by Divine standards.

YOMA 25A

(See also Yoma 35b and 47a)

A MOTHER'S TUNIC

Rav Huna bar Yehudah or alternatively Rav Shmuel bar Yehudah taught: After the Kohen Gadol *completed the initial series of Yom Kippur services inside the* Heichal *and Holy of Holies wearing the special four linen garments specific for these activities, he was able to replace those garments with a tunic that his mother made for him.*

THIS GEMARA IS QUOTED FROM A LENGTHIER DISCUSSION ON YOMA 35b. Please see there in this *sefer* regarding its commentary.

YOMA 29A

(see also Megillah 15b)

QUEEN ESTHER THE RIGHTEOUS

Rabbi Avahu said: Why did Rebbi (Rabbi Yehudah HaNasi) say that at dawn the sun's rays are diffused in all directions? It is based upon the posuk *in* Tehillim (22:1) :למנצח על אילת השחר, For the conductor, about the morning hind *(a type of deer or antelope).*

Just as this hind has antlers that diverge here and there (in all directions), so too does the morning sun (שחר) *shine in all directions.*

Rabbi Zeira said: Why is Esther compared to a morning hind? To teach us that just as the hind has a narrow womb, and is very desired by her mate every time just as she was the first time, so too Esther was as desirable to Achashveirosh every time just as she was the first time.

Rav Assi said: Why is Esther compared to a morning hind? To teach us that just as the morning sun comes at the end of the entire night, so too were the miraculous events at the time of Esther the conclusion of the epoch of miracles. But how could Purim represent the concluding miracle? What about Chanukah? (The story of Purim occurred between the two Temples; the Chanukah miracle transpired several hundred years later in the middle of the Second Temple period.) The Gemara answers that the Chanukah story (i.e. the Book of Hasmoneans or the Maccabees) is not incorporated as part of the Holy Writings (the twenty-four Holy Books that comprise Tanach*). Now this explanation accords with the opinion* *that* Esther *is included (as we in fact hold today). But what about the viewpoint that attests that Esther is not Biblically included as part of the* Tanach*? Why, according to this opinion, is Esther compared to a morning hind? The Gemara responds that this position expounds the word* שחר *as did Rabbi Binyamin bar Yefes in the name of Rabbi Elazar, as follows: Why are the prayers of the righteous compared to the morning hind? To teach us that just as the antlers of the hind continuously grow in its lifetime, so too the prayers of the righteous (i.e. Esther) will always be heard all the time they* daven.

THIS ALLEGORICAL GEMARA REQUIRES INTENSIVE STUDY IN ORDER FOR us to begin to comprehend the depths of the words of *Chazal.*

Rashi, quoting the Gemara in *Megillah* 15b, states that Esther was the author of this Psalm, which she recited to save the Jewish people when she went unsummoned to see her wicked husband, King Achashveirosh. *Rashi* notes that the female hind actually has no antlers; the Gemara just uses the species to make its point. *Hagahos Yavetz* disagrees, and says that *Rashi* erred here — the female does have antlers. *Ben Yehoyada* suggests that according to *Rashi,* the *posuk* should have mentioned the male hind if that is what was truly intended. Thus, he explains that the female term is specifically used here so as not to mistakenly think the *posuk* is referring to a ram (*ayil* — איל) rather than the hind (*ayal* —איל). By using the feminine form — אילת — no error can be made.

Maharsha questions the entire analogy. After all, usually the day is a reference to good things, whereas the night represents the conclusion of good and the onset of evil. Here, it is the exact opposite! *Maharsha* notes that the famous song, "And it was in the middle of the night," which is recited on Pesach night at the conclusion of the *Seder,* beautifully provides the answer. The liturgy there lists an array of amazing miracles that occurred at midnight, including the story of Achashveirosh being unable to sleep one night, and his summoning forth his aides to read for him — and miraculously the story of Mordechai saving his life is related. Thus it is very appropriate to use night as the analogy for miracles, with the early morning signifying its closure. This explanation likewise fits perfectly well into the Gemara regarding the exclusion of Chanukah from the *Tanach*. The poet here likewise does not relate the miracle of the lights of Chanukah, which of course occurred at night, even though he enumerates all the other nighttime miracles. *Chida* adds that Chanukah occurred after the period of prophecy and Divine Spirit, and thus could not be included as part of the Holy Scriptures.

Maharsha further states that the comparison with the sun is most appropriate. Each day the sun is renewed by Hashem, similar to the way that the hind's antlers are constantly growing.

Anaf Yosef comments that the morning hind appears just before the actual dawn. So too, the miracle of Esther and Purim presages the ultimate redemption. *Yefei Einayim* similarly contends that the ultimate redemption will come slowly, just as the dawn lasts a while before the sun actually appears and rises.

Ben Yehoyada and *Iyun Yaakov* both discuss the narrow womb of the hind. There is a downside to this anatomical configuration. Labor and delivery are more painful and arduous. What does Hashem do to enable the hind to give birth? He sends forth a snake to bite the hind and slightly swell the birth canal to facilitate delivery (see *Bava Basra* 16b). So too, Hashem sends us "snakes," in the guise of Amaleks, Hamans and all the vile anti-Semites of history, to spur the coming of Moshiach. Every year when we read *Megillas Esther,* it brings us that much closer to the final redemption.

Ben Yehoyada also comments that Esther specifically is described here as the dawn. In *halachah*, the dawn period potentially serves as both night and day. For example, if someone neglected to recite the evening *Shema,* he can still fulfill his obligation between dawn and sunrise. Likewise, if a (different) person will only have the opportunity to recite the morning *Shema* during this period, he too is permitted to say it then. The Book of *Esther* is similar in this respect. While the rest of the Holy Books will be somewhat diminished in their status in the time of Moshiach, *Esther* will retain its role and importance even then! It will still be read in the Future World, as it is read in our current existence!

Eitz Yosef opines that the entire world knew about Esther's miraculous events. After all, letters were sent out to all the communities of the known realm. This is alluded to by the analogy of the spreading antlers going in all directions.

Finally, the *Maharal,* as brought down in the *Inyana DeYoma,* states that the entire relationship between Esther and Achashveirosh was a miracle. Could you imagine two people with less in common? Esther, the holy and righteous wife of Mordechai, forced to marry the evil, lascivious, debauched Achashveirosh! I would add to this explanation that the Midrash comments in *Parshas Lech Lecha* that Esther was actually 75 years old at the time she wed Achashveirosh; and her appearance was not beautiful, but was indeed somewhat sickly. Yet, Hashem caused Achashveirosh to continuously love her as much each time as he did the first time. Truly an unbelievable miracle!

YOMA 35B

(See also Yoma 25a and 47a)

THE KOHEN GADOL'S MOTHER — A TUNIC OF LOVE

(The first part of this section, until the asterisk, is found on both pages 25a *and* 35b.*)*

Rav Huna bar Yehudah or alternatively Rav Shmuel bar Yehudah taught: After the Kohen Gadol *completed the initial series of Yom Kippur services inside the* Heichal *and Holy of Holies wearing the special four linen garments specific for these activities, he was able to replace those garments with a tunic that his mother made for him.(*) The only stipulation was that the* Kohen Gadol *donate this garment officially for Temple use. The Gemara queries: Is it not obvious that if he donated the clothing it is permitted? The Gemara points out that we might have thought that the* Kohen *would not donate the raiment with a full heart, and as such it would be invalid for the* Kohen Gadol *to perform the service with a privately owned garment. Therefore the Tanna teaches us that we need not be concerned that the High Priest did not fully transfer ownership.*

It is said about Rabbi Yishmael ben Pabi (a Second Temple period Kohen Gadol*) that his mother fashioned for him a tunic worth* 100 maneh. *(Previously, the Mishnah had mentioned that the standard requirement for this garment's value was either* 12 maneh *[Rebbi's opinion] or* 8 maneh *[Rabbi Meir]. This provides us with some perspective on the relatively great value of his mother's donation.) Rabbi Yishmael donned this garment and* *performed the Temple service in it, after first officially donating it to the public treasury. Similarly, they said about Rabbi Elazar ben Charsom (another Second Temple period* Kohen Gadol*) that his mother embroidered for him a tunic valued at* 20,000. *However, the other* Kohanim *did not allow him to perform the service wearing it because it was of such a delicate material that Rabbi Elazar appeared to be unclothed!*

We can all empathize with the tremendous happiness that a mother feels for her children when they succeed at their respective professions or achieve universal recognition. Certainly, this sense of *Yiddishe nachas* alone that a *Kohen Gadol's* mother undoubtedly had, would be sufficient reason for her to sew special expensive tunics out of pride and joy. *Rashi* (on *daf* 25a) comments that the mothers wished to demonstrate tremendous honor for the *mitzvah* of serving in the Temple. Alternatively, they wished to display their talents at cloth-making, or the splendor of their wealth. But this alone could not fully account for why the Gemara relates that it was specifically the mothers, and not wives, fathers or other relatives who rejoiced thus.

The *Ben Yehoyada* provides an elegant and beautiful explanation. The priestly garb serve many purposes, including some whose designs we know and understand, versus others of a more mystical and profound nature. When Yosef HaTzaddik was sold by his brothers into slavery in Egypt, he had his multi-colored distinctive cloak torn and dipped into blood. As a result, Hashem decreed that thereafter the *Kohen Gadol's* tunic will serve as an atonement for bloodshed by the Jewish people (see *Arachin* 16a). We also know that the Torah teaches us that under certain circumstances (outlined in greater detail in Gemara *Makkos*), a person who unintentionally kills a fellow Jew is expelled into exile. This banishment from his home to one of the special cities of refuge is not ordained for a set period of months or years, but is dependent upon the life span of the *Kohen Gadol.*

As long as the *Kohen Gadol* is alive, the unintentional murderer must remain inside the city of refuge. Our Rabbis comment that this is an appropriate punishment, as the rate of accidental deaths is somehow related to the *Kohen Gadol* and the example he sets, his saintly performance and his prayers for the Jewish nation. Naturally, if a person's sentence is dependent upon the *Kohen Gadol's* death, exiled people would constantly pray for his demise. Thus, the *Kohen Gadol's* mother would routinely assist in the provision of food and clothing to these exiled men, and ensure that their lives were comfortable and easy, making it not worth their while to pray for the premature death of the *Kohen Gadol* (see *Makkos* 11a). Thus, we can now comprehend that the weaving of the special priestly tunic fits perfectly into this concept. If the tunic atones for, and thereby prevents, unnecessary bloodshed, this is the most effective prophylaxis a *Kohen Gadol's* mother can perform. After all, if there is no accidental murder, then there will be no exiles in the cities of refuge to benefit from the *Kohen Gadol's* demise!

Finally, the *Maharsha* on *Yoma* 47a has an interesting suggestion regarding the identity of Rabbi Yishmael's mother. She is none other than the famous righteous Kimchis. See there in this *sefer* for further description of this novel woman.

YOMA 37A-B

(See also Succah 2b and Nazir 19b)

HILNI'S MENORAH

*(The Mishnah describes for us certain especially praiseworthy actions of several people regarding the Temple services.) ... Hilni, the mother of King Munbaz, made a golden "*mivreshes*" (menorah —* Rashi*;* Rambam *explains this as a block of gold;* Meiri *describes it as a gold window) for the entranceway to the* Heichal. *She also fashioned a golden tablet upon which was inscribed the* Sotah *passages* (Bamidbar 5:11-31). ... *The Sages recalled all those mentioned in the* Mishnah *with praise regarding the furnishings of the Temple and/or the Temple service.*

(The gemara further describes these people and their actions.) ... At the time the sun first shone in the morning, its rays would reflect off Hilni's menorah — and all the people would know that it was time to recite the morning Shema *prayer. ... From Hilni's tablet, we learn out that one is permitted to write down a single section of the Torah and use it as a book to teach a young child. (A technical discussion then ensues regarding whether indeed we can use Hilni's tablet as a conclusive proof.)*

THE RECITAL OF THE *KRIAS SHEMA* PRAYER EACH MORNING AT THE optimal time, and coupling it with the *Shemoneh Esrei* is a very important *mitzvah*. The Gemara in *Berachos* (9b) relates that saying *Shema* immediately prior to sunrise, followed by *Shemoneh Esrei* right afterwards, puts a smile on one's face all day. Hilni assisted many people in recognizing the appropriate time for prayers, and thus is described as extremely worthy of our remembrance. We all have the opportunity to do this daily, when we remind ourselves, our spouses, children and friends to *daven* in the correct time period.

Why couldn't the people in the Temple Courtyard simply look up and directly see for themselves the exact moment when the sun rose? Why was there a need for this surrogate marker? *Inyana DeYoma,* quoting from the *Shiurim BeAggados Chazal,* explains that the walls of the Temple obstructed the view of the initial moments of the sunrise. However, this *mivreshes* was located on the top of the *Heichal* at a height of 100 *amos* (approximately 150 to 200 feet high), and the reflected rays of the sun were therefore clearly visible to all. Therefore, they could not possibly miss out on realizing the optimal period to recite the *Shema.*

The *Sotah* chapter in *Parshas Naso* had to be copied, and then erased and mixed into the "bitter waters." It was then drunk by a woman suspected of committing adultery. This process is outlined in the Torah and discussed at great length in the Gemara in Tractate *Sotah.* Rather than requiring the taking out of a Holy Torah scroll each time this procedure had to be undertaken, Hilni donated this special tablet that would be used as a reminder of which verses had to be written down. Her actions resulted in honoring the Torah scroll — by not requiring it to be taken out unnecessarily from the Ark. Perhaps, this was an example of *middah keneged middah* — the suspected adulteress desecrated the Torah by her actions, and Hilni wished to demonstrate that certainly not all women acted in that fashion. Indeed, the *Iyun Yaakov* states that in the merit of Hilni's action of donating the menorah for the purest of motives, i.e. solely for the sanctification of Hashem's Name, she merited having her son become a king.

The Rabbis wanted to derive an important *halachah* from Hilni's action — that it is permissible to write down a small part of the Torah. The Gemara in *Gittin* (60a) has a discussion with opinions cited to the contrary regarding this ruling. We, of course, rule that one is permitted to do so.

Who were Hilni and her son King Munbaz? Their true identity is a matter of dispute, discussed and referenced in detail in the Schottenstein Edition of *Yoma* 37a. They were either of Hasmonean (possibly Herodean) descent and thus Jewish royalty, or alternatively some suggest they were righteous converts from the country of Adiabene, where they were the royal family.

Elsewhere in the Gemara, we are told additional snippets about these righteous individuals. In Tractate *Succah* (2b), we are told that she had seven young sons, all below the age of *bar mitzvah*, and she was interested in fulfilling the *mitzvah* of sitting in the *succah* with them. Furthermore, the Gemara there relates that she never did anything without the Rabbis' approval. In a Mishnah in *Nazir* (19b), Hilni is noted to have served a long period of *nezirus* (being a *nazir*: a person is obligated to refrain from drinking or eating wine or grape products; cutting one's hair; and becoming contaminated by certain types of ritual impurity related to the death of close relatives). Her term was only supposed to be for seven years, itself a very difficult and arduous task, yet it lasted either a total of fourteen or twenty-one years, to fulfill additional Rabbinical stringencies. She did so willingly, even though it demanded immense personal hardship.

Munbaz is also mentioned several times in *Shas*, and is certainly a "chip off his mother's block." One example: In *Bava Basra* (11a), after he dispersed an exceptional portion of his inherited wealth (from his father) to poor people at a time of horrific famine, he is chastised by other family members. They, more interested in preserving the inheritance for themselves, contrast his father's scrimping and frugality that led to an accumulation of great wealth, with Munbaz's magnanimous charity. Munbaz essentially replied that although his father collected for this world, he was investing and accumulating for the World to Come!

YOMA 47A

(See also Yoma 25a and 35b)

THE VIRTUOUS TZNIUS OF KIMCHIS

(The Gemara is in the midst of a discussion regarding the special ketores *(incense) service that the* Kohen Gadol *performed on Yom Kippur. The service involved the High Priest putting both his hands together and filling them up with the finely ground* ketores *for subsequent burning inside the Holy of Holies. The Mishnah had previously informed us that there was no fixed amount or minimal requirement of incense to be brought. Whatever size hands the* Kohen Gadol *had, that alone determined the proper amount to be gathered and offered.)*

It was said about Rabbi Yishmael ben Kimchis that his hands were so huge that he gathered up four kavim *(a vast measure) in his hands. He would remark: All women take* zered*; but my mother's* zered *rose to the roof. (*Rashi *— his mother's* zered *was superior to all the others.) The Gemara proffers two possible explanations regarding what* zered *actually is. Some say that* zered *is a type of cereal: As Rabbah bar Yonasan said in the name of Rabbi Yechiel that* zered *is a particularly therapeutic food for a sick person.*

And others say: Zered *refers to seed, as per the words of Rabbi Avahu, who stated: One* posuk *uses the word* ותזרני, you "girded" me with strength (Shmuel II 22:40). *Whereas a very similar* posuk *in* Tehillim (18:40) *uses the word* ותאזרני*, spelled with an extra* aleph *— even though the same idea is apparently intended. Rabbi Avahu reconciles the verses in the following manner:* ותזרני*, without the* aleph*, actually does not only mean* girded.

*Instead, since it is derived from a different root — זרה, *winnowing*, it can have a duel intent. Therefore, this is what David HaMelech (King David) purports in* Tehillim: *"Master of the World! You* winnowed *me* <u>and</u> girded *me with strength."*

*They further stated about Rabbi Yishmael ben Kimchis: One time (*Rashi *— on Yom Kippur) he was conversing with a certain Arab in the marketplace, when a drop of saliva from the Arab's mouth sprayed onto his (Rabbi Yishmael's) garment. Saliva of a non-Jew transmits a Rabbinically ordained ritual impurity, and thereby rendered Rabbi Yishmael ben Kimchis incapable of continuing the Yom Kippur service; his brother Yesheivav (*Eitz Yosef, *quoting different sources, states the brother's name was Yehudah) took his place instead. (*Meiri *notes that the* S'gan, *the vice-*Kohen Gadol, *normally takes over if the* Kohen Gadol *becomes incapacitated, and thus Yesheivav must have held this position.) It thus turned out that their mother, Kimchis, witnessed two of her sons performing the* Kohen Gadol's *service on the same day!*

Similarly, they further recounted in the Gemara: One time, Rabbi Yishmael went out to the marketplace and spoke with a certain lord. Likewise, a drop of saliva transmitting ritual impurity went from the lord's mouth onto Rabbi Yishmael's clothing, and his brother Yosef served in his place. Kimchis again was thus able to see two of her sons serving as Kohen Gadol *on the same day.*

Kimchis had seven sons, and each of them ended up serving as Kohen Gadol. *The wise men asked her what merit she had to deserve such wonderful* nachas *from her children. She replied that during her entire life, she never let even the beams of her house see her (uncovered) braided hair. The Sages responded that although many had done likewise, they did not merit such an outcome!*

Certainly, this is one of the most famous and intriguing stories about women in the entire *Shas*. Let us begin by understanding the basic details, and then analyze them from the proper Rabbinic perspective.

Rashi expounds that the *zered* plant is especially beneficial for health, based on a Gemara in *Berachos* (37a), as well as from the *Tosefta*. It was apparently typical pre-natal "standard care" to prescribe for pregnant women regular *zered* consumption, to maximize health and assure good pregnancy outcome. Rabbi Yishmael was attesting to the fact that his mother was especially careful in this regard, and provided optimal antenatal care. Indeed, he attributed his physical prowess to his mother's efforts.

The second explanation of *zered* is that it is a reference to seed. According to *Rashi* and other commentators, a child conceived is actually the end result of a very careful selection process. While Hashem always designates a specific seed to actually impregnate the mother, in Rabbi Yishmael's case there was an even finer selection process than usual, with the end result being Rabbi Yishmael, a unique individual. This is alluded to by the double meaning of the word *zered*, spelled with and without the *aleph*.

Rashi mentions that the stories with the spittle both took place on Yom Kippur itself. *Maharsha* is puzzled by this. How could the *Kohen Gadol*, after a week of separating himself from family and friends, living secluded inside the Temple itself, possibly have gone to the market on Yom Kippur, the holiest day of the year, when he has to enter the Holy of Holies? Thus, *Maharsha* concludes that both events actually occurred on *erev* Yom Kippur, and he marshals a Yerushalmi in *Yoma* to support his view. I would humbly question, however, why the *Maharsha's* bemusement with *Rashi's* understanding (that it is difficult to believe that the *Kohen Gadol* would leave the Temple on Yom Kippur itself) isn't just as problematic for the *Maharsha*. After all, *erev* Yom Kippur is also an unlikely time for the High Priest to be out shopping!

Nevertheless, the *Maharatz Chayes* comes to resolve the story as presented by *Rashi* in a different fashion. Quoting no less than three separate citations from the Yerushalmi — each with a different version of the events — he opines that indeed *Rashi* is correct. *Maharatz Chayes* points out that if the story took place on *erev* Yom Kippur, why couldn't Rabbi Yishmael have immersed and ritually purified himself prior to nightfall? *Tumah* of the saliva is only a light type of impurity that is removed by immersion and the coming of night. However, *Maharatz Chayes* himself remarks that possibly the escapade took place so close to dusk that there was no time to go to the *mikveh*. Furthermore, he brilliantly posits an innovative defense of *Rashi* from that very problematic Yerushalmi itself, which seemingly stated that the story occurred on *erev* Yom Kippur. What does that Gemara actually say? In the original source it states: עם מלך ערב יום כפור, *with an Arab king (on) Yom Kippur,* not, to a king on *erev* Yom Kippur. Rabbi Yishmael went to speak to an *Arab; the word is not erev!*

This explanation also decisively resolves the *Maharsha's* other difficulty: What was Rabbi Yishmael doing in the marketplace on Yom Kippur? The Arabian kings were in general friendly to the Hasmonean dynasty in the Second Temple period, and he went out of the Temple only to greet and give honor to the visiting Arab king. *Meiri* gives a similar response to this query, saying that the *Kohen Gadol* was permitted to leave the Temple in between services if he had a good reason to do so. *Meiri* further states that both stories occurred on the same day. Yesheivav became the acting *Kohen Gadol* in his brother's stead, and he too had to go out of the Temple later that day to see the Arab king regarding an important matter. He too became ritually contaminated, whereupon his brother Yosef took over. Kimchis was thus privileged to observe three of her sons serving on the same day! *Meiri* brings a proof from here to an important *halachah*. While the *Kohen Gadol* had to be secluded for a week prior to Yom Kippur, if for whatever reason he wasn't, as in the case of the replacement *Kohen Gadol*, the service could still go on as scheduled.

The exact identity of Rabbi Yishmael is also unclear. *Yefei Enayim* brings a *Tosefta* detailing that his name really was Rabbi Shimon. The *Vilna Gaon* disagrees, saying the version in the *Tosefta* is inaccurate, and the name provided in our Gemara is correct. *Maharsha* is troubled by the fact that Rabbi Yishmael's lineage is recorded by naming his mother, Kimchis, rather than the typical pattern of listing the name of a son and his father. He adds that Rabbi Yishmael was obviously a great man, yet we do not find his name on the short list of righteous *Kohanim Gedolim* in the Second Temple. (The Talmud had stated earlier in the tractate that there were only four righteous *Kohanim Gedolim* in the entire Second Temple period from the greater than 300 *Kohanim* who served in this role! See this *sefer*, *Yoma* 18a, for further discussion.) However, a Rabbi Yishmael *ben Pabi* is recorded as one of the four. *Maharsha* therefore concludes that Pabi and Kimchis were husband and wife — Rabbi Yishmael *ben Kimchis* and Rabbi Yishmael *ben Pabi* are one and the same person! Why then do we mention his lineage differently in the various *Gemaras*? To accentuate the fact that it was through Kimchis' merit (and not Pabi's) that Rabbi Yishmael became the *Kohen Gadol*. (Indeed, the Gemara on *Yoma* 25a and 35b details great acts of charity that Kimchis did.)

How does *Maharsha* derive this? Several explanations are proffered by the Sages. *Maharsha* suggests that the Talmud simply knew that Pabi was unworthy. Alternatively, it was possible that Pabi was not the father of all seven of her children. Maybe Pabi had died, Kimchis remarried, and she bore children from her second husband. (A regular *Kohen* is permitted to marry a widow, and his children are perfectly kosher and permitted to become the *Kohen Gadol*.) Thus, it was clear that it was Kimchis who was the source of the children's rise to greatness. *Otzar Balum*, however, questions this answer. Maybe Pabi was a hidden *tzaddik*? Maybe it was righteous grandparents of Pabi, and not the merit of Kimchis, that brought out such saintly children? And even if one would postulate that there were two husbands/fathers, maybe it was their combined merit that provided the impetus for Hashem giving Kimchis seven sons serving as the *Kohen Gadol*? So *Otzar Balum*, as well as the *Ben Yehoyada*, provide an alternative explanation — Pabi had other wives! Since the children of those wives did not become *Kohanim Gedolim*, it is perfectly obvious that it was solely in Kimchis' merit that they raised seven great sons.

Ben Yehoyada provides additional interpretations. Possibly Pabi died before these episodes. If he did not live to see the children become *Kohanim Gedolim,* it was clearly not due to his merit that they reached that lofty pinnacle. Secondly, Pabi himself was not a *Kohen Gadol.* If he was so righteous to merit seven sons serving in this capacity, then he too should have been selected as a *Kohen Gadol.* Furthermore, in the earlier Gemara in the tractate mentioning Rabbi Yishmael, Rabbi Yishmael is called after his father's name. Now, however, that we are aware of his special mother and her extreme modesty, which undoubtedly kept her out of the public eye and public recognition, we rightfully refer to him after his mother's lineage.

What indeed was truly so special about Kimchis? The Gemara extols her extraordinary *tznius* (modesty). *Halachah* requires a married woman to cover her hair in public. (For a detailed, referenced, and thorough discussion of this law, the reader is referred to the *Journal of Halacha and Contemporary Society,* Volume 30, page 81.) Kimchis, however, took the extra steps of being unusually modest in this respect even in the privacy of her own home, and when she was alone — when the *halachah* did not mandate such action. *Tosafos Yeshanim* comments that whenever she physically could, she covered her hair. *Rashi* and *Meiri* exhort that modesty, especially in Jewish women, is most essential. Based upon verses in *Tehillim,* women are promised exactly such lofty rewards if they fulfill this expectation. *Meiri* stipulates that their sons will grow up to become the greatest kings and prophets!

Ben Yehoyada remarks that the reward was yet another example of *middah keneged middah,* a principle we have often already seen in this *sefer.* Since Kimchis was careful in regard to *tznius,* so too did she merit her children going into the most *tzanua* of places, the Holy of Holies, where even the *Kohen Gadol* was only allowed to enter once a year on Yom Kippur. If we keep our actions and values modest and appropriate, Hashem will certainly repay us with precious eternal rewards.

Why then did the Gemara state that others have tried to be virtuous like Kimchis, but have failed? Because Kimchis acted solely for Hashem's sake, and not for the reward she would receive. Her pure motives, combined with her pure actions, were an unbeatable combination! A similar compliment is given to Hilni, detailed in this *sefer* (*Yoma* 37). Contrast this with the tragic story regarding the mother of Doeg ben Yosef on *Yoma* 38b, and we can truly appreciate how important proper Torah motivation is.

And lest one think that Kimchis only saw seven children become *Kohen Gadol* because they died one after the other, that is absolutely incorrect! That is exactly why the Gemara specifically relates what *appears* to be trivial episodes. They demonstrate that the seven children were only temporarily serving as *Kohanim Gedolim*, not that some died to allow the others to ascend to the position. *Iyun Yaakov* finds direct support for this from the language the Gemara employs. It says that her seven sons served as Kohen Gadol, not that they actually became *Kohanim Gedolim*.

Finally, the Yerushalmi in *Yoma* describes another illustration of Kimchis' righteousness. She never undressed in an immodest manner. We truly therefore see that Kimchis was one of the most special women of the Second Temple period, if not of all time. Through her virtuous actions and deeds, both physical and spiritual, we recognize the true optimal "Jewish pre- and post-natal care" necessary to guarantee wonderful and saintly children.

YOMA 66B

SPINDLES AND WEAVING—IS THIS THE WOMAN'S PLACE?

Similarly, a wise woman asked Rabbi Eliezer: Since the sinners involved in the infamous "Golden Calf" debacle all committed the same idol worship prohibition, why were they punished with different forms of death? (The Gemara subsequently relates that there were three distinct types of capital punishment meted out to the calf worshipers.) He replied to her, "There is no wisdom to a woman except with her spindle, and so it states in the posuk (Shemos 35:25): And every wise-hearted woman spun with her hands."

IT IS INCUMBENT UPON US TO UNDERSTAND AND EXPLAIN THE WORDS of the Sages, even when they are not written in a pure halachic sense. From the maxims and conversations of the great Rabbis we can truly comprehend the wisdom of the Torah, and better follow the path that Hashem wants us to take. It is especially important that we not belittle or dismiss the comments of the Sages through a lack of understanding of their words. The Gemara is a work that needs to be studied and appreciated on many levels. Understanding the simple literal translation of the text is just the first step in a multi-tiered process to truly comprehend the wisdom of the Talmud.

It is therefore absolutely crucial to fathom the response of Rabbi Eliezer in the context of the discussion that took place. We must not mistakenly look at his rejoinder and simply write it off as a misogynistic remark! Thus, I am appending the entire preceding discussion of the Gemara, to allow us to view Rabbi Eliezer's response in context.

The Gemara has been describing the Yom Kippur service in the *Beis HaMikdash.* A lottery was drawn for the purpose of assigning which one of two special sanctified goats would be brought as a sacrifice inside the Temple. The other goat was taken to a steep cliff, Azazel, located twelve *mil* [24,000 *amos*] outside the city of Yerushalayim, and pushed off this mountain, serving as an atonement for the sins of the Jewish people. The animal walked the distance led by a specially designated person, the *ish iti.* The Gemara is in the midst of a series of questions posed to Rabbi Eliezer regarding this goat, as well as other unrelated issues.

They asked Rabbi Eliezer: What is the *halachah* if the special Yom Kippur goat designated to be thrown off the Azazel cliff was too ill to traverse the twelve *mil* distance on its own power — is the *ish iti* permitted to carry it? He replied to them: The goat is strong enough to carry both you and me!

What if the *ish iti* took ill? Could they send the Azazel goat with a replacement? He replied: You and I will not need to send it. (*Rashi* — Why bother me regarding this query? You and I don't need to perform this service. Alternatively, *Tosafos Yeshanim* — You and I should only be so healthy!)

If the *ish iti* pushed the goat off the cliff, but it did not die, is he obligated to go down after it and kill it? Rabbi Eliezer responded: "*So may all your enemies get lost, Hashem*" (*Shoftim* 5:31). However, the Rabbis answered: If it became sick, the *ish iti* carried it on his shoulders; if the *ish iti* became ill, a replacement took the goat to the Azazel cliff; if when he pushed the goat over the cliff it did not die, the *ish iti* would go down and kill the animal.

They further asked Rabbi Eliezer: Is *Ploni* ("So-and-so") going to merit *Olam Haba,* the World to Come? He said to them: Perhaps you meant to ask me about *Ploni* (a different "So-and-so")? (The *Hagahos HaBach* adds: They then asked him: What about this [second] *Ploni*? He replied: What about the first *ploni*?)

The next several questions are actually profound historical questions that are couched in allegories. They asked him: Should a shepherd save a lamb from the lion? Rabbi Eliezer replied: You only asked me regarding the lamb. (Alternatively, *Hagahos HaBach* has the response: You only asked me regarding the lion.) They asked: Should the shepherd be saved from the lion? He replied to them: You only asked me about the shepherd. (Alternatively, *Hagahos HaBach:* You only asked me about the lamb.)

Again they asked: Does an illegitimate child (a *mamzer*) inherit his biological father? He replied: Does he have the obligation to perform *yibum*, the Levirate marriage, on his biological brother?

Further they asked: What is the law regarding plastering one's house? Rabbi Eliezer responded: What is the *halachah* regarding marking one's grave with lime?

Finally, the Gemara explains Rabbi Eliezer's puzzling and seemingly inappropriate responses. Because he did not answer them seriously, we must not think it was because he was incapable of doing so properly. Rabbi Eliezer was just putting them off with *non sequiturs*, because it was his rule to never say anything that he did not hear from his rebbi. It is at this point, after all of the above queries to Rabbi Eliezer, that the Talmud now relates the question of the wise woman.

This book is about stories of women mentioned in the Talmud. Yet, most of what is written above has nothing to do with women. Why did I transcribe nine seemingly unrelated queries posed to Rabbi Eliezer, before the question of the sagacious lady?

Rav Sherira Gaon, as brought down in the *Maharatz Chayes,* states that it would be a grave error to ascribe a straightforward meaning only to the last reply to the wise woman, while obviously understanding the first nine answers in an allegorical fashion. Thus, I wished for the reader to see for him/herself, in its literally translated form, the entire gamut of the discourse. This enables one to fully appreciate the Gemara's explanation of Rabbi Eliezer's action. No slight of women was intended by Rabbi Eliezer. This too was just another example of "pushing off the questioner" because Rabbi Eliezer had not heard the proper answer from his rebbi, and would not say anything on his own.

Rabbi Eliezer always responded in a manner that superficially had some semblance to the original question — maybe a similar word, theme or subject — but it can't be understood as a direct response and shouldn't be taken as its plain meaning would suggest. Indeed, the very example and *posuk* Rabbi Eliezer used in his reply to the wise woman actually expresses tremendous respect for a woman's wisdom. *Rashi* in *Chumash Shemos* (35:25) quotes the Gemara in *Shabbos* 74b which describes that women had an unbelievable skill and talent — חכמה יתירה, *extraordinary wisdom.* They were actually able to weave the wool while it was still attached to the animal's back! If Rabbi Eliezer truly wished to denigrate women, why did he choose to do so by quoting a *posuk* that praises them?

In truth, though, the *Maharatz Chayes* himself disagrees with this line of reasoning of *Rav Sherira Gaon*. He quotes the Yerushalmi in *Sotah* (Chapter 3, *Halachah* 4) that has our same question posed by a certain *matronisa* (noble woman; matron) to Rabbi Eliezer. After answering her with the same reply our Gemara describes, the Yerushalmi continues the story. After the woman left, Hyrkanus, Rabbi Eliezer's son, tells his father that he just caused them to lose the 300 *kor* (a very large amount) of tithes that the woman regularly gave them. She no longer would give those tithes to them, but will instead choose, as is her right, to give them to someone who does not anger her! (The commentators there suggest that Rabbi Eliezer and Hyrkanus were *Kohanim*, although the *Amudei Yerushalayim* disagrees.) Rabbi Eliezer retorted, "It is worthwhile to lose all the money and remain true to my teaching." Rabbi Eliezer's position was that it is not permissible to teach women certain subjects, and thus he could not respond directly to her query.

The halachic controversy regarding what is allowed and what is not permitted to be studied by women is a very involved and complex technical issue that is well beyond the scope of this volume. Readers are referred to an excellent dissertation on this subject by Rabbi Moshe Weinberger, in the *Journal of Halacha and Contemporary Society* (Volume 9, page 19). Suffice it to say, there are many varied and quite different opinions amongst the great halachic *poskim* (halachic decisors) as to what is the practical application of the law regarding this issue. Times play a very significant role in this halachic decision, as evidenced by the dramatic change in attitude toward formal women's education at the turn of the century with the introduction of the Bais Yaakov and other similar movements. Originally, these schools were extremely controversial; yet today, they are the mainstay of Orthodox transmission of our *mesorah*!

This book does not begin to address how to practically codify Jewish law; each reader must go to his/her own competent *posek* and determine what they are supposed to do.

One must always remember the famous dictum: אלו ואלו דברי אלקים חיים, *These and these are the words of a living G-d. Halachah* is not black and white; there is not always an absolute right answer in *halachah*. Different *valid* antithetical opinions can exist, with no diminution of the light of the Torah! One's own personal ruling, as dictated by one's competent halachic authority, environment, community and background, may be quite different from that of another equally observant Jew. Just look at the different customs involved in the laws of Pesach or *kashrus*! Yet, we respect each valid viewpoint as eternal Torah from Sinai, never dismissing out of hand a *valid* opinion that seems to conflict with secular, transitory "modern" theory.

Geon Yaakov (found in the *sefer Ein Yaakov*) takes a drastically different approach than the *Maharatz Chayes*. He posits three difficulties with perceiving the words of Rabbi Eliezer literally. First, why does the Gemara describe the woman as a wise person? If we are to dismiss her out of hand, why do we need to know she was intelligent? Second, how could Rabbi Eliezer so blithely ignore her question? After all, it indeed was an excellent question, as evidenced by the complex answer that both the Yerushalmi and our Gemara subsequently provide to the query. Third, if she wasn't really a learned and bright woman, why did Rabbi Eliezer answer her with a *posuk*? Because of these dilemmas, *Geon Yaakov* suggests that the conversation was actually much more profound than it appears at first blush. The sagacious woman was actually asking why all people who transgressed the prohibition of idol worship did not each receive the identical punishment. Their physical actions were identical; we should disregard their private thoughts and intentions as we do with most Jewish laws. A *beis din* cannot subjectively assess the frame of mind of the sinner. Either the witnesses saw the defendant commit the crime, or not! Rabbi Eliezer, recognizing the wisdom and fairness of her question, answered her with a *posuk* that indicated the reason she was incorrect. *And every wise hearted woman spun with her hands.* The accent is on the heart when it comes to idol worship. Here, intention is key. A person who is forced to commit this sin, or does so out of fear and/or other pressures, is not guilty of the same level of sin as the willful "believer" in the idol. Therefore, their punishments must differ as well. This is what Rabbi Eliezer truly meant with his response.

Ben Yehoyada has a novel approach. He also is puzzled by Rabbi Eliezer's reactions, and why he specifically quoted a *posuk* dealing with spindles and weaving. *Ben Yehoyada* understands the words at their face value, but gives additional insight into their meaning. Rabbi Eliezer told the wise woman that she may have tremendous understanding and wisdom in regard to general weaving theory and practice. Indeed the Torah clearly remarks that women have this knowledge. But her general cloth-making knowledge did not extend to a specific type of weaving scholarship — the understanding of the weaving of sin! She questioned why the different transgressors received different punishments despite committing the same crime. Rabbi Eliezer retorted: Just as you can't weave different size threads together on the loom and expect a smooth and even outcome, so too different size sins cannot be "woven together" if you desire a fair and even material. And it was only because she was such a wise and intelligent woman that he answered her in this subtle and covert fashion. Someone of her caliber would undoubtedly understand his hidden meaning.

I would humbly suggest that the opinions of *Rav Sherira Gaon, Geon Yaakov* and the *Ben Yehoyada* (which view women in a very positive sense), versus the less flattering understanding of the *Maharatz Chayes* and the Yerushalmi, are not actually at odds. This is based upon the slight difference in the text between the Yerushalmi and Bavli. Our Gemara refers to the woman as wise; the Yerushalmi calls her simply a *matronisa*. I believe that this is the crux of the matter. A *matronisa* was not necessarily a complementary term, and could suggest a woman concerned mostly with worldly, physical and material matters. To such a woman, Rabbi Eliezer's diatribe might be appropriate. But to the sagely lady of our Talmud, the deeper explanations of the commentaries are far more apt.

Meiri takes a more basic "human nature" approach to the issue. Rabbi Eliezer was simply upset at being asked all of these relatively unimportant questions that should have been more appropriately referred to the local rabbis, rather than himself as the senior rabbi in the area. (Such an idea has a basis in the Torah — the episode of Yisro telling Moshe Rabbeinu to appoint various layers of judges to ease the burden on the higher judicial decisors.) Rabbi Eliezer expressed this displeasure by his curt response —essentially telling her "go back to your work" — which in those days, for a woman, meant the spindle and weaving.

The other questions discussed in the section of the Gemara cited above do not deal with issues of women directly, and will not be explicated in detail here. The major Aggadic commentaries basically relate the animals to historical figures. The goat is a euphemism for the nation of Eisav, and how our sins are cast onto them when we merit atonement. The lamb is a reference to Batsheva, the wife of David HaMelech; the shepherd symbolizes her first husband Uriah; and the lion represents David HaMelech. That entire episode (in Chapter 12 of *Shmuel II*) is discussed in great detail in different places in the Talmud. Finally, the allusions to the *two ploni*s is a reference to David's sons, Shlomo HaMelech and Avshalom. *Iyun Yaakov* explains that allegories are used instead of the real names of the individuals themselves, in order to protect their reputations and not embarrass those great Torah personages.

YOMA 82B

PREGNANCY AND FASTING IN THE TALMUD

(The Mishnah stated that under certain conditions, a pregnant woman who smells a particular food on Yom Kippur may be in danger if she is not given that food to eat. She is thus permitted to eat that food until she feels better.)

There was a pregnant woman who smelled a certain food on Yom Kippur and felt herself to be in danger. The people came to Rebbi (Rabbi Yehudah HaNasi) and asked him the halachah. Rebbi told them to whisper in her ear, "Today is Yom Kippur." They whispered to her, and she felt relieved (without having tasted the food). Rebbi quoted the posuk *from* Yirmiyahu (1:5) *about her fetus:* Before I formed you in the womb, I knew you. *This fetus eventually was born and grew up to become the great Rabbi Yochanan.*

There was another pregnant woman who smelled a certain food on Yom Kippur and felt herself in danger. The people came before Rabbi Chanina and asked him the halachah. Rabbi Chanina told them to whisper in her ear, "Today is Yom Kippur." They whispered to her, but she was not relieved, and they were required to feed her. Rabbi Chanina quoted the posuk *from* Tehillim (58:4) *about this fetus:* The wicked are estranged from the womb. *This fetus eventually was born and grew up to become Shabtai, the evil hoarder of produce.*

THROUGHOUT THIS GEMARA, *RASHI* IS OF THE OPINION THAT IT IS THE fetus inside the pregnant mother who is actually somehow able to smell the food in question. Thereafter, if the mother does not partake of the food, both mother and fetus would theoretically be at risk of death or miscarriage. *Siach Yitzchak* supports *Rashi's* opinion based upon the Mishnah's usage of the word עוברה שהריחה to describe the mother, implying mother as well as fetus, rather than the more commonly used term מעוברת. However, according to most other major authorities, and the simple understanding brought down in the *Shulchan Aruch*, it is the mother who smells the food.

The *Shaar HaTziyun* notes a potential ramification: According to *Rashi*, the fetus therefore must be at least forty days into its evolution. Otherwise, its organs would be insufficiently developed, and how then could it smell? It is quite interesting that the Gemara and early halachic authorities (several thousand years prior to modern science's discovery of this fact) note that at forty days of life the fetus changes its status — from previously being a mere "watery substance" to now becoming a more significant entity. Not that the Torah needs scientific validation or confirmation, but it has only been recently recognized by embryologists that at day forty of maturation the embryonic tissues reach a milestone of development and growth. At that time, the external and internal features are first fully recognizable as human. Indeed, at this stage, the growing child is no longer referred to as an "embryo"; instead the term "fetus" is now used.

The *posuk* from *Yirmiyahu* describes how Hashem designated Yirmiyahu to become a great Navi even prior to his birth. So too, this special fetus was ordained to grow up to be the great redactor of the Talmud Yerushalmi, Rabbi Yochanan. *Rashi* in *Yirmiyahu* adds that the *posuk* also refers to how Hashem showed Adam HaRishon all of the souls that would be brought into this world, as well as who would be the prophets and leaders of each generation.

We can certainly understand the reward of having a son such as Rabbi Yochanan. But what was so ignoble about Shabtai the amasser of produce? Why is that necessarily a bad thing? *Rashi* comments that Shabtai was an infamous hoarder of food. He would buy up the available supply in its entirety, and then drive up the prices by refusing to sell too much. By the economics of supply and demand, he artificially raised the cost-of-living index, especially and severely hurting the poorest members of society. This is expressly prohibited; no wonder the Gemara cites him as an example of a wicked person. *Inyana DeYoma*, quoting the *Shiurim BeAggados*, states that the fetus (Shabtai) was unwilling to give up his own desire to taste the food, even though it went against the wishes of his mother. In my opinion, this is very similar to his actions later in life, where the adult Shabtai put his own wants and personal monetary aspirations ahead of the common good. *Maharsha* further comments that smell is the most spiritual of the five senses. The saintly Rabbi Yochanan was able to be satisfied with this superior ethereal pleasure, as opposed to the more base Shabtai who demanded the physical corporeal pleasure of taste instead.

What is uniquely characteristic about Rabbi Yochanan that his personality is featured in this episode? *Tosefes Yom HaKippurim* brings the Gemara in *Taanis* (11a) that remarks that a person who takes upon himself fasts is holy. And the *posuk* in our Gemara from *Yirmiyahu* 1:5 concludes: *before you left the womb you were sanctified.* (*Rabbeinu Chananel* actually lists this part of the verse in our Gemara instead of the quoted first part of the *posuk*.) This fits in perfectly with the Gemara in *Berachos* (20a) that calls Rabbi Yochanan a holy man. His fasting prior to birth helped towards his eventual subjugation of his evil inclination, and he became sanctified.

The *She'arim Metzuyanim BaHalachah* points out an important lesson we can learn from the action of the Rabbis. They said to whisper quietly in the woman's ear. This is a practical application of the saged words of *Koheles* (9:17): *Wise words given pleasantly are listened to.* Don't noisily run over and yell for all to hear: "It's Yom Kippur! How can you possibly eat?" Instead, walk over unobtrusively, and in a calm and confidential manner gently remind the person that the action is prohibited. Indeed, *Meiri* opines that we should tell pregnant women in distress from fasting on Yom Kippur that in the merit of their not eating, they will have wonderful children.

Finally, the *Rosh* iterates that the rabbi in the second story was not Rabbi Chanina, but was in fact none less than Rabbi Yochanan himself, the "fetus" of the first story! *Yefei Einayim* quotes the Yerushalmi though, that attributes both stories to Rabbi Tarfon, and comments that both incidents occurred at the same time.

Yoma 83b

(see also Chullin 106a)

THE MURDER OF KIDOR'S WIFE

Rabbi Meir, Rabbi Yehudah and Rabbi Yose were traveling on the road together. Rabbi Meir always scrutinized the name of the hotel owner at which they would stay, whereas Rabbi Yehudah and Rabbi Yose did not. One time, when they reached a certain area erev *Shabbos, they searched (asked) for and were successful in obtaining lodging for Shabbos. They asked the hotel proprietor his name, and he replied, "Kidor." Rabbi Meir said (to himself) that this person is a wicked man, based upon the* posuk: כי דור תהפכת המה — they are a generation of reversals (Devarim 32:20). *(Rabbi Meir read into the man's name Kidor —* כי דור *— a deeper meaning suggested by the* posuk.*) However, Rabbi Yehudah and Rabbi Yose took no cognizance of this interesting wordplay and deposited their wallets with the hotelier. Rabbi Meir did not entrust him with his purse.*

Instead, Rabbi Meir went and placed the wallet by the grave of Kidor's father. That night, Kidor dreamt of his father appearing to him and telling him to take the purse lying by his head. In the morning, the puzzled Kidor asked the rabbis (according to the Bach, *only Rabbi Meir) the significance of his dream. They (*Bach *— Rabbi Meir) responded that Friday night dreams are unreliable. Rabbi Meir then left and stayed by the grave the rest of Shabbos in order to safeguard his possessions. He brought the money back once Shabbos was over.*

The next morning, when Rabbi Yehudah and Rabbi Yose asked for their wallets back, Kidor denied ever receiving them. Rabbi Meir asked the other rabbis why they weren't more careful in investigating names. In turn, they asked Rabbi Meir why he hadn't warned them. Rabbi Meir responded that he only said to examine names to see if suspicion is appropriate, and not to automatically establish the hotel owner as evil. The rabbis then joined with Kidor for a drink. They noticed that he had some lentils in his mustache. They subsequently went to Kidor's house where they told his wife that Kidor wanted her to return their wallets. As proof, they told her that Kidor told them to say that the couple had lentils at breakfast. The wife assumed this was a strong proof that Kidor wanted to give back the wallets, and so she returned their purses to them. The rabbis went and confronted Kidor, who then went home and murdered his wife. Based upon this incident, the rabbis taught in a Baraisa*: First waters (washing hands before eating) led to a man being fed non-kosher pigs' meat; last waters (in preparation for* Bircas HaMazon*) resulted in a murder.*

THIS STORY IS FOUND AS WELL IN THE *MIDRASH TANCHUMA* (*BALAK* 15) and the *Midrash Rabbah* (*Balak* 21). The underlying theme of this anecdote is to teach us the importance of observing fully even the lightest of *mitzvos*. Oft times it appears to the average person that a certain *mitzvah* is not especially important or essential to his *Yiddishkeit*, and this (G-d forbid) leads to a certain laxity in observance, or even worse, outright disregard for the precept. Therefore, this narrative reminds us of the supreme significance of even (what appears to be) a lowly ritual such as washing one's hands after eating. This is indeed the *halachah*, as brought down in *Shulchan Aruch Orach Chaim* 181. Furthermore, even a relatively less paramount *mitzvah* still has the potential for prolonging life, as is evidenced by Kidor's wife. If only her husband had been scrupulous in his observance of washing one's hand (and lips/mustache area) after eating, she might have been saved from death. Obviously, she did not die solely because her husband didn't wash; she must have been deserving of punishment for reasons not discussed in the Gemara. Yet, if her husband had been zealous in observance, maybe that merit would have saved her life. Indeed, there is a *minhag*, based upon this Gemara, that after washing *mayim achronim*, one washes the mouth/mustache area with one's wet hands before drying them.

The *Yefei Einayim* quotes the Yerushalmi (*Berachos* 58b) where a slightly different ending is given. According to the *Perush MiBaal Sefer Charedim,* three people died as a result of Kidor being exposed as a crook: his wife, her son who came to her defense but was killed by Kidor in the process, and finally Kidor himself. After realizing what had just transpired, he climbed up to the roof of the building and threw himself off, committing suicide.

A third version is suggested in the Gemara in *Chullin* 106a. An argument is brought down between two Amoraim. One opinion ends the story as does our Gemara; the second version though has Kidor simply divorcing his wife, not killing her.

Maharsha questions how Rabbi Meir stayed at Kidor's hotel in the first place if he was so concerned with the evil portent of his name. He suggests a practical reason. It was too close to Shabbos to look for alternate lodging at that time. *Ben Yehoyada* gives an answer from a halachic perspective. To tell his colleagues that Kidor was bad and they should not stay there would have involved a transgression of the prohibition of not speaking evil about one's fellow man. After all, Rabbi Meir did not know for certain that Kidor was wicked, it was only hinted at by his name. Were Rabbi Meir to have recommended going elsewhere, he would have been guilty of speaking *loshon hara.*

What was the significance of the *posuk:* כי דור תהפכת המה, *they are a generation of reversals? Maharsha* comments that originally the Torah was to have been given on Mount Sinai after

1,000 generations had passed. Instead, Hashem gave it after only 26, because Hashem in His mercy saw that the world could not survive that long without the Torah. What happened to the souls of those additional 974 generations that were supposed to have been created prior to the receiving of the Torah? Hashem deposited them throughout all of the subsequent years. Kidor was apparently one of those "souls of reversal."

Maharsha further notes that the rabbis apparently did not observe the lentils on his mustache until they were in the store. They brought Kidor there to get him intoxicated, based upon the well-known teaching that wine loosens the lips. *Ben Yehoyada* suggests that the drinking washed his mustache and allowed them to only then first see the lentils.

According to the *Bach's* version, why did Kidor only ask Rabbi Meir about the significance of his dream? *Ben Yehoyada* provides three posssible explanations. As is clear from the reverential tone with which Rabbi Yehudah and Rabbi Yose addressed Rabbi Meir, he was the greatest of the three. (This is corroborated in *Eruvin* 13b where the greatness of Rabbi Meir is discussed.) Kidor recognized this, and thus went straight to the leader. Alternatively, Kidor did not want to bring up the subject of wallets around the other two rabbis. After all, he was planning on stealing theirs, so better not to mention the subject at all. Thus he discussed his dream only with Rabbi Meir. Thirdly, Kidor was actually attempting to usurp Rabbi Meir's purse as well! He suspected his dream was in fact accurate. He went to Rabbi Meir to ascertain if he would be able to detect a change in his facial expressions that would prove this when he told him the story. But Rabbi Meir was too smart for him, and did not reveal anything, thereby convincing Kidor that the opposite was true. Rabbi Meir insisted that the dream was just a mistake.

Finally, what is the Gemara alluding to with the reference that a man was fed pork because of "first waters" — because he did not wash his hands (*netilas yadayim*) prior to eating? From the Gemara in *Chullin* and the Midrash cited above, *Rashi* relates the following: Once during a period of severe religious persecution against the Jews by the local governing authority, a Jewish butcher had a store. Normally, it is prohibited for a Jewish person to have a business involving the selling of swine. However, here he had to sell all types of meat or else he would have been forced to close. Indeed, people were so oppressed that they were afraid to even ask for the kosher meat. But when a person came into the store, sat down and washed *netilas yadayim* prior to eating, the butcher recognized that he was Jewish and served him only kosher food. One time a Jew came in and did not wash *netilas yadayim*. The store owner mistakenly assumed he was a gentile and served him ham. Thus, the lack of performance of *netilas yadayim* led to the consumption of pork.

Yoma 84a

Rabbi Yochanan and the Matronisa's Remedy

Rabbi Yochanan suffered from a severe mouth disease called tzefidna. *He sought the professional services of a certain* matronisa *(*Rashi *— a gentile woman who was a professional healer). She gave him a salve which was applied on Thursday and again on Friday. Rabbi Yochanan asked her for medicine for Shabbos as well. She told him that he would not need any more treatment. He persisted and asked her what to do if, indeed, he would need it. The* matronisa *insisted that Rabbi Yochanan swear to her that he would not reveal her secret remedy to anyone. Rabbi Yochanan swore to the G-d of Israel that he would not reveal this therapy, and she told him its ingredients. The next day, at his public shiur, Rabbi Yochanan disseminated the secret of the ingredients to everyone.*

The Gemara asks: How could he do this, for he had sworn to Hashem that he would not divulge the information? The Gemara explains that he only swore that <u>*to Hashem*</u> *he would not reveal the remedy, but not that he wouldn't tell all the people. But still, what about the desecration of the Name of Hashem he would cause? After all, the* matronisa *didn't know that, and she would rightly assume that he violated his oath. The Gemara responds that Rabbi Yochanan informed her of his intent right from the beginning, as soon as she told him the potion recipe.*

THE *YEFEI EINAYIM* QUOTES A YERUSHALMI THAT PROVIDES THE conclusion to our Gemara's story. One opinion there states that the *matronisa* committed suicide when she heard that her previously exclusive remedy was now made public. However, other Amoraim state that she was so impressed with the lack of pecuniary interest on the part of Rabbi Yochanan — that he was willing to dispense the medical information to everyone free of charge — that she converted to Judaism. The *Korban HaEidah* in the Yerushalmi comments that the woman remarked how the Jews were the type of people to whom it is worthy to become attached.

It is still difficult to understand and accept how Rabbi Yochanan did what he did. The woman specifically told him not to tell; she in fact was doing him a tremendous favor by revealing her trade secret so that he would not have to come to her on Shabbos! Even though he may not have technically transgressed either swearing falsely or *chillul Hashem* (desecration of the Name of Hashem), how could Rabbi Yochanan so blithely simply turn around and disregard her wishes?

I believe the answer lies in the context of the Gemara. One has to always be especially careful in interpreting a Talmudic text by analyzing it within its full context and by becoming totally familiar with the background setting. Our Bavli is in the midst of a long discussion dealing with what one is permitted to do to potentially save even one life. One is required to even desecrate the holy Shabbos if there is even a possibility that a Jewish life might be saved. In this framework, Rabbi Yochanan's behavior is not so puzzling. The Gemara relates that the *tzefidna* illness is potentially life threatening. Perhaps Rabbi Yochanan assessed that individuals were not always able to obtain the prescribed cure due to its unavailability and their lack of knowledge. It is therefore possible, that for future *pikuach nefesh* (life threatening) situations, Rabbi Yochanan considered his actions commendable. Indeed, the second approach of the Yerushalmi supports this, as the *matronisa* herself recognized Rabbi Yochanan's selfless humanitarian public-health interest.

מסכת סוכה

SUCCAH

SUCCAH

SUCCAH 2B

(see also Yoma 37a-b; Nazir 19b)

HILNI THE QUEEN

Rabbi Yehudah said: It is told of Hilni (Helene) the Queen in the city of Lod, that she had built a succah *that was more than* 20 *cubits (approximately* 30 *to* 40 *feet) high. When the Elders (Rabbis) came to visit her, they did not say a word to her. They did not require her to lower the* s'chach *of her* succah *— the roof — to a height of no more than* 20 amos *above its floor.*

Rabbi Yehudah brought this story/episode as proof to his opinion that there is no upper limit to the height of a succah.

The Chachamim *(who limit the height to* 20 amos*) said to him: From there you bring proof? Hilni is a woman, and women are exempt from the obligation to sit in the* succah *because it is a time-related* mitzvah *(a* mitzvah *which is fulfilled at a specific time). The Rabbis did not reproach her for having an invalid* succah *because she was not obligated to have a* succah.

Rabbi Yehudah replied to the Rabbis. What about her seven sons — they are obligated to fulfill the mitzvah*? And furthermore, Hilni did nothing without the consent of the Rabbis.*

The Gemara interjects — why was it necessary for Rabbi Yehudah to add this second statement — that all of Hilni's actions met with the Rabbis' approval? To this the Gemara answers: Perchance you will say that all seven of Hilni's sons were under the age of bar-mitzvah, *and minors do not have a Torah obligation to fulfill the* mitzvah *of* succah, *and that is why Hilni did not have a proper* succah *made. That would not explain Hilni's action. For it is impossible that there was not at least one of her sons who "did not need his mother constantly" (i.e. the minimum age at which there is a Rabbinical requirement to observe the mitzvah of* succah*). Should you suggest that maybe Hilni was not careful to observe Rabbinical ordinances, Rabbi Yehudah comes along and tells us that all of Hilni's actions were fully in accordance with the Sages' wishes.*

The Gemara then continues with a detailed halachic discourse (not pertinent for this sefer's *deliberation), ultimately explaining how the opinions of both Rabbi Yehudah and the* Chachamim *(regarding the height of kosher* s'chach*) are consistent with the dimensions of Hilni's* succah*).*

WHO WAS HILNI? HER IDENTITY IS A MATTER OF DISPUTE, discussed in detail in the Schottenstein Edition of *Yoma*, 37a. She was either of Hasmonean (possibly Herodean) descent and thus Jewish royalty, or a righteous convert from the country of Adiabene, where she was from the royal family. The Gemara in *Yoma* 37a-b (see this *sefer*) and elsewhere discusses other merits of Hilni and her family. The *Yefei Einayim* quotes the Yerushalmi's slightly different version of our story which notes that all seven of her sons were great Torah scholars (which would indicate that they were adults). One of them, Munbaz, is favorably mentioned by the Rabbis in other places in *Shas* as well (see this *sefer*, *Yoma* 37a).

The *Ritva* on Tractate *Succah* (printed in the back of the second volume of the *Rashba*) derives an important halachic requirement from this story regarding the *mitzvah* of *chinuch* (educating children). People frequently err and presume that a minor should be taught how to perform a *mitzvah* by simply going through the proper motions. But, one need not give the minor a kosher *esrog*. It is sufficient to give him a lemon and have him shake the *lulav* and lemon in the correct way. *Ritva* says this is not so. To properly fulfil the commandment of *chinuch*, one must give the child the appropriate kosher objects, as well as have him do what an adult is required to do. Hilni could not have educated her young sons by placing them in an invalid *succah* to teach them that it is a *mitzvah* to sit in a *succah*!

The *Pnei Yehoshua* and others cite our Gemara as a proof that the *mitzvah* of *chinuch* is not only incumbent upon the father (as other halachic authorities contend), but is also an obligation which falls on the mother. Alternatively, he comments that in a situation where there is no father, the obligation to educate a child in the path of the Torah falls upon the Rabbis and all Jewish males. Hilni always conducted herself with the Sages in mind. For she knew that it was the Rabbis themselves who were required to see that her sons were receiving a proper *chinuch*. Thus Rabbi Yehudah's contention is that she constructed a valid *succah* so that the Rabbis would be able to fulfill their *chinuch* obligation!

If Hilni was not obligated by *halachah* to perform the *mitzvah*, then what was she doing in the *succah* when all the Elders came to visit? *Ben Yehoyada* proposes that she wanted to be near her children to assist and help them when necessary. *Maharatz Chayes* explains why she would not be transgressing the precept of *bal tosif* — that it is forbidden to add to the Torah. If Hilni was not obligated to sit in the *succah*, but did so anyway, isn't this tantamount to transgressing *bal tosif*? *Maharatz Chayes* says that since she was taking care of her children it was permissible. *Bal tosif* applies only when one intends to create a new obligation. However, a woman who wishes to sit in a *succah* (or perform any of the time-dependent *mitzvos* with the exception of *tzitzis* and *tefillin*) may do so as a אינו מצווה ועושה, *a voluntary deed,* for which she will receive reward. (See *Eruvin* 96a-b and *Succah* 11a for further discussion of time-dependent *mitzvos*, women, *tzitzis* and *tefillin.*)

But we are left with a question from *Tosafos* in *Pesachim.* Why did the Rabbis not institute a Rabbinical requirement for women to sit in the *succah.* After all, women are obligated to eat matzah on Pesach because they, too, were involved in the redemption from Egypt. (Indeed, we have already mentioned that the Gemara reminds us that it was through the women's righteousness that we were redeemed!) Similarly, women are obligated to hear *Megillas Esther* on Purim and light the menorah on Chanukah because of the preeminent role women played in the miracles of Purim and Chanukah. Since women were involved in the redemption from Egypt, and also benefited from the *succos* we sat in during the forty years of wandering in the desert, why wasn't a Rabbinical edict established to require women to sit in the *succah*?

The *Al HaDaf* publication gives the answer of the *Vilna Gaon.* We sit in the *succah* to commemorate the return of the "Clouds of Glory" that had been previously withdrawn by Hashem because of the sin of the Golden Calf. Upon Moshe Rabbeinu's return from his first forty-day period in heaven, he smashed the *Luchos* (the two Tablets bearing the Ten Commandments) when he witnessed that cataclysmic event (*Shemos* 32:19). That tragedy transpired on the 17th of Tammuz, and is one of the reasons we fast that day. Moshe Rabbeinu subsequently returned to heaven to (successfully) plead for mercy on our behalf. He went up a third and final time to receive the second set of *Luchos,* returning on Yom Kippur, the 10th of the month of Tishrei. Five days later, after following various instructions from Hashem, the "Clouds of Glory" reappeared at the Jewish encampment, signifying forgiveness for the sin of the Golden Calf. The *Chasam Sofer* adds that it is this return of the clouds that we commemorate with the holiday of Succos.

Who was embroiled in the sin of the Golden Calf? Only the men. The commentaries relate that the women absolutely refused to donate any of their gold or jewelry to the cause of idol worship; the Calf was forged from precious metals of the men! The Israelite women were on a loftier spiritual plane; they never participated in the dreadful sin. The "Clouds of Glory" therefore never left the women of Israel and their return carried no special significance to these righteous women. Consequently, the Sages perceived no special need to decree that women sit in the *succah* (which commemorates the return of the "Clouds"). They, who sinned, require expiation and remembrance. The women, who did not, are exempt from the Torah obligation and even any Rabbinical one.

SUCCAH 11A

MAY A WOMAN WEAR TZITZIS?

(The Gemara is in the midst of a detailed discussion regarding acceptable formation of a succah's s'chach. S'chach *must be made for the* succah *for shade purposes, and cannot already have been in existence as a roof for a different reason. As part of a long dialectic proving this point, the Gemara compares* s'chach *to* tzitzis.*)*

Rav Amram Chasida (the pious) placed tzitzis *on the cloak of "the people who lived in his house" (*Rashi — *his wife).*

WITHOUT DELVING INTO THE COMPLICATED HALACHIC DEBATE, RAV Amram placed *tzitzis* on his wife's garment because in his opinion, there is an obligation to wear *tzitzis* even during the night. As a result, *tzitzis* are time independent. One is always required (all day and night) to have *tzitzis* on a four-cornered cloak. As with all time independent positive *mitzvos*, both men and women are equally obligated in the *mitzvah*.

We, of course, do not accept Rav Amram's view as the practical *halachah*, but it raises an interesting question. Granted, women are indeed exempt from *tzitzis*, a time-dependent commandment, as we just once again saw on the preceding *daf* (*Succah* 2b) in this *sefer*.

But why can't women wear *tzitzis* at least as a אינה מצווה ועושה, *a voluntary meritorious act?* Indeed, if one reads the opening remarks of this section in the *Shulchan Aruch Orach Chaim* (17:2), that is in fact how *Rama* initially suggests the strict *halachah* to be.

However, *Rama* then continues his comments and explains that today a woman who wears *tzitzis* has the "appearance of arrogance." Practically, he therefore is *posek* that it is improper for a woman to wear *tzitzis*. This is different than other time-dependent *mitzvos*, which the *Rama* permits women to perform even with a *berachah*! Why?

Intrinsically, there is no automatic obligation even for a man to wear *tzitzis*. The Torah prescribes that if a man is wearing a four-cornered garment, only then must he attach *tzitzis* to it. But absent such clothing, there exists no Biblical requirement to own and/or wear such garb. This is as opposed to other *mitzvos*, such as shaking a *lulav* and *esrog*, where a person is required to seek out and purchase the four species to fulfill the Torah commandment. Thus, in the latter case, a women too can perform the *mitzvah* of her own volition if she so desires, without giving the appearance of arrogance. But with tzitzis, if a woman were to go out of her way to perform this mitzvah, she would appear haughty, and arrogant. Arrogance is a ghastly trait. We find numerous other examples (not to wash our hands *netilas yadayim* before eating fruit, not reciting the *Shema* on a wedding night, etc.) where the *poskim* instruct us not to proceed with what on the surface appears to be a meritorious positive commandment, for the reason that it will give the appearance of arrogance. Indeed, two great prophetesses, Devorah and Chuldah were reprimanded for exhibition, even a very small measure of our arrogance (see comments to Megillah 14a and b for a further discussion of this).

Finally, why does Rav Amram use the curious terminology "the people who lived in his house" to describe his wife? The *Tosafos Yom Tov* and others explain that a true woman of valor is best represented by the house. Rabbi Yochanan often referred to his wife in a very positive manner as "his house." A wife in Judaism is the foundation, the house of the marriage, our tradition, and everything we hold dear.

SUCCAH 27B

(See also Rosh Hashanah 16b)

ELISHA AND THE WOMAN OF SHUNEIM

Rabbi Yitzchak said: From where do we know that a person is obligated to visit his rebbi during the "regel" *(the holidays of Pesach, Succos and Shavuos)? This is learned from a* posuk *in* Melachim II *(*4:23*). The husband of the woman of Shuneim asked her,* "Why are you going today to visit the prophet Elisha? It is not the New Moon, nor is it Shabbos."

THE FOURTH CHAPTER IN *MELACHIM II* DESCRIBES THE FAMOUS STORY of how the prophet Elisha miraculously resuscitated a young child. Elisha was a frequent guest at the house of a childless couple. They treated Elisha with great respect and generosity, setting up a special guest room solely for his use. Elisha inquired how he could repay their kindness. The wife, a woman from Shuneim, implored not for financial nor material gain. Yet, with Elisha's prayers, they subsequently merited the birth of a son.

Several years later, while the young boy was with his father, he was suddenly stricken with a severe headache, and collapsed. His father quickly returned home, where the Shuneim woman realized that their son was dead. She placed the deceased child in the holy Elisha's bed in his private room, and she posthaste sought out the prophet to help obtain Divine intercession and intervention. Her husband, not realizing what had truly transpired, asked why she was running to Elisha, for it was not a New Moon nor a holiday. Subsequently, Elisha performed certain maneuvers (remarkably similar to mouth-to-mouth resuscitation), and Hashem returned life to the child.

The Gemara derives an important halachic concept from the actions of the Shuneim woman and the question posed by her husband. From here we derive the obligation to visit with one's teacher or mentor on the holidays. But the commentators wonder how this is evident from the *posuk* cited. The *posuk* only mentions Rosh Chodesh (the New Moon) and Shabbos. And why is Rosh Chodesh listed before Shabbos? Usually we enumerate the more frequently occurring event first? *Eitz Yosef* and *Ben Yehoyada* explain that Shabbos in this context does not mean Shabbos itself, but actually signifies all of the *Shalosh Regalim* (the three festivals: Pesach, Shavuos and Succos). The Torah itself sometimes uses the word Shabbos and festival interchangeably. This also accounts for the order of the events listed in the *posuk* too. Rosh Chodesh occurs more regularly than the festivals, and is thus appropriately listed first in the verse.

Who was the Shuneim woman? *Rashi* and *Radak* in *Melachim II* inform us that she was the sister of Avishag of Shuneim, the young lady who warmed (comforted) David HaMelech in his old age (see *Melachim I,* Chapter 1). Thus she must have had great merit since she was quite old at the time of this story. *Radak* adds that she was a G-d-fearing woman, superior to other women in the performance of acts of kindness. Her husband was either the prophet Iddo according to some commentators, or the Navi Oded. Yet she, rather than her prophet husband, was the vehicle Hashem chose through which to manifest the great miracle of resuscitation. Clearly, she was an extraordinary woman.

And who was the little boy? The *Zohar* informs us that the young child grew up to become the Navi Chabakkuk, one of the twelve prophets of the Book of *Trei Asar.*

Succah 28a-b

THE SUCCAH AND THE NEWBORN

The Mishnah relates that Shammai the Elder cut a hole in the roof, and placed s'cach *over the bed of his recently post-partum daughter-in-law, in order to allow her baby son to observe the* mitzvah *of sitting in the* succah. *The Gemara asks: Is this not in opposition to the law previously stated in our Mishnah that exempts very young children from the* mitzvah*? And even where the boys are obligated Rabbinically to sit in the* succah, *that is only because of the principle of* chinuch, *to teach our children, which is incumbent on the parent. This* mitzvah *of* chinuch *only begins at an age when the child can understand the precept! The Gemara responds that Shammai was especially stringent.*

How does the Gemara's response that Shammai was especially stringent answer the question? If there is no obligation save that of *chinuch*, and the infant newborn is certainly not of sufficient mental capacity to understand the commandment, what was Shammai being stringent about? He was accomplishing nothing with this stringency! *Maharsha* and other commentators supply an explanation. Shammai indeed would not have built the *succah* just for the mother and her newborn, as they both were fully exempt. (See the preceding *succah* sections in this *sefer* regarding why women are not obligated.) However, Shammai's daughter-in-law had another young son. While he was still strongly attached to, and needed his mother, this small boy was capable of some understanding of the concept of *succah*. And it was for this other child that Shammai constructed the *succah*. While he was stringent in the performance of *chinuch* of children, Shammai was still quite cognizant of the special needs of a young child for its mother. Shammai made certain that he was able to fulfill both commitments without compromising either.

SUCCAH 31A

A STOLEN SUCCAH

A certain elderly lady went before Rav Nachman and informed him that the Reish Galusa *(Exilarch, head of the Jewish community in the Babylonian exile) and all the Rabbis staying in his house were sitting in a stolen* succah. *(*Rashi *explains that the stewards of the* Reish Galusa, *unbeknownst to him, misappropriated the woman's lumber and used it to build the* Reish Galusa's *succah.) She screamed that the wood be returned to her, but Rav Nachman ignored her. She said to Rav Nachman, "A woman descended from a 'father who had* 318 *servants' is screaming before you, and you ignore her?" Rav Nachman said to the students, "This woman is a 'yeller'; she is entitled to claim only the value of the wood stolen from her."*

ACCORDING TO RASHI, A "FATHER WHO HAD 318 SERVANTS" IS A reference to the elderly woman's great ancestor, Avraham Avinu. As described in *Bereishis* 14:14, Avraham Avinu took with him 318 assistants to battle the four kings who had captured his nephew Lot. (Others explain that it really wasn't 318 men, but it was just his trusty servant Eliezer, whose name in *gematria* adds up to 318.) Ritva postulates that her reference to 318 attendants is not necessarily alluding to Avraham. She actually had a very wealthy father who had that many domestics.

Before we can even try and understand the puzzling reaction of Rav Nachman, we must familiarize ourselves with an important *halachah*. A person who steals is obligated to return the stolen item itself. However, to encourage recalcitrant thieves to repent and do *teshuvah*, the Rabbis permitted a burglar to repay just the value of the stolen property if the goods themselves were not easily accessible. For example, a crook might be reluctant to return the exact stolen ten-dollar beam that he placed in the foundation of a ten-million-dollar apartment house! Rather than try and directly confront this basic human reality, *Chazal* decreed that in cases where restoration of the illicitly obtained possession presented unusual hardship, it was acceptable for the thief to simply repay the value of the theft.

The servants of the *Reish Galusa* inappropriately and wrongly stole the wood of the elderly lady. However, once the wood was built into a structure, even a relatively temporary one such as a *succah*, this principle of "encouraging repentance" applies. Thus, the *Reish Galusa* was not obligated to knock down the *succah* and return her property. Indeed, this rule is taught elsewhere. The halachic point that our Gemara (in Tractate *Succah*) is establishing is that a *succah* during the holiday of Succos is deemed a permanent structure included in this rule of encouraging repentance. However, once the holiday concludes, and the *succah* is being taken apart, then they would indeed have to return the specific stolen lumber. *Meiri* adds that the *Reish Galusa* offered to pay the woman for the wood, otherwise they could not have fulfilled the *mitzvah* by sitting in a "stolen" *succah*. However, the elderly lady did not wish to accept this as payment; she insisted on the return of the wood itself. In this case, the *Reish Galusa* and the Rabbis could fulfill their *succah* obligation even without paying (yet) for the value of the wood. *Rabbi Akiva Eiger* is of the opinion, however, that even if the thief has not yet given back the monetary worth, or if he has not even expressed his interest in doing so, as long as he eventually does pay the victim back, the *mitzvah* is fulfilled. However, the *Beis Yosef* writes (based on his understanding of *Rashi*) that even if the crook never pays the money back, he still can fulfill his obligation of sitting in the *succah* with the stolen piece.

Still, this does not fully explain the seeming indifference of Rav Nachman to the elderly woman's plight. The *sefer Aggados HaShas Mishnas Yosef* brings down a beautiful insight from the *Kesav Sofer* regarding this incident. The elderly lady was obviously poor; she had no servants to go out and purchase new wood for her. She thus would be forced to go out to the market herself to obtain the lumber. In essence, she remarked to Rav Nachman, "I do not have 318 servants like Avraham Avinu. Yet, I am still a king's daughter. All Jewish woman have the status of princesses. And doesn't *Tehillim* (45:14) state: כל כבודה בת מלך פנימה, *All the honor for a woman is inside?* Isn't a woman supposed to act modestly in her endeavors? If the house of the *Reish Galusa* does not return my wood to me, I will be forced to go out publicly, in the open marketplace, and purchase it myself. That's a lessening of my honor! Therefore the principle of 'encouraging repentance' should not apply in my case."

Rav Nachman ignored her. Her very actions demonstrated her true disinterest in observing the high ideals of David HaMelech in *sefer Tehillim*. Rav Nachman instructed the students: Look, she is a screamer, a yeller. She does not act modestly. If she had truly been a righteous woman and approached us in a modest fashion, then she would have been correct in requesting that we abrogate the special repentance rule to protect her modesty. But obviously, she is not concerned with her modesty, as evidenced by her screaming at us. Thus, she is entitled only to the value of the wood. Furthermore, she is not entitled to any additional recompense to hire servants to obtain the lumber for her. This is implicit in Rav Nachman's language — she is <u>only</u> entitled to the value of the wood.

The *Aruch LaNer* postulates a slightly different scenario and explanation for Rav Nachman's actions. The woman came to Rav Nachman on the first day of Succos, when they were all sitting in the *succah*. She demanded that the wood be returned immediately. Of course, Rav Nachman could not convene a judicial court right then because one is not permitted to judge monetary matters on Yom Tov. She mistook his silence for condoning the deeds of the thieving servants. She therefore screamed at the Rabbis — Avraham Avinu was very proactive regarding his servants to prevent them from misappropriating items not belonging to them. Why aren't you as zealous in scrutinizing the *Reish Galusa*'s staff? Her public yelling and screaming was causing embarrassment to the assembled Rabbis, so Rav Nachman was forced to address her financial concerns on Yom Tov. However, he did not wish to do so directly. He thus spoke to his students, as if he were teaching them a *halachah* (not a practical judicial ruling on a real case) and told them, and indirectly also the elderly woman, what the *halachah* was in such a case.

SUCCAH 52A

ABAYE AND HIS YETZER HARA

Abaye overheard a man tell a certain woman, "Let us arise early and travel together on the road." Abaye thought: I will follow them to prevent them from committing a prohibited act. Abaye followed behind them for a distance of three parsahs *(*24,000 amos*). As they reached the point in the road where their paths diverged and they were forced to go in separate directions, Abaye heard them conversing. "Our paths are far apart, and we can no longer travel together, but the company would have been very pleasant." They departed (without sinning). Abaye remarked: If my "enemy" were here, he would have been unable to restrain himself from committing a transgression. Whereupon Abaye went and leaned against the door bolt and was distressed. Along came an old man and taught Abaye: Whoever is greater than his fellow man, so too is his evil inclination greater.*

R*ASHI* EXPLAINS THAT ABAYE'S ENEMY WAS A REFERENCE TO HIS own *yetzer hara* (evil inclination). The Gemara earlier related that "enemy" is one of the seven names by which the evil inclination is called. Abaye was essentially acknowledging that he might not have so successfully passed this difficult task of not transgressing with the woman had they been alone on the road.

The *Divrei Shaul* comments that the man and woman were unaware that they were being tailed by Abaye, and thus they truly did not sin because it was wrong, not because they were watched.

Maharsha notes that the potential for sin was great. The "pleasant company" made the long trip seem like just a short jaunt, even though they actually traveled together for quite a distance. *Ginzei Yosef* adds that they knew each other well; they were not strangers and thus were more likely to sin.

Given all this, why was Abaye so distressed and concerned that he might not have acted as properly had he been the man in the situation? Abaye was one of the leading sages of his time, a righteous scholar, who, the Gemara elsewhere relates, was supposed to die at a young age (he was from the House of Eli, which had been cursed with early deaths). Yet, because of his extraordinary meritorious acts of kindness, in addition to his great Torah learning, he lived until the age of 60. Why was he distressed now?

Gur Aryeh answers that Abaye knew he also would not have sinned. But Abaye reasoned, this was only because he felt that he would be protected due to his great merits. Otherwise, Abaye felt it would have been beyond human ability to restrain himself. Yet, these relatively unlearned and non-saintly simple man and woman were able to do just that! It was this fact that caused Abaye distress. He thought that he might not have overcome the *yetzer hara* on his own, yet a plain person was able to do so.

This Gemara (as well as the entire *daf* not discussed here), is informing us of a crucial Judaic principle. The daily tests Hashem provides for us in many shapes and guises are individualized. What appears as a great temptation to one would be easily overcome by another. Each person has his/her own fortitude and strengths that Hashem implanted inside him, including the ability to pass the tests Hashem demands of him. Yes, for some people certain actions would be unattainable and therefore not expected. For others, the mere passing of the same test in a minimal fashion would be deemed a failure — they should have succeeded with the flying colors expected of them!

Abaye was reminded of this by the old man (a term the Gemara often, but not always, uses as an allusion for Eliyahu HaNavi). My rebbeim have taught me, in the name of many great sages, including the *Vilna Gaon*, that every person is given his own personal *yetzer hara* — evil inclination. To some, on Judgment Day, it will appear like a gigantic mountain. They will step back in amazement and exclaim, "How could I ever have overcome that huge elevation?" Yet, to others, the evil inclination will appear as a razor-thin hair. Those wicked people will mumble in disbelief, "How could I not have easily vaulted over such a slim line?" (see *Succah* 52a).

Mishnas Yosef in *Aggados HaShas* expounds this further. Hashem has to make each individual's trials fair. However, with every passing righteous deed a person performs, he becomes that much greater. It would soon be no contest if the person's evil inclination did not grow as well. Thus a *tzaddik's yetzer hara* is constantly increasing in power, commensurate with the growth the righteous person gains by performing acts of holiness. Conversely, the *yetzer hara* of an evil person would quickly overpower him if it were not downsized regularly! Each wicked deed makes him/her that much feebler, unable to combat his or her baseline *yetzer hara*. Therefore Hashem constantly shrinks this inclination to maintain a fair test. Thus, Eliyahu told Abaye, "Do not be surprised and amazed that the simple couple were able to defeat their evil inclination. It was not the same strength as yours. For them, it was the appropriate size, and they are to be praised for their victory."

SUCCAH 52B

(see also Yoma 18a, Gittin 56a, and Yevamos 61a)

MARTA'S STRONG SON

Come and hear a Baraisa *(discussing the fantastic events of the* Simchas Beis HaShoeva, *the festival of the water-drawing celebrated during the holiday of Succos): The young* Kohanim *would carry thirty-*log *(a certain significant measure) pitchers containing oil up to (menorahs at) the top of fifty-*amos *high ladders ... It was taught in another* Baraisa*: And these (the young* Kohanim*) were more praiseworthy (*Rashi *— stronger) than the son of Marta bas Baitus. It was said about the son of Marta bas Baitus that he could take (carry) two thighs of a large ox that was worth* 1,000 zuz *and walk heel to toe up the ramp of the altar (to perform the necessary sacrificial activity by himself). But his fellow* Kohanim *would not permit him to do so, because of the verse:* In the multitude of people is the glory of the King *(*Mishlei 14:28*).*

Why were the young Kohanim *more praiseworthy? It can't be purely because of the weights involved, because the ox thighs were much heavier than the oil pitchers. Rather, it was the fact that the* Kohanim *had to carry their load straight up steep ladders, whereas Marta's son hauled his burden up a long but shallow incline to the top of the Altar.*

MARTA HAS BEEN DISCUSSED IN DETAIL IN THIS *SEFER* (*YOMA* 18a), and is mentioned in other places in the Gemara (listed there as well). She merited having an exceptionally strong son, as illustrated in our Gemara. *Rashi* comments that a person carrying a heavy burden usually walks very swiftly, to shorten the time he has to bear the load. But Marta's son was able to lift the two large thighs of this huge animal by himself. And yet, despite the weight of the animal's sacrificial parts, he was still able to walk at a very slow and leisurely pace. The *Otzar Mefarshei HaTalmud* notes that he did this specifically to show off his physical strength. This is of particular interest, as Marta was also interested in superficial titles and physical aggrandizement, as outlined previously on *Yoma* 18a. The apple does not fall far from the tree.

We learn a very important principle from this episode. Even though one person would have been physically capable of bringing the sacrificial parts to the Altar, the Rabbis preferred that the *mitzvah* be performed by several individuals instead. The greater the involvement of more of the Jewish people in any sacred act, the better. We Jews are all one unit, one single entity, albeit with many integral parts. The more the parts work in unison, the greater the spiritual elevation that ensues. One person performing a *mitzvah* alone is wonderful; a whole group of Jews doing the same thing together is exponentially superior!

Succah 56b

Bilgah's Chutzpah

The Rabbis taught in a Baraisa*: There was a story involving Miriam the daughter of Bilgah, who went and married a non-Jewish officer of one of the Greek kings. When the Greeks entered into the Sanctuary (Holy Temple) area, she kicked with her sandal on the top of the Altar, and remarked: "Wolf! Wolf! Until when will you stop consuming the money of the Jewish people, yet you do not stand by them in their time of oppression?" Subsequently (after the Maccabees defeated the Greeks and recaptured the Temple —* Rashi*), when the Rabbis heard about her comments, they permanently attached the (slaughtering) ring of Bilgah to the Temple floor, and sealed off Bilgah's "window" (cubby). Others explain that the reason these penalties were imposed on the watch of Bilgah was because they (the watch of Bilgah) were tardy in arriving for their Temple service. As such, the watch of Yesheivav, their brother* Kohanim*, took their place and served in their stead ...*

The Gemara asks: It is clearly understood according to the second explanation (i.e. that the entire watch delayed in coming to the Temple service) that the whole watch deserved to be punished. But, according to the first viewpoint (that a single woman from the family of Bilgah became an apostate), is this a reason to punish the entire Bilgah group of Kohanim*? Abaye responds: Yes! As the popular aphorism states: The public utterances of a young child represent the words of either the mother or father (that the child overheard in the house). The Gemara* *persists in questioning: And because of a single father or mother, should the entire watch be punished? Again Abaye responds: Yes! Woe is to the wicked person, woe is to his neighbor. Similarly, (when) it is good for the righteous person, so it is good for his neighbor.*

All of the *Kohanim*, and indeed the Levites as well as the rest of the Israelites, were originally divided up into eight and subsequently twenty-four groups to regularly perform the Temple service requirements in a rotation. These twenty-four divisions or "watches" alternated one week at a time in the performance of these duties. Bilgah was the name of the fifteenth such group of *Kohanim*. *Ben Yehoyada* points out that Miriam was obviously not the actual daughter of Bilgah. The watches were so named after the original group leaders, who lived hundreds of years previously during the time of the First Temple. *Rashi* points out that this story occurred in the Second Temple period during the time of the Maccabees. Since Miriam was from the family of Bilgah, the Gemara thus refers to her as Bilgah's daughter.

Intermarriage and apostasy are among the most severe transgressions that a person can commit. Yet, the Gemara and commentators do not ascribe the degradation of the family of Bilgah to these sins. Instead, they note that it was her disrespectful treatment of the Temple, her rebellious attitude and "chutzpah" in her diatribe against Hashem that sealed her family's shame and denigration. No longer would they have their own ring to slaughter the Holy Temple sacrifices. No, *Meiri* opines, they would have to borrow a different group's station every time they ritually slaughtered a sacrifice. Alternatively, they actually physically restrained and held down the struggling animal by hand (without benefit of the special slaughtering ring) because of Miriam's disrespectful blasphemous comments. Likewise, Bilgah had their cubby (containing the essential sacrificial tools and clothing) permanently sealed off, furthering their humiliation because of Miriam.

Maharsha explains that Miriam specifically referred to the Altar as a wolf, because wolves commonly killed sheep, and each day a lamb was offered as the daily morning and evening required sacrifice — the *korban tamid*. Since there were thus two lambs each day, Miriam called the Altar two times "wolf," symbolizing this sacrifice and her disrespect toward it. *Ben Yehoyada* exposits that the double usage is an allusion to both the First and Second Temples; the wolf analogy is a reference to the tribe of Binyamin whose symbol (as stated by our forefather Yaakov Avinu) was a wolf. Miriam felt that it was worthless to offer sacrifices to Hashem, and that they were just a financial drain on the Jewish people. And if we always performed the *tamid* offering with such diligence, and if it was truly so important, then why didn't Hashem help the Jews in times of distress?

This is an age-old question, which many commentators have answered with various ideas and thoughts. The simplest answer, in my opinion, is an idea expressed by *Tosafos* in *Berachos* (55a) regarding *davening*. When a person prays to Hashem, and sincerely and joyously accepts whatever answer Hashem provides to his *tefillos* without complaint, this person is considered truly righteous. But a person who *davens* with seeming great piety and resolve, and then declares: Now, Hashem, You <u>have</u> to do what I requested <u>because</u> I *davened* with such concentration — well, such a person is just begging for trouble. So too Miriam. Her chutzpah in expecting Hashem to help and save the Jewish people, just because they performed certain rituals — and then kicking the Altar in disgust, when in her opinion, the Jewish people were not protected as she saw fit — was totally inappropriate. Permanent punishment in this setting was necessary to demonstrate to us for all time that the ways of Hashem are often unfathomable. We should never presume to ascribe cause and effect without direct Divine interpretation.

This Gemara also teaches us a second equally important lesson. We must always be critically cognizant of what we say in front of our children. What appears to us as innocent conversation decrying a leader, rabbi or Jewish law, can be totally misunderstood, misconstrued and then repeated and acted out in a horrible fashion by our children. And, the Gemara says, we bear responsibility for such actions, even though the resulting damage was never our intent. Children are sponges that soak up our every action and deed; they assimilate much from what we say, as well as from what we don't express. The consequences can be shocking, permanent and unfortunately quite tragic.

מסכת ביצה

BEITZAH

BEITZAH

BEITZAH 13B

PROVING THE HALACHAH

The Gemara is in the midst of an involved discourse regarding the permissibility of certain activities on Shabbos and Yom Tov. As part of the countering argument (prohibiting one to peel more than one kernel of barley at a time), the Talmud states the following: Is that so (that one is allowed to prepare only one barley at a time)? Didn't Rav's wife peel cupfuls of barley for him on Shabbos? And didn't Rav Chiya's wife peel cupfuls of barley for him on Shabbos? Based on these women's actions, the Gemara resolves the discussion in a totally different manner.

IT IS INTERESTING TO REALIZE THAT THE GEMARA BRINGS AN uncontested proof from the wives of these great Rabbis. Obviously, not only did their husbands know the law, but the women as well were well versed in the intricacies of the complex laws of Shabbos food preparation — the Talmud adduced a proof from their actions! Similarly, we recognize that Rav and Rav Chiya obviously concurred with the practice of their wives, or the Gemara would certainly have told us otherwise. This similar theme is present in many places in the Talmud (e.g. *Beitzah* 29b in this *sefer*).

Elsewhere, in *Yevamos* 63a, the Gemara relates that Rav and his wife did not get along very well. Whenever Rav asked for a certain dish, his wife brought him something else. Yet, despite the difficulties that they may have had in their personal relationship, their contentions never spilled over into halachic areas. If Rav had disagreed with his wife's actions, she certainly wouldn't have performed these activities on Shabbos; and Rav never would have condoned or allowed her to continue doing a prohibited labor.

Beitzah 25b

(See also Berachos 51b and Shabbos 54b)

Yalta's Glorious Carriage

The Rabbis taught in a Baraisa*: On Yom Tov, a blind person may not go out carrying a cane; a shepherd is not permitted to carry his pouch; and one is not permitted to go out being carried in a seat — neither a man nor a woman. The Gemara asks: Is this (the latter case) really so? But Rabbi Yaakov the son of Idi sent (the following statement): There was an old man in our neighborhood, and he would be carried out in a special folding chair. They came and asked Rabbi Yehoshua ben Levi (if this is allowed) and he said: If the public needs him, it is permitted. The Gemara then lists several similar cases where indeed this ruling was relied upon in actual practice, and concludes: Where there is a public need, it is permitted to carry a person in a chair; otherwise, it is prohibited to do so on Yom Tov ...*

Chama bar Adda met Rabbi Zerika, and asked him if it is permitted to carry someone on a seat on Yom Tov. Rabbi Zerika answered him: This is what Rav Ami said: It is allowed as long as one does not carry the seat on the shoulders. What does this mean? Rav Yosef the son of Rava stated that it means using an alunki*. (*Rashi *explains that it is prohibited to carry via an* alunki *— it is not permitted to have two men face each other, and place their hands on the opposite person's shoulders and carry the seat in between them on their outstretched arms.) Is this so? But didn't Rav Nachman permit his wife Yalta to be carried in this fashion on Yom Tov? The*

Gemara replies: Yalta is different. She feared she would fall down if her chair were carried in the regular manner, and thus it was permitted to carry her via the alunki. *Similarly, Ameimar and Mar Zutra were carried in this fashion on the Shabbos before a Yom Tov (when they would be teaching the laws of the holiday) because of their fear. And others explained the reason was because of the pressure of the crowds.*

R*ASHI* COMMENTS THAT THE THREE ACTIVITIES MENTIONED IN THE *Baraisa* are prohibited because they resemble work done during the week, and permitting their use on Yom Tov would denigrate the holiday. (It should be noted that a totally blind person who absolutely requires a cane to ambulate is not included in this ruling.)

Yalta, the famous wife of Rabbi Nachman ben Yaakov, is described elsewhere in this *sefer*, and in the Gemara in *Chullin* 109b, as a very knowledgeable, bright woman. She was the daughter of the Exilarch Rabbah bar Avahu, who was the prime rebbi and mentor of her husband, Rabbi Nachman. They were privileged to have three great children that we know about, Mar Zutra (himself mentioned in our Gemara above), Rabbah and Ravin, all of whom are mentioned prominently in the Talmud.

Menachem Meishiv Nefesh points out that carrying a seat in the normal fashion was more dangerous, and carried a greater risk that the occupant of the chair would be dropped. *Rashash* appears troubled by the entire discussion. He asks: How could fear itself be a reason to allow Yalta to be carried. If she was so afraid, she should have walked, or not traveled in the first place! This problem is echoed by various commentators below.

Rashi states that the "needs of the public" refers to giving a public Torah discourse. *Meiri* contends that any communal need would satisfy this requirement. *Tosafos* add that when the Gemara remarked that Yalta is different — she can be carried via the *alunki* — it meant she was also terrified of falling, in addition to the fact that many people needed her on Yom Tov. Whether this was to give a *shiur* for women, or for some other important public task, *Tosafos* does not state.

Meiri disagrees however. When it says that Yalta was different, it implies that she was able to be carried via an *alunki* if she was afraid. It isn't necessary to invoke that she was needed for public service as well. The *Rashba* posits that fear alone would not normally be sufficient reason to carry a man or a woman on Yom Tov. However, Yalta was different. She was such an important woman — the daughter of the Exilarch — plus, she was needed by the public, so she could be carried via an *alunki*. But a man in the same setting would not be permitted to be carried. How then were Ameimar and Mar Zutra (her son!) able to be carried? Only because there was an additional fear and concern regarding their special situation. *Rashi* explains that many people came to their public discourse. As all the populace rose out of respect, the multitude of rising humanity would disorient their carriers and significantly increase the risk of falling. *Maharam Schif* adds that the great commotion and crowd magnitude precipitated unusual jostling, escalating their risk if they were carried in the normal fashion. Alternatively, it was much faster to carry them via an *alunki*. If there was a more rapid entrance and departure, the public would only have to remain standing for a shorter period. Because of this respect for the public welfare, the shortest and swiftest mechanism to bring the scholars in and out of the lecture hall was utilized.

The *Shitah Mekubetzes* provides a similar explanation to the *Rashba*, based upon the Talmud Yerushalmi and the *Re'ah*. Since Yalta was such an important person, she always traveled in this glorified fashion, even during the week. Thus the Rabbis permitted her, but nobody else, to travel with the *alunki* on Yom Tov, even if there was no communal necessity to do so. Others were only permitted to be carried in this way if there was a public need.

The *Ran* has a slightly different approach. The reason Yalta was carried via *alunki* was to prevent her from being pushed in the public areas, and/or to protect her from getting filthy from the dirt roads. Thus, even without public need, she was permitted to be carried this way.

A textual controversy is found in the *Rosh*. Two versions of our Gemara are proffered. The Rosh himself has the language: A woman is different; because she is afraid of falling, she is permitted to be carried. But the *Tiferes Shmuel* and the *Korban Nesanel* provide an alternate reading in the *Rosh*, one similar to our Gemara's version. They have the text "'Yalta' is different." In any event, we clearly see that *Chazal* gave a special Rabbinical dispensation to certain women or possibly even all females based upon their special status.

BEITZAH 29B

ZEALOUS OBSERVANCE

*(The Gemara is in the midst of a discussion regarding permissible food preparation activities on Yom Tov. Under selected circumstances, certain preparations were permitted only if a change was implemented from the normal weekday performance of that act.) The wife of Rav Yosef would resift the flour on Yom Tov with a slight change from the normal way she performed sifting during the week. She would use the back of the sieve rather than its front side. Rav Yosef said to her: See, I require well-sifted flour — you can therefore sift in a regular fashion without any change (*Rashi*). Similarly, the wife of Rav Ashi resifted the flour using the underside of the table (*Rashi*). (*Tosafos *explain this as the top flat part of the table. This was considered an unusual way to sift, since normally a trough was used.) Rav Ashi commented: My wife is the daughter of Rami bar Chama; Rami was very zealous and careful in his actions. If she did not see this practice in her father's house, she would not have done this.*

WE SEE YET ANOTHER EXAMPLE OF THE GEMARA BRINGING practical halachic decisions based upon the actions of respected women. It is a common misconception among some to minimize the role of women as transmitters and teachers of Jewish law and custom. Indeed the opposite has always been true. Our *mesorah* has always been carefully passed from mother to daughter. Women have always been considered authentic, absolutely reliable transmitters of Torah and Rabbinical law. In fact, these women were more stringent than required by law (at least in the viewpoints of some authorities).

The *Korban Nesanel* (and others) suggest that the father of Rav Ashi's wife was actually Rami bar Abba (not Chama) as our text describes the lineage. Rami bar Chama in fact lived many years prior to Rav Ashi. Moreover, the Gemara (*Chullin* 111a) specifically states that Rami bar Abba was Rav Ashi's father-in-law. The *Encyclopedia LeChachmei HaTalmud VeHaGeonim* states that there were two different Rami bar Abbas. One was a third-generation Amora scholar, and the other was the fifth-generation Amora Rami bar Abba — the father-in-law of our Gemara's Rav Ashi — who lived during the sixth and last Amoraic generation (6th century C.E.). Alternatively, this work suggests that there was indeed only one Rami bar Abba. He was a great man and merited living a very long period of time!

Beitzah 32b

(See also Beitzah 13b)

MORE ZEALOUS OBSERVANCE

*The wife of Rav Chiya had a half-brick fall (*Rashi *— from the oven wall) into her oven on Yom Tov. Rav Chiya told her: See, I require especially high quality bread (and therefore it is permissible to clean out the oven —* Rashi*).*

This Gemara is very similar to the Gemara cited in the preceding section (*Beitzah* 29b). We frequently find that the Gemara demonstrates a halachic point by describing an actual case. Here, the wife personally followed the more stringent opinion, but the law states that the activity is permitted. In a different case in *Beitzah* 13b, the wives took the lenient position, and the Gemara used their acts as a strong proof as to what is demanded by *halachah*.

מסכת תענית

TAANIS

TAANIS

TAANIS 5B

(see also Megillah 14b-15a; Zevachim 116b)

RACHAV'S BEAUTY

> *Rav Yitzchak said (to Rav Nachman), "Whoever says the name 'Rachav, Rachav,' will immediately 'become impure.'" Rav Nachman remarked back to Rav Yitzchak, "I say it ('Rachav, Rachav') without any concern." Rav Yitzchak replied to him, "I made my remark only regarding someone who knows her and recognizes her."*

RACHAV IS ONE OF THE MOST INTRIGUING FEMALE FIGURES mentioned in the *Tanach* and Gemara. She is described in the Gemara in *Megillah* 15a as one of the four most beautiful women who ever lived. (The other three are Sarah [the wife of Avraham], Avigayil [wife of David HaMelech], and Esther.) *Zevachim* 116b relates that she became an infamous harlot when she was only 10 years old, from the time the Jewish nation left Egypt and throughout the next forty years that they traveled in the desert. The Gemara relates that every ruler and prince had sinned with her. Nevertheless, she ultimately did *teshuvah*, and actually converted and married the leader of the Jewish people, Yehoshua bin Nun! The Gemara recounts that with the same articles with which she sinned, she did *teshuvah*. When the two spies, Pinchas and Kalev, were sent by Yehoshua to explore Yericho and the surrounding land, Rachav saved their lives by hiding them. She covered Kalev with the same bed (flax) she used for immoral purposes, and let them down her window (which faced the exterior wall of the city) with the same ropes she had previously used to secretly allow entry to her boudoir! Yehoshua recognized her true potential and greatness, and married her after she converted.

Their subsequent progeny included eight (the Midrash [*Ruth Rabbah* 2] writes ten) *Kohanim* who were prophets, and one prophetess (Chulda). (Yehoshua was not a *Kohen* himself. They had only female children. When their daughters subsequently married, their progeny followed the house of the husband.) Rachav's repentance was so complete and sincere that the Midrash (*Ruth Rabbah* 2a; *Koheles Rabbah* 50; 4,6) states that she merited the Divine Spirit. The Yerushalmi (*Berachos* 2:8, page 20a) compares her to that other great convert, Yisro, Moshe's father-in-law. *Midrash Rabbah* (3:2) further notes that both Yisro and Rachav themselves were not originally destined for glory by Hashem. However, through their own internal goodness they became closely attached to Hashem and the Jewish people. About them the Midrash opines: Praiseworthy are those who were not chosen by Hashem, but nevertheless, on their own volition, come close to Him.

The Yerushalmi elsewhere in *Berachos* (4:4, page 35a) remarks: Her actions were so meritorious that she was able to not only save her immediate family from the miraculous destruction of Yericho (described in the beginning of the Book of *Yehoshua*), but her merits were sufficient to even save any individuals that were married to somebody from her family as well! When he was punished with a fatal illness, King Chizkiyahu prayed "towards a wall" to plead with Hashem to save his life. What wall? Rabbi Yehoshua ben Levi remarks: None other than the wall of Rachav, once used for sin, but ultimately used to save the lives of Pinchas and Kalev.

While very interesting, what is Rav Yitzchak's purpose in telling us this information regarding the legendary beauty of Rachav? She had lived hundreds of years earlier, and nobody was around who actually knew her. *Rabbi Yaakov Emden* remarks that the Gemara is teaching us an important lesson. Anyone who knows a women who is beautiful as was Rachav, must be very vigilant so as not to come to transgression. *Ben Yehoyada* likewise queries the significance of the Gemara. After all, nobody in the time of the Gemara had known or had seen Rachav. Therefore the purpose is to warn us. We must be especially zealous in our conduct with our wives during times of ritual impurity when they are not permitted to us. This is deduced from the repetition of her name, "Rachav, Rachav," a sign of endearment. *Iyun Yaakov* suggests that possibly one could transgress from just seeing a picture of her! And why did the Gemara specifically choose Rachav as the example? The thought of her would also remind one of her occupation, and this would increase the risk of sinning. We learn from this Gemara how very careful a person living in our modern immoral world must be. We must constantly be on our guard against the perpetual stream of inappropriate sights to which we are exposed in the routine secular environment!

Ben Yehoyada further asks: How could Rav Yitzchak have taught this rule? In stating the law, he had to mention her name — wasn't he afraid of the potential adverse outcome himself? The answer is simple. Rav Yitzchak did not know her or recognize her, and thus was immune to her captivation. *Tosafos* indeed comment that the mere mention of her name only caused impurity in those who had sinned with her or had actually seen her.

Taanis 9a

(see also Bava Metzia 84a)

Rabbi Yochanan's Sister — A Glaring Glance

(The Gemara just related one story about Rabbi Yochanan and his nephew, the son of his deceased brother-in-law Reish Lakish [Rabbi Shimon ben Lakish]. A second anecdote is told.)

And furthermore, Rabbi Yochanan found the son of Reish Lakish sitting and saying the following verse: The foolishness of a person perverts his way, but in his heart he blames Hashem for this (Mishlei 19:3). *Rabbi Yochanan sat and wondered, "Is there anything written in the* Kesuvim *(Writings) that is not alluded to in the Torah (Pentateuch) itself?" His nephew replied to him, "Is it not alluded to? Does it not state (regarding when Yosef secretly returned the money that his brothers had paid for their grain on their first trip to Egypt):* And their hearts left them, and they trembled to each other saying, 'What has Hashem done to us?' *(i.e. isn't this essentially the idea of the* posuk *in* Mishlei*?)" Rabbi Yochanan lifted his eye(lids). The boy's mother (Rabbi Yochanan's sister) took the boy away. She said to her son, "Go away from Rabbi Yochanan, so he shouldn't do to you as he did to your father."*

The Gemara in *Bava Metzia* (84a) and elsewhere provides some details explaining the relationship between Rabbi Yochanan, his sister, and Reish Lakish. At that time, Rabbi

Yochanan had glared askance at Reish Lakish and thereby indirectly caused his premature demise. Rabbi Yochanan's sister was very concerned that the same disaster should not be repeated to their son as well. Ultimately, Rabbi Yochanan became so distraught over his role in Reish Lakish's demise that he suffered a breakdown and died, himself quite broken.

Rabbi Yochanan is also described in that Gemara in *Bava Metzia* as being most beautiful in appearance. That was not inconsistent with his being quite obese, so much so that he had to lift his eyelids with a silver fork in order to see (*Bava Kamma* 117a). *Rashi* explains that he lifted his eyelids to see who it was that said such a sharp response.

Why didn't Rabbi Yochanan know the *posuk* in the Torah to which the verse in *Mishlei* alluded? *Ben Yehoyada* proposes that he really knew the answer, but he was just checking to see if his nephew knew of the *posuk* and its reference. *Menachem Meishiv Nefesh* also suggests that Rabbi Yochanan was indeed familiar with the source of the idea expressed by Shlomo HaMelech in *Mishlei*. He was just surprised that the child bypassed a verse from the Torah and instead quoted a *posuk* from the later *Kesuvim*. His nephew replied, "Do you think that I do not know the verse in the Torah? I intentionally chose the later *posuk*. The verse in *Chumash* portrays the holy *shevatim* (brothers) in a derogatory light. They sinned against their brother Yosef, and now they have the *chutzpah* to complain to Hashem as to why He caused them to get into this situation." His nephew therefore preferred not to use this earlier source to illustrate the concept. However, Rabbi Yochanan misunderstood this reply as being derisive — he thought that his nephew was talking to him in an inappropriate, mocking fashion, thinking that Rabbi Yochanan did not know the *posuk*. He raised his eyes to look at him, and that is when the boy's mother became concerned, because it was just such a look that Rabbi Yochanan gave Reish Lakish that led to his untimely death.

TAANIS 9AA

MIRIAM'S MIRACLES

*Rabbi Yose ben Rabbi Yehudah taught a lesson about three wonderful supporters who arose for the Jewish nation; they were Moshe, Aharon and Miriam. And three wonderful presents were given to Israel because of them. And they were the well, the cloud and the manna. The well came about in the merit of Miriam; the cloud in the merit of Aharon; the manna in the merit of Moshe. When Miriam died, the well disappeared, as it states (*Bamidbar 20:1*):* and Miriam died there, *followed immediately by the verse* and there was no water for the community. *The well subsequently returned through the merit of Moshe and Aharon. (The Gemara continues to relate that similarly, the cloud disappeared when Aharon passed away, and returned in the merit of Moshe. At Moshe's death, all three [the well, the cloud, and the manna] disappeared, never to openly return.)*

MIRIAM THE PROPHETESS, THE OLDER SISTER OF MOSHE AND Aharon, the famous daughter of Yocheved and Amram, is undoubtedly one of the most prominent women described in all of the Torah. It was she who caused her parents, and therefore all of the Jewish couples, to remarry (see *Sotah* 12a). They had all separated and decided to forgo procreation, rather than give in to Pharaoh's horrendous decree of throwing the male newborns into the Nile. The then only 6-year-old Miriam boldly declared that their voluntary separation was a fate worse than that which Pharaoh had decreed. Pharaoh had decreed only that the male children should be thrown into the river. But by divorcing, they were mandating that no Jewish children (male or female) would survive (be born). This argument was accepted, all the couples remarried, and this ensured the successful propagation of our people. It was Miriam, along with her mother Yocheved in their roles as chief midwives, who courageously defied the wicked Pharaoh and saved the Jewish babies despite his orders to the contrary. It was Miriam who later gathered the women after the miraculous splitting of the Red Sea and led them in singing praises to Hashem. And it was in the great merit of Miriam that the Jewish people had water during their forty-year sojourn in the arid, barren desert. The "well of Miriam," as it is known, was actually a large mobile rock that gave out water (twelve streams, one for each tribe, according to a Midrash) and rolled with the Jewish people to wherever they camped. Its waters were miraculous in many ways. Just as the manna was well known for its ability to taste like any food the consumer desired, so too the well of Miriam tasted like any beverage the imbiber wished. *Benayahu* (*Ben Yehoyada*) adds that the water not only quenched their parched throats in the hot desert climate, but it had many other therapeutic benefits as well, amongst them the ability to augment and increase memory powers. Indeed, he remarks, it is well known that the well of Miriam is hidden in the Tiberias Sea in Northern Israel *to this very day*. And great *tzaddikim* throughout the ages have located it and drunk from it! It is said that the Holy Arizal gave his student Rabbi Chaim Vital a drink from it, and this contributed to his legendary powers of recall.

Rashi points out that it was exactly this departure of the well of Miriam that precipitated the tragic episode of Moshe hitting the rock to bring forth water, instead of speaking to it. It was this "transgression" that caused Moshe to be banned by Hashem from entering the land of Israel.

The *Maharsha* asks a very basic question. If the well (and subsequently the cloud) was able to be returned in the merit of Moshe, why did it depart after the death of Miriam, albeit only for a while? *Maharsha* explains that this is to show us the primacy of Miriam in precipitating this miracle. *Ahavas Eisan* (a commentary in the *sefer Ein Yaakov*) posits that while the well did return because of Moshe, the miracle was not the same. There was something lacking, although he does not state exactly what was missing. The *Eitz Yosef,* quoting the *Shelah,* gives a similar answer. There is less of a miracle involved in returning something that was already present versus creating something *de novo*. In his parallel commentary, the *Anaf Yosef,* he adds that this follows the principle of *middah keneged middah*. Because Miriam helped save the Jewish babies, and was the supplier of food and water to the newborns in Egypt, Hashem provided the Jewish people with water in the desert as a payback for her kindness. In a similar vein, the *Iyun Yaakov* exposits the famous second Mishnah of *Pirkei Avos* as describing these three leaders in the desert. Shimon HaTzadik states (*Avos* 1:2) that the world exists because of three things: Torah, service, and the performance of acts of *chessed* (kindness). Torah is equated with Moshe, service is associated with Aharon, and *chessed* is represented by Miriam, as exemplified by her work as a midwife in Egypt.

TAANIS 18A

(see also Rosh Hashanah 19a)

WISE ADVICE

(The Tanna Chananyah ben Chizkiyah wrote Megillas Taanis. *It describes many minor holidays that the Sages established during the Second Temple era to commemorate miracles and great events that occurred to the Jewish people. The Gemara essentially directly quotes here the exact same Gemara found previously in Rosh Hashanah 19a.)*

On the twenty-eighth day of the month of Adar, good news was brought to the Jews. (An evil decree was lifted.) They would not have to stop learning Torah. The secular (non-Jewish) government had originally decreed that Jews were forbidden to engage in Bible study, were not permitted to circumcise their children, and were required to desecrate the Shabbos. What did Yehudah ben Shamua and his colleagues do (about this harsh law)? They went and sought counsel from a certain non-Jewish matronisa *(noblewoman), who was frequently visited by many senior officials of the Roman government. This* matronisa *told Rabbi Yehudah and the Rabbis to go out and demonstrate in the nighttime. They followed her advice, and protested and cried out against the evil decrees. They said:* אי שמים*, For Heaven's sake! Aren't we your brothers? Aren't we the sons of the same father (Yitzchak)? Aren't we the sons of the same mother (Rivkah)? Why are we singled out from all the other nations under Roman rule to have such harsh decrees promulgated against us? The demonstration was* *successful. The Romans abolished those anti-Jewish laws, and the Rabbis established the twenty-eighth of Adar as a (minor) holiday.*

THE COMMENTARY FOR THIS GEMARA IS FOUND IN THIS *SEFER* IN *Rosh Hashanah* 19a.

TAANIS 23B

RABBI MANI'S WIFE — CHANNAH

(The Gemara is in the midst of a series of fascinating stories about the extraordinary and miraculous abilities of various Sages of the Talmud. Rabbi Yitzchak ben Elyashiv was such a person.)

Rav Mani related to Rabbi Yitzchak ben Elyashiv: The person of my household (i.e. my wife) is not satisfactory to me (Rashi — *Rav Mani was stating that his wife was not pretty). Rabbi Yitzchak asked him, "What is her name?" (Rav Mani replied), "Channah." (Rabbi Yitzchak declared), "Let Channah become beautiful," and indeed, she became beautiful. (Subsequently, Rav Mani returned to Rabbi Yitzchak) and complained that his wife had become too overbearing and critical of him. Rabbi Yitzchak decreed: "If so, then let her return to her darkness," and Channah reverted to her darkness (i.e. to her being uncomely).*

NO STORY IS RELATED IN THE GEMARA UNLESS THERE IS A PURPOSE and/or message to teach us. *Rashi* specifically states that she became overbearing because of her excessive beauty. *Rabbi Yaakov Emden* writes that the Gemara is reminding us that sometimes beauty can be bad. The woman's character was adversely affected by the improvement in her physical features. We must always be very much on guard against the haughtiness that can sometimes come with great comeliness. Physical beauty is a gift from Hashem, and if we flaunt the gift over others, it can, *chas veshalom*, quickly be taken away.

Ben Yehoyada notes that once the wife of Rav Mani became haughty, the only solution was for her now to lose her beauty, and not to have Rabbi Yitzchak pray that the character flaw of haughtiness disappear. The reason is that having the weakness of being haughty disappear would not provide a permanent solution. Each day the *yetzer hara* renews itself in the battle for our souls. Rabbi Yitzchak would have had to *daven* each day specifically for her to be less arrogant, and that would have been a prolonged and difficult situation. It was simpler to remove the cause rather than to try and alleviate its effect daily. This is an important lesson for us. Battles against the evil inclination are not fought and won (or lost) in one confrontation. Continuous striving for improvement is imperative, or we risk the loss of everything we have so diligently gained previously.

Why did Rabbi Yitzchak need to know her name before he could pray for her? *Ben Yehoyada* remarks that this demonstrates to us that Rabbi Yitzchak did not mingle with the wife of any other man. He did not know her name and he was not familiar with the appearance of even another scholar's wife. He lived a totally pure lifestyle.

With this approach, I would like to suggest a second answer as to the *Ben Yehoyada's* question as to why Rabbi Yitzchak asked for her name before *davening* on her behalf. When one is in the presence of a sick person, one can *daven* directly to Hashem for their recovery without mentioning the ill person's name. *Chazal* tell us that the *Shechinah* is present at the head of the sickbed, and it is clear for whom you are praying. However, when making a *mi sheberach* (the *tefillah* for a sick person to be cured) in shul, the custom is to specifically mention the name of the afflicted person. Perhaps here too, Rabbi Yitzchak needed to know her name for his *mi sheberach* to work!

Benayahu and *Anaf Yosef* both argue that it is inconceivable that Rav Mani would go to the great Rabbi Yitzchak and complain about physical beauty. They suggest that, in actuality, Channah must have had a serious disfiguring skin condition, albeit not a life-threatening one. Rav Mani requested that Rabbi Yitzchak pray for her to receive a *refuah sheleimah* (complete cure). However, when she acted haughtily thereafter, Rabbi Yitzchak prayed for her condition to relapse.

Likewise, the *Eitz Yosef* commentary in the *Ein Yaakov* does not take this narrative literally. He proposes that it is an allegory discussing the trait of jealousy. He cites the *sefer Mechir Yayin* who notes that it would be absurd to understand that miracles would be performed simply because Rav Mani desired that his wife be more beautiful.

Rather, Rav Mani was inquiring about how to rid himself of the trait of jealousy, which he referred to as "Channah." Channah is a Biblical name and figure associated with jealousy. The great and righteous mother of the Navi Shmuel, Channah, prayed to Hashem for a child because she was very jealous of her co-wife Penninah who had children, while she didn't (see this *sefer*, *Berachos* 31a-b for details of that famous story). Rabbi Yitzchak told him that the corrective measure would be to distance himself to an extreme, and not to express any jealousy toward anyone for a prescribed time. "Let yourself become beautiful in regards to Channah (jealousy)" — by ridding yourself of it totally. Later, when Rav Mani felt that he had succeeded, he reported to Rabbi Yitzchak that he felt he could now "rebel against his jealousy," and control it. He asked his mentor if he should revert back to a middle-ground where he could at least exercise "the jealousy of sages." Rabbi Yitzchak then concurred that Rav Mani could begin to utilize jealousy, albeit in a limited manner.

Taanis 24a

Rabbi Yose and His Daughter's Death

(The Gemara is in the midst of a discussion of various great Talmudic figures. Rabbi Yose ben Yukras was a great tzaddik *capable of performing miracles and extraordinary feats. However, the Gemara just commented that even a great sage like Rav Yose bar Avin was afraid to stay and learn with him — out of fear of his very exacting and harsh standards. In that story, the Gemara related that Rabbi Yose ben Yukras induced the premature death of his own son. Our narrative describes what transpired to his daughter.)*

What is the story about his (Rabbi Yose ben Yukras') daughter? He had a most beautiful daughter. One day, he saw a certain man who was making a hole in the bushes (destroying a fence of trees surrounding Rabbi Yose's house — Rashi*) to be able to look at the beautiful girl. Rabbi Yose asked the man what he was doing. He replied, "My dear rebbi! If I am not meritorious enough to marry her, can't I at least merit to gaze upon her?" Rabbi Yose said to her, "My daughter, you are causing much distress to people. Return to your dust, and do not be a stumbling block for mankind."*

IT IS ESSENTIALLY IMPOSSIBLE FOR US TO COMPREHEND THE ACTIONS OF Rabbi Yose. How could a father treat his beloved daughter in this fashion? Indeed, *Maharsha* provides a very direct and straightforward explanation — Rabbi Yose was in error! He acted improperly in condemning his daughter. He brings a proof to this from Avraham and Sarah and the Biblical episodes where Pharaoh, and subsequently Avimelech, kidnaped Sarah because of her great beauty. It is no sin to be beautiful, and Sarah (and the daughter in our Gemara) were totally blameless regarding the improper actions of those men.

Ben Yehoyada adds that the reason that Rabbi Yose didn't make his daughter less beautiful (rather than inducing her premature death) was because he felt that it was wrong for a person to blatantly change nature in this fashion. After all, in the previous narrative regarding his son, the reason he got angry with his son was because he used his Torah talents to change nature. Rabbi Yose felt that for that he deserved an early death. How could Rabbi Yose himself thereby justify causing a similar change in nature — for nothing more than his own benefit? Therefore, he was willing to stand by his principles even if it meant losing his own daughter as a result. *Ben Yehoyada* further comments that death is an inevitable outcome, and thus was not considered meddling with nature.

Obviously, Rabbi Yose functioned on a different plane than we do. His approach, that of the מדת הדין, *strict and exacting justice*, is not one under which the rest of the world can operate. We must therefore continuously thank the Creator of the world for changing His attribute for guiding this world from the מדת הדין to that of the מדת הרחמים, *the aspect of mercy.*

Taanis 24a

A Daughter's Trousseau

A story about Elazar Ish Birta (according to some versions, including the Ein Yaakov, *this is Rabbi Eliezer Ish Bartusa). Whenever the administrators of charity would see him, they would hide from him, because he would donate to them whatever money he was holding. One day, while he was going to the market to purchase a trousseau for his daughter, the charity administrators saw him and hid from him. He ran after them, (found them), and made them swear to tell him for what they were collecting. They told him (they were collecting) for an orphan boy and girl (to be married to each other —* Rashi*). He said to them, "By the Temple service! (an oath), they have priority over my own daughter!" He took all that he had with him and gave it to them. He was left with one* zuz *(coin of the realm). He bought with it wheat, and brought it (home) and tossed it into his storage room (granary). When his wife came, she asked her (their) daughter, "What did your father bring?" She replied, "Whatever he brought, he threw in the storage room." She (Elazar's wife) tried to open the door of the granary and saw that it was filled with grain — bulging out of the pipes (hinges) of the door — and the door couldn't open because of the wheat. His daughter went to the Beis Midrash and said to her father, "Come and see what the One Who loves you (Hashem) has done for you!" He replied to her, "It (the grain) is as sanctified property to you — and you have no share in it except as one of the impoverished people of Israel."*

ELAZAR ISH BIRTA WAS UNDOUBTEDLY AN EXTREMELY GENEROUS AND charitable person. But how was he able to give away all of his funds to charity? Doesn't that transgress the decree established by the Rabbis of Usha (*Kesubos* 50a) prohibiting excessive charity? *Ben Yehoyada* suggests simply that the enactment of Usha arose subsequent to our story. *Gevuras Ari* quotes the Gemara (*Arachin* 28a) which brings down an opinion that does not hold from this enactment of the Rabbis of Usha, and the *Gevuras Ari* says that Elazar presumably held like this opinion. Thus, he was not restricted to the rule of giving only up to one-fifth of his money, and he, in fact, chose to donate nearly all of his money.

Ben Yehoyada himself brings another suggestion of the *Gevuras Ari*, that the Elazar mentioned is an Amora, but he himself does not think that this is the case.

Why did Elazar Ish Birta think that the needs of the orphans had priority over those of his own daughter? After all, there are *halachos* about everything, including to whom and how much one can donate to charity. The *halachah* states that *tzedakah* to one's own family member takes precedence over charity to a non-relative. *Maharsha, Anaf Yosef* and *Ben Yehoyada* all comment that Elazar obviously had other funds available at home. Although he gave them almost everything on his person, he did not exceed the total Rabbinical limitations. *Iyun Yaakov* opines that Elazar considered this case an exception to the rule. He could always obtain other monies for his daughter's trousseau, but there was no one to pay for the wedding of these two orphans, and thus they had halachic priority.

Elazar did not want his daughter to benefit from the miracle; thus he considered the grain to be sanctified and thereby off-limits. Yet, if he considered this grain halachically consecrated, why were the poor permitted to use it? And why was his daughter not entitled to benefit from it as any poor person? *Menachem Meishiv Nefesh* writes that since the miracle was not done for the poor people, they were permitted to benefit from it. And since his own daughter was now also poor, she shouldn't be considered less worthy than them! (*Iyun Yaakov* as well expresses a similar sentiment.) *Ben Yehoyada* and *Rabbi Yaakov Emden* introduce an important general rule when it comes to miraculous acts. One is allowed to receive benefit from them only when certain pre-conditions exist. Namely, if there was already something physical in existence before the miracle, then benefit is allowed. This is proven from various historical events: i.e. the famous story of Eliyahu (Elijah) the prophet providing the woman of Tzorfas with voluminous oil and flour, miraculously produced from the small amount that she already had; the miracle of Chanukah, whereby the small container of oil miraculously lasted all eight days, etc. (see *Melachim I* 17:14)

Why did Elazar request that the *tzedakah* collectors swear to tell the truth? They were quite aware of Elazar's prodigious generosity — it certainly is not a common complaint today of charity collectors that they have to hide from donors who give too lavishly! Elazar wanted to make sure they did not minimize the true needs of the orphans.

Why did Elazar specifically purchase wheat with the last *zuz*? *Benayahu* remarks that Elazar did not consider his daughter's plans to be married as failed due to his dispensing of the funds. He had full confidence that due to his having performed a *mitzvah*, everything would succeed, and he purchased wheat as part of the provisions for the wedding and guest needs associated with it. He maintained total belief in Hashem's ability to provide for them no matter what.

Wheat is made into bread, and women are compared to bread for a variety of reasons. *Chazal* (see *Bava Metzia* 59a) inform us that financial blessing and bounty (bread) come to a house only because of women. This, remarks the *Benayahu*, explains their ancient Baghdad custom of placing long candles studded with wheat kernels in front of a *kallah*. Also, the *gematria* (numerical value) of חטים (wheat) is sixty-seven. This is the same value as בינה (wisdom). The Gemara in *Niddah* (45b) states that women possess בינה יתירה, *extra wisdom*, as compared to men.

Elazar was comparing his daughter to the wheat in other ways as well. Wheat is unique among produce in that it is the only ground-growing item whose *berachah* (blessing) — בורא פרי האדמה — changes to a higher *berachah* — בורא מיני מזונות — when it undergoes a transformation. Other types of produce are usually reduced to a more general, less specific blessing if altered. So too, is a woman. When she changes from being single to becoming married, a young lady undergoes a spiritual uplifting in the process. May all woman and men merit reaching this elevated state!

Finally, in his *Ben Yehoyada* commentary, this great Baghdad scholar expresses the idea that our Gemara too represents an example of *middah keneged middah*. Elazar Ish Birta did the *mitzvah* of giving *tzedakah* wholeheartedly, without any restraint. So too, Hashem blessed his granary to the bursting point, without any restraint.

TAANIS 24B

(see also Zevachim 116b; Niddah 20a)

IFRA HURMIZ RECOGNIZES HASHEM

There was a certain man who was sentenced to lashes in the Beis Din *(court) of Rava because he had relations with a Cuthite woman. Rava administered lashes to the man and he (the man) died. The matter became known to the house of* Shvur Malka — *King Shapur (the Persian emperor of the Sassanid dynasty that ruled Israel, Persia and Mesopotamia from* 241-272 *C.E. [Schottenstein Edition,* Taanis 24b *note* 17 *and* Succah 53a *note* 24*]). The king wanted to cause Rava pain (i.e. to punish him for meting out capital punishment). However, his mother, Ifra Hurmiz, told him not to get into any dealings (quarrels) with the Jews. She warned him that all that they ask from their Master (Hashem), He grants them. King Shapur asked her for an example of what G-d does for them. (She told him that) they pray for mercy and the rains come. He remained skeptical and wondered whether precipitation arrived only because it was the natural time for rain. Rather, he declared that they should pray for mercy now in the Tammuz (summer, non-rainy) season, and all would see if the rain would fall! She then sent to Rava and advised him to have the Jews focus their thoughts, and pray for mercy that the rain should come. Rava* davened *for mercy, but no rains came. He said before Hashem, "Master of the universe!* G-d, with our ears we have heard, our fathers have recounted to us the actions You have wrought in their days, the days of old (Tehillim 44:2). *However, we have never seen (such miracles) with our own eyes!"*

*Rains (then) came (with such an amount) that the gutters in Tzippori (*Ein Yaakov *reads Mechoza) flowed water all the way to the river Diglas (Tigris). (That night) Rava's father appeared to him in a dream and said to him, "Is there anyone who has caused so much trouble to Heaven (has anyone ever bothered Hashem to change nature so drastically)?" His father further remarked, "Change your sleeping place (tonight)." Rava changed his place. The next day, he discovered slash marks of knives imprinted over his (previous sleeping place's) bed.*

R*ASHI* IN NIDDAH (20B) DESCRIBES IFRA HURMIZ AS A RIGHTEOUS gentile woman. This explains why she remarked to her son how wise the Rabbis were. *Rashi* here (and elsewhere) explains that the name Ifra means "grace"; Hurmiz was the name of a beautiful demon; i.e. she had the attractiveness of this demon. *Rashi* notes that even though she was a non-Jew, nonetheless she observed the laws of marital/ritual purity, and sent sacrifices for Hashem. (*Shitah Mekubetzes* writes that she sent Rava very expensive special meat. Possibly this is because Rava lived well after the destruction of the Second Temple when Jews were [and still are] forbidden to bring sacrifices to Hashem.) *Rashi* comments that she was very close to converting to Judaism. She obviously recognized that the Jewish people have a special relationship with Hashem. Starting up with the Jews when Hashem is shining upon them is foolhardy. She was not too proud to warn her son that even a powerful monarch like him has no chance against the Almighty. To his credit, King Shapur followed his mother's sagacious advice. The Gemara in *Moed Katan* (26a) relates how Shapur told the Amora Shmuel that he never killed any Jews. (Commentators there explain that he never killed them without a reason or provocation. He did kill 12,000 Jews once during a rebellion.) Moreover, he himself became somewhat knowledgeable in Jewish laws and practices. The Gemara in *Avodah Zarah* (76b) recounts how he *kashered* a knife prior to slicing an *esrog* for Rav Yehudah to eat; in *Succah* (53a) he is described as participating in the great pomp and circumstances surrounding the *Simchas Beis Hashoeva,* the festival of the water-drawing, on Succos. Indeed, one of the titles of respect by which Shmuel was referred to was *Shvur Malka* (see *Bava Basra* 115b).

Maharsha explains that Rava quoted the *posuk* in *Tehillim* that describes how the Navi Shmuel successfully beseeched Hashem for rain (*Shmuel I* 12:17,18). Rava considered his predicament identical to that of Shmuel. Both were trying to save the Jewish people from trouble: Shmuel from famine and drought, Rava from King Shapur. *Rashi* explains, however, that the demons felt Rava acted inappropriately, and therefore they sought his death, as evidenced by the vicious attack on his bed. *Menachem Meishiv Nefesh* ponders, however, what was Rava's crime? What else should he have done? Granted, asking Hashem to perform a miracle is not something one undertakes at a whim; the physical laws of the universe are not to be wistfully disregarded. Yet, if the king could be convincingly persuaded once and for all that the Jews were not to be trifled with, then it was worth "troubling" Hashem to alter nature. *Menachem Meishiv Nefesh* therefore postulates that there was an easier way out. Rava should simply have *davened* that King Shapur have a change of heart. This would have been a "less unnatural" way of preserving the peace. Alternatively, *Ben Yehoyada* suggests that to avert a problem with Shapur it would have been sufficient if it had just rained a little. Since it never rained in the summer, any precipitation would have confirmed Ifra's opinion, and voided any possible conflict. Rava, however, requested rains like in the days of Shmuel. It was this excessive display that "angered" the Heavens. Rava's father, however, was able to warn him. He appeared to him at the very beginning of the night as soon as he fell asleep, before the demons were able to do their damage. In the dream, he told him to switch his bedroom, because the demons were only given permission to harm Rava in a specific location.

The *Mesoras HaShas* and the *Maharatz Chayes* both comment that the version found in the *Ein Yaakov* (that the city mentioned should be Mechoza rather than Tzippori) is more correct. *Maharatz Chayes* explains that Rava lived in Mechoza, and that this Babylonian town was located relatively near the Tigris River. To suggest that the waters flowed all the way from Tzippori (in Israel) to Bavel would be harder to understand.

Taanis 25a

Rabbi Chanina ben Dosa's Righteous Wife and Daughter

(The Gemara on 24b *informs us about the greatness of the saintly Tanna Rabbi Chanina ben Dosa. He was extremely poor, and lived on the most meager of resources, yet in his merit, the whole world was supported. The Gemara in* Berachos (61b) *terms him a complete* tzaddik, *yet few (if any) actual technical halachic statements are attributed to him anywhere in the Gemara. He taught by example, and the Talmud is replete with these. Our Gemara continues to relate a series of additional stories about him, his family and neighbors. We will only describe here the ones that involve his wife, daughter or female neighbors, in keeping with the theme of this* sefer. *The first such story actually begins with the last few words on 24b.)*

The wife of Rabbi Chanina ben Dosa was accustomed to heating up her oven every erev *Shabbos, wherein she would throw a smoke-causing substance because of embarrassment. (All her neighbors were "cooking up a storm" preparing for Shabbos, yet she was so poor that she had almost nothing to bake — Rashi.) She had a bad neighbor who said (to herself), "Let's see, I know that they (Rabbi Chanina ben Dosa and his wife) have nothing (in their house) at all. So what is all that smoke coming from her oven?" She went and knocked on their door. Rabbi Chanina ben Dosa's wife was embarrassed, and went up to escape to an inner room. A miracle was wrought for her; when the neighbor entered, she saw an oven full of bread and a trough filled with dough. The neighbor called to Rabbi Chanina ben Dosa's wife, "Mrs. So-and-so, Mrs. So-and-so! Bring a baker's shovel (the special cooking implement they would use to remove the bread from the walls of the oven where they were placed) because your bread is getting burnt." Rabbi Chanina ben Dosa's wife replied, "Indeed, that is why I went upstairs (i.e. to get the tool)." A Tanna taught: She indeed had gone to bring the shovel, as she was very accustomed to having miracles performed.*

WHY WAS THE NEIGHBOR DESCRIBED AS A BAD PERSON? GRANTED, she was nosy and acted improperly in investigating Rabbi Chanina ben Dosa's oven, but does this make her a rotten individual? The commentators emphatically declare that indeed, this behavior exposed a flawed and evil character! How could somebody live next door to a family, especially one so righteous, know that they are in dire straits and impoverished, yet not go over there to help out and bring food and necessities to them! A neighbor who can witness that, yet only is concerned with why smoke is pouring out of their empty stove, is truly a sinister person.

Rabbi Chanina ben Dosa's wife claimed to the nosy neighbor that she had actually gone upstairs to get the shovel. How could Rabbi Chanina ben Dosa's wife have lied? And let us not think that maybe she was not on the same level of saintliness as her husband. Our Gemara specifically mentions that she was accustomed to miracles. Furthermore, in *Bava Basra* (74b) it describes how Rabbi Yochanan once went out to sea on a boat. While far out in the ocean, they beheld a beautiful jewel-studded chest (with unknown fabulous treasures inside) that was protected by circling fish. They sent out a diver to retrieve it, but Rabbi Yochanan said to leave it alone, as he declared, "That is the treaure chest belonging to the wife of Rabbi Chanina ben Dosa; it is specially reserved for *tzaddikim* in the World to Come." So, how could she have seemingly fabricated such a mistruth?

Eitz Yosef and the *Sfas Emes* provide an identical answer. She was not prevaricating at all! She knew that Hashem never allowed her to be embarrassed, and as such He would certainly perform a miracle on her behalf. Thus she truly went upstairs looking for the baker's tool to scrape the bread off her oven. *Maharsha* and *Menachem Meishiv Nefesh* suggest that the simple fact that she even had a shovel was a miracle. On her own, she never would have needed it. They were so impoverished that there was no need for any cooking equipment. But since she regularly had miracles performed for her, she kept one handy just in case. Alternatively, maybe they had a shovel, but certainly the trough for the dough appeared miraculously.

The *Yavetz* (*Rabbi Yaakov Emden*) explains how she was allowed to benefit from the bread and dough, even though they were miracles. (This was also expounded and attributed as well to the *Ben Yehoyada* on the previous *daf* — *Taanis* 24aa.) There must have already been at least a little flour and dough in the trough and oven respectively. Therefore, the miracle was not totally "something from nothing." People are permitted to benefit from miracles of this nature, as was illustrated by Eliyahu and the woman of Tzorfas (see *Melachim I* 17:14).

The Talmud Yerushalmi (*Demai* 1:3) recounts another interesting story about this holy couple. Rabbi Chanina ben Dosa's wife was very careful to only serve food that had been properly tithed. One *erev* Shabbos, she obtained some spices right before Shabbos, but she did not have an opportunity to take off the proper tithes before Shabbos began. She then forgot about it. That night at the meal, Rabbi Chanina ben Dosa reached for the spice. Hashem made the table break so that he did not get it and accidentally use it. His wife, realizing what had transpired, explained to her husband that it was *tevel*, untithed. He made the necessary apportioning in a manner that was permissible on Shabbos. Miraculously, the table fixed itself, and they went on with their meal. For people like Rabbi Chanina ben Dosa and his wife, the presence of Hashem was a truly tangible thing that pervaded their every move and action. Both of them are role models for the ages.

Rabbi Chanina ben Dosa's wife said to him, "For how much longer are we to continue to suffer so much?" When he asked her what they should do, (she replied), "Pray to Hashem for mercy that He provide us with something." Rabbi Chanina ben Dosa davened *for mercy and something like the palm of a hand miraculously appeared, and he was given one golden leg of a table. He (others have the version* <u>*she*</u>*) saw in a dream that in the future world, the righteous* tzaddikim *are eating at golden tables that have three legs, whereas Rabbi Chanina ben Dosa was eating at a table with only two legs. He said (others have the version* <u>*she*</u> *replied), "Are you content that everyone else is eating at a complete (three-legged) table, while we eat at a defective (missing a leg) table?" She said to him, "What shall we do?" "Let us pray for mercy that they should take it back." He prayed for mercy, and they took it back. A Tanna taught: The last miracle (i.e. returning the leg) was greater than the first (receiving it). For we have a tradition that Hashem gives, but He does not take back.*

M*AHARSHA* EXPLAINS, BASED UPON THE MISHNAH IN *PIRKEI AVOS* (1:2), that the three-legged table represents the three legs upon which the world stands: the Torah, the Service of Hashem (*davening* and Temple work) and *gemillas chessed* (acts of kindness and charity). By asking Hashem to provide them with reward in this world, they lost out on the full benefit of their *tefillos*, and thus that particular leg was diminished. Alternatively, the *Anaf Yosef* postulates that the three legs represent three character traits of the righteous, as described in various Talmudic and Midrashic sources. Namely, the ability to be silent even in the face of someone who wronged you, the ability to accept painful suffering from Hashem *with gladness*, and the ability to always serve Hashem in happiness. By asking Hashem to remove their suffering, they were in essence giving up one of those legs, and their table was thus missing that piece.

This story at first glance appears out of character. After living a lifetime of poverty and selfless sacrifice, was Rabbi Chanina ben Dosa's wife suddenly concerned with material possessions? Was she truly troubled and distressed because of a lack of physical goods? Both the *Menachem Meishiv Nefesh* and the *Anaf Yosef* quote from the *Yaaros Devash* which provides us with tremendous insight into the way the righteous view this world. *Chas veshalom*, do not think for even a second that Rabbi Chanina ben Dosa's wife cared for worldly material products. That was not what distressed her. Instead, she was greatly troubled by her (perceived) lack of being able to donate to charity. She felt truly distressed and pained because she often had to turn other poverty-stricken individuals away without satisfying their hunger and distress. She would literally give them her last morsel of food, even at the risk of leaving herself and her family with nothing. Yet, she felt terrible that she could not do more. Finally, she approached her husband and demanded that he pray to Hashem so they could perform the mitzvah of *gemillas chessed* to perfection.

This however, was their mistake, which they quickly recognized. God does not require a person to become rich. The *mitzvah* of charity is based upon one's means. A person can fulfil the precept by giving the appropriate percentage of his income to charity. Rabbi Chanina ben Dosa and his wife indeed gave much more than required, much more than could ever be expected. They already performed the *mitzvah* to perfection. Plus, when a *tzaddik* desires to observe a commandment, but is not physically able to do so, Hashem considers his good intentions as completion of the act. Thus, by giving them the golden leg, they were actually diminishing their accomplishments. For some of the charitable acts they would now discharge with their new funds, would undoubtedly be bestowed upon unscrupulous and/or undeserving charlatans. When one gives charity to a person not truly in need, one does not receive the same credit (if indeed one receives any reward — see *Bava Basra* 9b) as he does by donating to a deserving pauper. Rabbi Chanina ben Dosa and his wife therefore begged Hashem to take the leg back, and restore their fulfillment of this third leg (*gemillas chessed*) to its previous elevated status.

One (Friday) evening during twilight, Rabbi Chanina ben Dosa saw that his daughter was sad. He asked her, "Why are you sad?" She told him that a container of vinegar was accidently switched with a container of oil, and she had lit the Shabbos lamp using it (the vinegar). Rabbi Chanina ben Dosa said to her, "My daughter, why do you care (why does that bother you)? The One Who said to the oil it should light, He will say to the vinegar, and it will light." A Tanna taught: It stayed lit continuously all day that entire day (Shabbos), even until they used it to light the Havdalah (candle).

R*ASHI* MAINTAINS THAT THE VINEGAR LAMP ITSELF WAS NOT USED FOR *Havdalah* because one is not permitted to benefit from a commodity obtained from a miracle. The *Yavetz*, cited above on this *daf*, questions this. Why was *Rashi* forced to say this? Hadn't they already benefited from the light all Shabbos long? Furthermore, since the vinegar lamp was not a total miracle, they should have been allowed to benefit from it.

Menachem Meishiv Nefesh therefore adduces that *Rashi* must contend that since this miracle allowed them to perform a *mitzvah*, it was permitted to utilize the light of the candle on Shabbos (since fulfillment of a *mitzvah* is technically not considered personal benefit). However, once Shabbos was over, they had another option (i.e. lighting a second candle) that was preferable to continuing to benefit directly from the miracle. *Ben Yehoyada* thinks this a forced answer and posits a simple, yet brilliant solution. That was the daughter's candle. Obviously, Rabbi Chanina ben Dosa's wife lit her own (oil) Shabbos lights too! They received enjoyment on Shabbos from these candles, not the miracle vinegar lights.

Once the daughter fulfilled the precept of Shabbos candle-lighting, why did Hashem continue the miracle? Why didn't they burn out? *Maharsha* suggests that Hashem wanted to publicize the miracle. If you truly believe that Hashem controls the world and nature, then it really is no more surprising that a vinegar candle lights than one filled with oil!

Ben Yehoyada delves deeper into understanding the story. Why was the daughter sad? After all, the candle obviously was already lit, she saw the miracle performed, and she was used to seeing such events in her parents' home. Why the sad face? *Ben Yehoyada* explains. The daughter was concerned that she was losing some of her merit in the World to Come. After all, normally, if we are given something from Heaven that is above and beyond the usual (or what we deserve), it has to come with a price tag — i.e. a deduction from our account in the True World. Rabbi Chanina ben Dosa consoled his daughter, however, by explaining to her that they were above the normal rules. By them, it truly made no difference if oil or vinegar was lit. They so totally and completely believed that everything occurred in this world absolutely only because Hashem decreed it, that everything was miraculous yet "normal" at the same time. Thus, he encouraged her not to be distraught over any loss of merit. There was none. And the proof was that if Hashem had provided an undeserved benefit and was "taking it off" her account, it wouldn't be fair if He kept the miracle going longer than necessary. Once the mitzvah was fulfilled, the miracle should have stopped. Since it continued throughout Shabbos, obviously, it was not going to be deducted from her merits.

Rabbi Chanina ben Dosa had a certain neighbor who was building a house, but the beams "did not reach" (i.e. they were too short for the length they were to span). She (the neighbor) came before him, and said to Rabbi Chanina ben Dosa, "I have built my house but the beams do not reach." He said to her, "What is your name?" She replied *to him, "*איכו *—* Aiku.*" Rabbi Chanina ben Dosa declared: "Aiku, let your beams elongate (i.e. reach the necessary length to be used in the house)." A Tanna taught: They elongated (so much so) that they stuck out one cubit on this side, and one cubit on this (the other) side. And some report that additional sections became added (miraculously —* Rashi*). It was taught in a* Baraisa*: Pelimo says: "I saw that very house myself, and its beams protruded one cubit to this side, and one cubit to this side, and people told me that this was the house which was roofed (covered) by Rabbi Chanina ben Dosa with his prayers."*

THE STRETCHING OF THE BEAMS BEYOND THE NECESSARY LENGTH puzzles *Maharsha*. What purpose was there in having the beams extend beyond the dimensions of the house? He explains that this greatly publicized the miracle. Everyone who would subsequently see this house would question why the beams project out so much on each side. This would result in a retelling of the story, reiterating the greatness of Hashem's humble servant Rabbi Chanina ben Dosa, resulting in further *kiddush Hashem*, sanctification of G-d's glorious Name. This is perfectly illustrated by the immediate comments of Pelimo, who lived a century later! Even a hundred years after the rest of Rabbi Chanina ben Dosa's generation had died out and been long forgotten, people were still noticing the strange house and then talking about Rabbi Chanina ben Dosa and his miraculous prayers and deeds.

Benayahu provides additional background information about the narrative. The woman neighbor who built the house was extremely sincere and devout in her belief in Hashem and the Sages. When her gentile construction workers told her the beams were too short, she remained calm and felt that this presented no problem. She knew that she could simply speak to her rabbi neighbor and he would solve the problem. The gentile workers scoffed and poked fun at her — how could the rabbi possibly help her out of this predicament? Nevertheless, she went to Rabbi Chanina ben Dosa and asked for his help. He asked her name, to see if he could get some insight into her character. The כו represents a short form of one of the Names of Hashem, and אי is the numerical value of another of Hashem's Holy Names. Convinced that the woman was truly righteous and sincere, Rabbi Chanina ben Dosa prayed so that a *kiddush Hashem* would occur.

Again, why was there no problem with benefiting from the miracle in this case? *Ben Yehoyada* states that since she just dwelled in the house, but did not get benefit directly from the miracle into her body, it was not a problem.

TAANIS 26B/31A

(see also Bava Basra 121)

TU B'AV — SHIDDUCHIM AND CELEBRATION

(Mishnah, 26b:) *Rabban Shimon ben Gamliel said: There never were as great holidays for Israel as the fifteenth of Av ("Tu B'Av") and Yom Kippur; on these days the daughters of Yerushalayim would go out in white garments that were borrowed so as not to embarrass one who had none. All the garments required ritual immersion (in a mikveh). And the daughters of Yerushalayim would go out and dance in the vineyards. And what would they say?* "Bochur *(young man), lift up your eyes and see what you choose for yourself. Do not 'put your eyes on' (i.e. look at) beauty; 'put your eyes on' family.* Grace is false and beauty is vain, a woman who fears Hashem should be praised (Mishlei 31:30). *And (the verse) says:* Give her the fruits of her hand, and let her be praised in the gates with her deeds *(ibid.* 31:31*)."*

(Gemara, 31a:) *The Rabbis taught in a* Baraisa*: The daughter of the king would borrow from the daughter of the* Kohen Gadol. *The daughter of the* Kohen Gadol *from the* Vice Kohen Gadol. *And the daughter of the* Vice Kohen Gadol *from the daughter of the* Kohen *annointed for battle. And the daughter of the* Kohen *annointed for battle from the daughter of an ordinary* Kohen. *And all Jews would borrow one from the other, in order not to embarrass someone who had none (beautiful clothing to wear).*

Rabbi Elazar said that even folded garments lying in a chest (required immersion — so as not to embarrass anyone whose garments might have become ritually impure — Rashi*).*

A Tanna taught: Whoever did not have a wife would turn there (to the vineyard where the maidens were, to find his mate). The Rabbis taught in a Baraisa*: The beautiful ones (i.e. the women) amongst them, what would they say? " 'Put your eyes on' (look at) beauty, because a woman is only for beauty." What did the woman with distinguished lineage say? " 'Put you eyes on' family (lineage), because a woman is for sons (i.e. childbearing)." (The version in the* Ein Yaakov *adds one more group. The rich girls would proclaim: " 'Put your eyes on' wealth.") What would the ugly ones amongst them say? "Take your purchase (i.e. find your mate) for the sake of Heaven, but only (on the condition) that you crown us with gold (jewelry)."*

THIS GEMARA IS UNDOUBTEDLY WELL KNOWN TO MANY BECAUSE OF its superficial resemblance to secular customs involving "role reversals," e.g. "Sadie Hawkins Day." Nothing could be further from the truth. Let us see how *Chazal* understand this Mishnah and the associated Gemara. (I have chosen to place the discussion of both together to achieve a more uniform picture and understanding, even though they are separated by several pages of unrelated text.)

The Gemara (*Taanis* 30b and *Bava Basra* 121a-b) elaborates as to why Yom Kippur is so special. After all, it is the day that Moshe returned with the Second *Luchos* (Ten Commandments), and it is designated forever as a time that Hashem forgives us for our sins. But what is so special about Tu B'Av? Various Sages in the Talmud proffer a total of six reasons.

(1) On Tu B'Av, women were first permitted to marry men from outside their *shevet* (tribe). Until the generation of Jews who

entered Eretz Yisrael died out, it was forbidden for a woman to marry a man from a different *shevet*. Why? The five righteous daughters of Tzelaphchad (a man who died without any male children) implored Moshe not to have them lose their share in Eretz Yisrael. Just because their father had no male children — why should they not receive their father's portion? Moshe inquired from Hashem as to the law, and indeed, was told that the Torah mandates that a daughter inherits her father if there are no male children. However, since a husband inherits his wife at her death, the portion of the land originally assigned to one *shevet* (i.e. her father's *shevet*) would now perforce be transferred to another (i.e. the husband's *shevet*). To solve this dilemma, the Torah states that women were only permitted to marry a husband within their father's tribe (*Bamidbar* 36:6-9). However, the Rabbis deduced through Biblical exegesis that this law pertained solely to that generation. This elucidation was first derived on Tu B'Av, and this was a great cause for celebration.

(2) The tragic story outlined in *Shoftim* Chapter 21 regarding the concubine of Givah resulted in the ostracization of all existing members of the tribe of Binyamin. The few surviving males were restricted from marrying with the other Israelites. However, on Tu B'Av, the Rabbis derived that this prohibition too was only applicable for a limited period of time, and the 600 remaining men, including future King Shaul, were saved from eradication. Hence, a great celebration was declared.

(3) On Tu B'Av, the generation of the *midbar* (desert) stopped dying. As a punishment for accepting the *lashon hara* (evil report) from the spies that Moshe had sent to investigate Eretz Yisrael, Hashem decreed that all men between the ages of 20 and 60 would die (prior to the Jews entering the land of Israel). Each year on Tishah B'Av (that was the day the spies returned and spoke their *lashon hara*), the men of that generation would dig graves and actually lie down in them and spend the night in them! A percentage of them did not arise the next morning, and this was how the punishment was meted out. Every Tishah B'Av for the remaining forty years that the Jews wandered in the desert, this

gruesome scenario would recur. Finally, in the fortieth year, nobody passed away. The people naturally assumed that they had miscalculated the date, and repeated their steps the next night. Again, no one expired. (Hashem made a miracle within a miracle. Even the elderly who were supposed to die naturally did not succumb during this period to highlight this fact.) The same procedure was followed every night until Tu B'Av. At that juncture, the people saw that the moon was full and that they could not possibly have miscalculated the dates — and they recognized that the ghastly decree was over. They greatly rejoiced and celebrated Tu B'Av as a holiday.

(4) On Tu B'Av, Hoshea ben Elah, the last monarch of the Northern Kingdom of Israel (where the ten northern tribes resided) removed the roadblocks and guards from the roads exiting his kingdom. People were now able to travel freely and choose to worship in the *Beis HaMikdash* in Yerushalayim.

(5) Fifty-two years after the destruction of the Second *Beis HaMikdash,* the Jewish forces suffered a final blow that sealed their fate. The great city of city of Beitar was defeated, and along with it any last hope for immediate salvation. The cruel Roman conquerors did not permit the Jews to bury their dead from the battle; they remained out in the fields for seven years. Miraculously, the bodies did not decay. On Tu B'Av, when they were finally allowed to bury them, the Rabbis sang praise to Hashem for this miracle. At that time they established the fourth (and only Rabbinical) blessing of the Grace After Meals entitled הטוב והמטיב. הטוב (the Good) since the bodies did not decay; והמטיב (and the One Who does good) since they were allowed to be buried.

(6) On Tu B'Av, it was no longer required each year to chop wood to stockpile for the fire upon the Altar of the *Beis HaMikdash*. The summer heat was beginning to dissipate at that time, and wood chopped after that date annually would insufficiently dry out to assure that any worms inside would die. Thus they stopped cutting wood at this juncture, and celebrated the extra free time that they now could devote to learning Torah

as a result. *Rashbam* (*Bava Basra* 121b) notes that they made a celebration upon completing a *mitzvah,* and, accordingly, some bring this as a source for making a festive meal and celebration to commemorate the completion of a *mesechta* of Gemara. Indeed, this is one of the few practical *halachos* brought down in *Shulchan Aruch* (*Yoreh Deah* 246:23) still applicable today for Tu B'Av. A person is required to increase his evening Torah study time from Tu B'Av and onward. *Ben Yehoyada* adds that we should have realized this from the actions of our mothers. They get up regularly in the middle of the night to take care of their responsibilities (the young children), so too should the men arise early and go to sleep late to discharge their Torah duties.

Ben Yehoyada writes that we see from our Gemara that Tu B'Av was especially designated for *shidduchim*. The women of Israel became permitted then to marry outside of their tribe. Since on that day the available pool of bachelors greatly increased, the Rabbis recognized in Tu B'Av an opportune time to arrange *shidduchim*. The other great events listed above were only of secondary importance in establishing this as a day for the men and women to gather and look for *shidduchim*. And *Ben Yehoyada* explains that this is why the Mishnah gave top billing to Tu B'Av. Shouldn't Yom Kippur have been listed first? The answer is that since the roots of the *minhag* (custom) were on Tu B'Av, it is given priority in mention. Indeed, the Rabbis were originally unhappy about permitting such social events on Yom Kippur, but they ultimately decided not to protest. Nothing should diminish the chances of a *shidduch* being arranged. If they tampered with the custom, even one Jewish couple might not meet, and that would be too steep a price to pay to protect the solemnity of the day.

The *Ohr HaChaim HaKadosh* in *Chumash* (*Bamidbar* 36:9) notes that the five daughters of Tzelaphchad themselves were actually not included in the original decree restricting marriage to one's *shevet*. However, recognizing that this was the will of Hashem, they took upon themselves the obligation to marry only within their tribe! The Gemara in *Bava Basra* (119b) describes them as great Torah scholars.

The *Kli Yakar* on *Parshas Shelach* (*Bamidbar* 13:2) uses the daughters of Tzelaphchad as the basis for an absolutely unbelievable commentary. *Parshas Shelach* begins with Hashem instructing Moshe to send spies to investigate the land. Many commentators give varied explanations for the unusual language that the Torah employs: שלח לך אנשים, *Send for yourself men (to scout out the land)*. *Kli Yakar* writes: Hashem said to Moshe: You chose to send men; I would have chosen women instead!! For women love the land of Eretz Yisrael more than men, as evidenced by the daughters of Tzelaphchad. Plus, women were not at all involved in the sin of the spies, and were not included in the resulting punishment (i.e. dying out in the desert). Only the men between the ages 20 and 60 died. Furthermore, we know from many other commentators that the women likewise had no role in the sin of the Golden Calf. The women refused to donate their jewelry for the construction of the idol. Again, only men were involved in that disastrous escapade. It is therefore not surprising to hear that Hashem would have preferred that women go instead of the male spies which Moshe sent!

All women, wealthy and poor, regal and common were required to exchange garments to prevent the impoverished and "have nots" from being embarrassed. Similarly, all garments had to be ritually immersed — even if they were absolutely *tahor* (pure). Again, this was done so as not to embarrass women who were currently (a) *tamei* (ritually unclean; whose clothing was thus possibly *tamei* as well) or (b) unknowledgable regarding the ritual purity laws (their clothing is always suspected of being impure). *Chazal* are teaching us that everybody has to be very much aware of the terrible hurt and possible distress that can result from embarrassment. This is especially so when we are dealing with weighty matters like marriage and *shidduchim*.

The *Meiri, Ran, Raavad* and *Ritva* all quote the Talmud Yerushalmi and provide a different reason why the women were required to first immerse all their clothing in a *mikveh*. All their garments needed immersion, even the ones they were not using.

Why? This would encourage them to lend everything they owned. Once they already had to take all their good clothing out of mothballs and immerse them, they would be less reluctant to lend these items to their less fortunate friends.

White garments specifically were worn because they represented purity and simplicity. Alternatively, *Maharsha* opines that they were less expensive than colored clothing, and thus everybody had such garments. Therefore nobody would be embarrassed and unable to wear the appropriate outfit of the day.

Sfas Emes notes that "higher caste" women lent their garments to their "lower" colleagues. This was to further ensure that no one would be embarrassed by having to ask their "superiors" for a loan. *Ben Yehoyada* suggests that an additional important lesson is taught here as well. Always compare your material wealth with those less fortunate than yourself; you will be much happier, and satisfied with what you possess. If we would only appreciate the goodness Hashem has bestowed upon us without always comparing ourselves to somebody who has more, life would be so much more pleasant.

The Mishnah and the *Baraisa* are in agreement that the women expressed various thoughts (through *pesukim* in *Mishlei*) that highlighted their personal attributes. These verses are commonly said today as part of the Friday night Shabbos meal — in the *Aishes Chayil* song.

The *Ein Yaakov* appends a text to our Gemara from the *Nachal Eshkol; Korban Nesanel* advances a similar theme. When the Mishnah concludes: וכן הוא אומר, *And similarly it says,* the Mishnah is not simply quoting the verse in *Shir HaShirim*. Rather, it is quoting the call of the young men who gathered in the vineyards to find wives. The women who possessed physical beauty or who came from illustrious families insisted that they be credited for those features. The ladies who lacked these qualities proudly quoted the verse from *Mishlei*, and justified their own desirability "for the sake of Heaven." There were also eligible bachelors as well, who were themselves not endowed with wealth nor with physically attractive features. What did these men have to offer to a potential spouse? The Mishnah concludes by telling us that even such a young man had a sales pitch. וכן הוא אומר, *Also he* (the eligible young man) would say: *Go forth and gaze, O daughter of Zion, upon King Shlomo adorned with the crown* (*Shir HaShirim* 3:11) There are three crowns of glory: that of kingship, that of priesthood, and that of Torah. Only one person achieves kingship. However, the men who had achieved Torah scholarship offered this as a powerful advantage. Even without money and without being particularly handsome, a young man who possesses Torah can offer joy and a sense of tranquility to a marriage.

The Mishnah concludes that the *pasuk* cited above alludes to the day of King Shlomo's wedding, which is parallel to the receiving of the Torah at Sinai and the marriage of *Klal Yisrael* to Hashem. The men who were *Kohanim* proudly announced their heritage, as the ones who served in the *Beis HaMikdash*. Once again, the symbolism is to the day on which Shlomo had a gladdened heart — when the *Beis HaMikdash* was opened.

Why was lineage considered a virtue? Besides the obvious answer, *Eitz Yosef* remarks that the Holy Divine Presence alights on a prestigious family. *Rashi* notes that there will be many people eager to marry into this family, and the *Elyah Rabbah* opines that she is more likely to raise her own children well if she comes from good stock herself.

The Talmud uses interesting language when discussing what the women remarked to the men: שא נא, *Please lift up* (*your eyes*). *Ben Yehoyada* points out a very interesting play on words here. נא also means raw or uncooked. Only when you are "raw," i.e. unmarried, can you raise your eyes to look for a pleasing *shidduch*. But once you are married, no more looking!

Why did the ordinary young women add the apparently gratuitous remark that their husbands should adorn them with gold? *Rashi* notes that this refers to after the wedding, and is an unrelated statement. *Elyah Rabbah* disagrees, and comments that the women are saying that a little jewelry can make an unattractive woman that much prettier. *Yavetz* and *Eitz Yosef* both cite the Gemara in *Nedarim* (66a) where Rabbi Yishmael laments that all Jewish women are beautiful; it is only the terrible ravages of poverty that prevent their beauty from being developed. This is what the women intended to convey when asking their future husbands to shower them with gold. If that is what concerns you (i.e. an attractive appearing wife), that can be easily remedied.

Ben Yehoyada takes a different approach. The latter group of women is telling their prospective spouses to get married because that is the *mitzvah* of Hashem. No other considerations should enter their mind. They should not think about riches or beauty. However, maybe some of the men want a poor, less physically attractive or less prestigious woman, so they will not have to spend a lot of money "maintaining" her in the style to which she is accustomed. They think they are saving money and therefore are willing to accept such a *shidduch*. Therefore, these women declare: Marry us for Heaven's sake, and prove it by showering us with gold, to demonstrate that you didn't marry us out of stinginess.

Maharsha and *Eitz Yosef* comment that we see from this Gemara a proof to the *halachah* that a person must see their mate before getting married (*Kiddushin* 41a). If not, it is possible that one partner may have a blemish that will prevent the couple from reaching proper marital bliss. Therefore, the bride and groom are obligated to at least meet prior to the wedding. Obviously, different communities within the Torah-abiding world fulfill this requirement in different fashions.

Finally, not all commentators understand our Gemara literally. The *Eitz Yosef* vehemently states that it would have been a great breach in modesty for the young men and women to commingle in this fashion. Many other great Rabbis (brought down in the *Al HaDaf* [*Taanis* 31]) also find it difficult to believe that the sexes mixed so freely, especially on Yom Kippur, the holiest holiday of the year! Therefore, the *sefer Tzefiras HaTzadik* proposes that these events did not transpire until Yom Kippur was over. The great *Reb Tzadok HaKohen* suggests that in the days of the *Beis HaMikdash,* the *yetzer hara* was powerless to tempt people with sexual immorality on Yom Kippur. (Note: This is alluded to by the *gematria* of השטן, which equals 364. For 364 days of the year the *yetzer hara* [the שטן] has power over us, but not on the 365th day — Yom Kippur!)

Others interpret the Gemara allegorically. *Tiferes Yisrael* says the *bochur* is a depiction of Hashem; the young women represent the Jewish people. After Yom Kippur we are beautiful (i.e. without sin). And even if not, then we at least have our great lineage of the patriarchs and matriarchs. And even if we are ugly (i.e. sinners) Hashem turns our sins into gold jewelry through our *teshuvah* (repentance). Similarly, the *Mishnas Yosef* says that the vineyard represents the Jewish nation approaching Hashem for forgiveness on Yom Kippur. The beautiful women represent the *tzaddikim*; the prestigious maidens (those of important lineage) are the average Jews who can advance towards Hashem only through the merit of their saintly ancestors. And finally, the transgressors are compared to the ugly girls. They ask Hashem to forgive them for Heaven's sake alone.

Mishnas Yosef further brings down the *Shaar Yissachar* who notes that there are forty days between Tu B'Av and the onset of creation. (Creation began according to one opinion on the twenty-fifth day of Elul. Man was thus created on Rosh Hashanah according to this view.) Forty is a special number in Jewish lore. Forty days before a male child is conceived, a Heavenly voice calls out "the daughter of So and so will marry this child." Hashem is the ultimate *shadchan* (marriage arranger). And Moshe spent forty days in Heaven receiving the first *Luchos*, and another forty days thereafter receiving getting the second set. Thus, the period of introspection and self-assessment begins on Tu B'Av — the start of the ימים נוראים, the days of awe — and concludes on Yom Kippur.

מסכת מגילה

MEGILLAH

MEGILLAH

MEGILLAH 7A

(see also Pesachim 117a; Yoma 29b; Megillah 13a; 13aa; 14a-b; 15a; 15b; 16a)

ESTHER'S REQUEST FOR THE MEGILLAH

*Rav Shmuel bar Yehudah said: Esther submitted the following to the Sages: Establish me for all generations (i.e. establish an everlasting name for the festival of Purim and the reading of the Megillah). They replied to her: You will incite the wrath of the nations against us (i.e. by reminding them of our role in their downfall). Esther sent back to them: I am already written in the chronicles of the Kings of Persia and Media (*Rashi *— they can see for themselves what is already written down anyway in their historical annals) ...*

Esther submitted (a second request) to the Sages: Write me (i.e. the story of the miracle of Purim) for all generations. (The Gemara then goes through a technical discussion as to why the Rabbis originally did not want to accede to her request, but subsequently it was proven to be correct to include the Book of Megillas Esther *among the twenty-four Holy Scrolls of the* Tanach.*)*

THE GREAT QUEEN ESTHER "HATZADEKES" (THE RIGHTEOUS — SEE *Megillah* 10b where she is referred to by this name, which is only very rarely used by the Rabbis) is discussed in great detail throughout *Mesechta Megillah*. We will only discuss those Gemaras that depict her in a story or narrative.

This short account describes Esther's desire that the story of Purim be established as a Rabbinical holiday for all generations. Even when the Rabbis decreed that Purim be established, Esther still was not totally satisfied until it was actually incorporated into the Holy text of our people, the *Tanach*. The book was written with Divine inspiration, and remains with us today as one of the amazing accounts of the miracles performed by Hashem for the Jewish people.

Megillah 9a-b

(see also Megillah 14a-b; 15a)

Sarah's Laugh

(The Gemara is in the midst of the famous story of the Egyptian king Ptolemy who sequestered seventy-two Rabbis in separate houses and had them translate the Holy Bible into Greek — the famous Septuagint. Hashem Divinely ordained that the Sages make the exact same "emendations" to the text, to prevent possible misinterpretations and misunderstandings from occurring, as the work would now be available without the benefit of the Gemara and the great commentators. The following are two such emendations regarding women in the Torah.)

"And Sarah laughed amongst her relatives" (instead of the correct And Sarah laughed to herself [Bereishis 18:12]).

(In regard to the list of non-kosher animals with one of the two kosher signs), they wrote "the short-legged animal," and they did not write "and Arneves *— the rabbit"* (Vayikra 11:6), *because the wife (*Rabbi Akiva Eiger *in the* Gilyon HaShas, *based on the Yerushalmi and the Midrash, says the text should read* mother*) of Ptolemy was named "*Arneves *— rabbit." This change was made in order that Ptolemy not say that the Jews are making fun of him by having his wife's name appear in the Torah as a name of a non-kosher animal.*

Regarding the first emendation listed above, *Maharsha* comments that the Rabbis were afraid that Ptolemy would raise a question. We know that Avraham also reacted by laughing when Hashem told him that at the age of 100 years he would become a father. Why, then, was only Sarah criticized and rebuked for laughing at this fact? *Chazal* realized that Ptolemy would not understand that Avraham laughed a chuckle of joy and gladness; Sarah, however, chortled in ridicule. Alternatively, *Ben Yehoyada* suggests that Avraham was happy for both of them, whereas Sarah snickered at the idea that an old man like Avraham could still father a child. Thus, the Rabbis changed the literal translation to clearly reflect the different reactions of Sarah and Avraham, and to clarify why Hashem only criticized Sarah. Ptolemy would now understand that Sarah deserved rebuke because she laughed publicly, whereas Avraham who laughed privately did not err so egregiously.

Eitz Yosef reconciles the version of our Gemara with the text of the Yerushalmi. There were really two Ptolemys. One was the father of the other (similar to the Senior and Junior usage in modern secular society). Thus, one Ptolemy had a mother with the name “Arneves” (rabbit), while at the same time the senior Ptolemy had a wife of that appellation.

Why were seventy-two Sages chosen? *Ben Yehoyada* states that this exemplified the Divine kindness involved in the miracle. The gematria of חסד, *kindness*, is seventy-two.

Megillah 10b

(see also Megillah 25a-b; Sotah 10b)

The Modesty and Rewards of Tamar

Rabbi Levi said: This statement is a tradition that has been passed down to us from our fathers: Amotz and Amatziah were brothers. What does this tell us? As Rabbi Shmuel bar Nachmani said in the name of Rabbi Yonasan: Every bride who is modest in her father-in-law's house will merit having kings and prophets descending from her. From where do we know this? From Tamar, as it is written: And Yehudah (Judah) saw her (Tamar) and thought she was a harlot because she had covered her face (Bereishis 38:15). *Now, because she had covered her face, that is why he thought she was a harlot? Rather, because she (Tamar) had always covered her face in her father-in-law's (Judah's) house out of modesty, and he did know what she looked like, she merited, and kings and prophets descended from her. We see that she merited to have kings as descendants because King David was her descendant. Prophets, because Rabbi Levi said: The following statement is a tradition that has been passed down to us from our fathers: Amotz and Amatziah were brothers. And Amotz was the father of Yeshaya as it is written* The vision of *Yeshaya* (Isaiah) son of Amotz (Yeshaya 1:1). *(Thus, Isaiah was a nephew of Amatziah, who, like all kings of Judah, was a descendant of Tamar.)*

We will not discuss here the justification for Tamar to have relations with Yehudah in this fashion. One is referred to the commentators on this section of the Torah for greater insight and all the details of the story. Tamar was willing to sacrifice her life and her unborn twin sons to save Yehudah from embarrassment. Suffice it to say that the Rabbis all write that Tamar had full right to have acted in this seemingly improper fashion. Either she was fulfilling the Levirate marriage that Yehudah neglected to fulfill, or she saw through the Divine Spirit that she was destined to be the mother of Yehudah's children and the matriarch of the future kings of Yehudah, David HaMelech and Moshiach. In any event, the *Chumash* itself bears witness to this, as Yehudah ultimately remarks, "*Tamar was more righteous than I was*" (*Bereishis* 38:26).

Rashi in *Sotah* 10b states that Yehudah suspected that the harlot really was Tamar. However, since he said that she conducted herself in a manner of *tznius* (modesty), he concluded that this woman could not be her. *Maharsha* (also in *Sotah* 10b) explains that it is impossible to read and understand the verse literally — "because she covered her face, he knew she was a harlot." The exact opposite is true! A harlot exposes herself and does not cover her body. Further, *Eitz Yosef* (also there) notes that Yehudah should have recognized her voice even if her face was covered. Thus here, Tamar did not cover her face. Yehudah therefore determined that this lady was a harlot, but he did not recognize her as Tamar. In reality, Tamar never went about uncovered in Yehudah's house. *Iyun Yaakov* similarly comments (also in *Sotah* 10b) that the words in the *posuk* specifically state that he saw her face, so obviously it cannot be that she was veiled. Instead, it clearly refers to her previous practice while she lived in the house of Yehudah while married to his son.

Ben Yehoyada adds that the Gemara specifically uses the language "all" women who dress/act modestly will be rewarded with descendants who are kings and prophets. But how can this be? Granted, there were many prophets (the Gemara later in *Megillah* 14a comments that there were twice the number of prophets as those who left Egypt — i.e. 1,200,000 prophets in the history of the Jews). But there can only be *one* king! He answers that the blessing of descendants who will be kings refers to Talmudic scholars. The Gemara elsewhere notes that the Rabbinic Sages are "regally crowned" when they become the heads of an academy. It is such progeny that every woman who acts modestly will deserve and enjoy. Alternatively, the "all" implies that even women who are not so beautiful — but cover themselves up because they are ashamed of their bodies or have a blemish — will also merit reward. Even though they are not dressing in a manner of *tznius* for the right reason, Hashem will grant them the blessing. Similarly, even if their father-in-law insists on this mode of *tznius* dress, as undoubtedly Yehudah did, the women will still receive the same reward for dressing appropriately.

Why does the Gemara state that every "bride" will be so rewarded? *Ben Yehoyada* remarks that this teaches women that even from *day one* of their marriage they must act modestly. Furthermore, this is especially true for a bride, upon whom all eyes are trained. She must be particularly unpretentious and unassuming in her actions and dress.

Finally, *Ben Yehoyada* points out that this reward is yet another example of the *middah keneged middah* principle. A prophet and a king need to be notably modest in their behavior. It is necessary for a prophet to be secluded to receive the Divine Spirit. And a king must distance himself from the common folk and act in a very formal and modest fashion. Furthermore, a king makes rules and laws regulating dress and modesty, and is the embodiment of government. People fear the king and obey the rules because of him. Likewise, a prophet constantly preaches and implores people to act decently and modestly to prevent lewdness. Thus, it is a most fitting reward for a woman who herself acts modestly to further beget modesty, by having children who are kings and prophets.

MEGILLAH 12A-B

(see also Megillah 15a)

EVIL VASHTI

Queen Vashti also made a feast for the women in the royal house of King Achashveirosh (Esther 1:9). *The* Megillah *should have said that Vashti's banquet took place in the women's house (a more private location, not frequented by men —* Maharsha*). Rava said: Both of them (Achashveirosh and Vashti) intended to commit immoral acts. And so goes the popular adage: He with large pumpkins and his wife with small pumpkins (i.e. the man and his wife both engage in the same behavior).*

On the seventh day, when the king's heart was merry with wine ... *(ibid.* 1:10*). Until now his heart was not merry with wine (the seventh day of the feast)? (Why state that the king was drunk* on the seventh day*?) Rava says: The seventh day was the Sabbath. For when Jews eat and drink, they begin discussing words of Torah and words of praise to Hashem. But idolaters who eat and drink begin discussing only indecent matters. And so it was at the feast of that wicked one (Achashveirosh). These would say that the Median women were the most beautiful, while these would say that the Persian women are the most beautiful. Achashveirosh said to them: "The vessel that I use (i.e. my wife, Vashti) is neither Median nor Persian, but Chaldean (yet she is the most beautiful). Is it your wish to see her?" They said to him that they did want to see her, but provided that she be unclothed.*

For with the measure that a man measures, they (the Heavenly tribunal) measure out to him (i.e. middah keneged middah*). This teaches that the wicked Vashti used to bring Jewish girls and strip them of their clothes and make them work on the Sabbath. (Therefore,* middah keneged middah, *as her punishment from G-d, she was ordered by Achashveirosh to appear unclothed on the Sabbath.) Thus, it is written:* After these things, when the wrath of King Achashveirosh subsided, he remembered Vashti and what she had done, and what had been decreed upon her *(ibid.* 2:1*) — as she had done, so it was decreed upon her.*

And Queen Vashti refused ... *(ibid.* 1:12*). Now, let us see. She was a lewd woman, as the master said, both (Achashveirosh and Vashti) intended to act immorally. So, what is the reason she did not come (when Achashveirosh ordered her to appear unclothed)? Rabbi Yose bar Chanina said: This teaches that she broke out in leprosy (and thus did not want to appear unclothed). In a* Baraisa *it was taught: The Angel Gavriel came and made her have a tail.*

"And the king became greatly incensed by her refusal (and his anger burned within him)" (ibid. 1:12*). Why did his anger burn within him so much (as evidenced by the repetition of the animosity)? Rava said: Because Vashti sent him a message. "You stable boy of my father (Belshazar). My father drank wine the equivalent of what a thousand people drink, and did not get drunk, whereas that man (i.e. Achashveirosh) became foolish from his wine." (Therefore) immediately,* and his anger burned within him *(ibid.* 1:12*).*

E*ITZ YOSEF* OPINES THAT THE "KING" REFERRED TO AT THE VERY beginning of our Gemara is not solely Achashveirosh, but it is actually a reference to Hashem. Every place in the *Megillah* where the word "King" is used by itself, it actually contains a hidden reference to the true King of Kings, Hashem. And thus when the *posuk* says the wine gladdened the King's heart on the seventh day, it refers to the Shabbos *Kiddush* and the Torah learning at the Shabbos table.

Maharsha and *Menachem Meishiv Nefesh* both comment that Achashveirosh and Vashti had the same depraved intents. Thus, both plotted and connived to have their respective parties near each other to facilitate their immoral plans. *Anaf Yosef* notes that that the *Midrash Esther* gives the "credit" for this to Haman — he was the force behind the close proximity of the carousing. Haman recognized that Hashem despises lewdness. By having the gatherings close to each other, he was hoping that the Jews would sin as well. They would then deserve to be punished, and his plan would be successful. Haman was even the one who suggested that the Jews should be invited to these affairs!

Our Gemara contrasts the difference between the gentile nations and the Jews. We eat and drink and then learn Torah; they eat and drink but then commit acts of lewdness. This idea is expressed in our Shabbos *Minchah* prayer. *Chazal* tell us that before we take out the Torah, we daven "*V'ani tefillasi*" ("And my prayer"). This is to reiterate this very point. We are commanded to eat and drink on the Shabbos, yet nevertheless we come back to shul to pray the afternoon service.

The principle of *middah keneged middah* is clearly at work in this narrative. Vashti caused so much pain and suffering to the young Jewish maidens, and she is repaid in kind.

Maharsha notes that not only did she make them work while unclothed on Shabbos, but she was also excessively cruel to them. They were forced to spin wool which is especially discomforting and painful to do while unclothed. The girls refused to work on Shabbos, according to the *Iyun Yaakov*, and thus she had them killed. *Middah keneged middah*, she was also killed. The *Kosev* in the *Ein Yaakov* adds that a tail is a repulsive appendage, and it was especially effective in diminishing her beauty. *Ben Yehoyada* further writes that just as she treated the women like animals (i.e. made them work unclothed), so too, *middah keneged middah*, she grew the tail of an animal. And the three letters of the word tail (זנב) are a discrete *gematria* reference to her lineage. She took great pride that she was a descendant of the infamous (a) Nebuchadnezar, (b) Belshazar, and (c) Evil-Merodach. Thus she was shown that lineage's true worth — a repulsive tail!

Not all agree that Gavriel "made her a tail." The *Aruch* (quoted by *Maharsha*) says that the word זנב (literally: tail) could refer to any appendage. *Maharsha* himself though wonders why the *Aruch* doesn't translate the word as it usually is used — a tail.

Iyun Yaakov states that Vashti caused her own demise. If she hadn't been interested in immorality, nobody ever would have had the nerve or audacity to suggest that the queen appear unclothed. Also, her proximity to the men permitted the punishment (i.e. her death) to be carried out right away, with no opportunity for delay. Had she not been so close, maybe he would have had a chance to change his mind. *Eitz Yosef* adds from the *Vilna Gaon* that the men were able to hear the women talking because they were so close, and this gave them the idea to act with depravity. *Geon Yaakov* adds that Vashti refused to go to Achashveirosh on the pretense that no Jews would be there — it was Shabbos. Why bother going if the whole purpose of going (i.e. to get the Jewish people to sin) is not able to be accomplished? Thus *Chazal* nickname Vashti a little "pig." Just as the pig tries to demonstrate that it is a kosher animal because it has one of the two signs of *kashrus* (split hooves), so too Vashti tried to express the idea she was going only because she had an ulterior motive. Otherwise, she never would do such immorality. But in reality, like the pig, she was a faker and a charlatan.

Ben Yehoyada provides additional insight. How did the men dare to suggest to Achashveirosh that the king's wife appear unclothed? They realized that the king steered the conversation to the beauty of their wives, so he could ask them to show off their spouses. If one were indeed prettier than Vashti, he would take her for himself. They therefore commented that it was an unfair beauty contest. After all, fancy royal clothing and jewelry make a person appear much more beautiful. (See this *sefer*, *Taanis* 26b/31a.) Thus, they suggested what they thought was an absurdity. To make the comparisons fair, everyone's wife would have to appear unclothed! But Achashveirosh was only too happy to comply. It did not concern him in the least that Vashti would be discomforted. All he desired was to satisfy his own carnal needs. *Benayahu* further writes that he intended to have relations with her publicly. Achashveirosh was so arrogant and debauched that the surrounding people were no more significant to him than animals — they did not even rate as humans, in front of whom to be embarrassed. This is why Vashti called him a stable boy. He really was the son of Darius, the Median king. But he acted like a horse (a very promiscuous animal) and thus she called him a stable boy.

Why didn't Vashti simply tell Achashveirosh the truth about why she could not appear? *Ben Yehoyada* suggests that if she answered him politely, he would have come to her anyway. Therefore she forestalled that possibility by her sharp retort. Why wasn't she afraid he would kill her? She knew he was madly in love with her, and never dreamed he would act so impetuously. Hashem, of course, was controlling the events, and the cruel Achashveirosh indeed had her killed immediately.

Maharsha and others say that the double language of the *posuk* (*And the king became greatly incensed by her refusal* and *his anger burned within him*) signifies the extreme wrath Achashveirosh felt. *Eitz Yosef* comments that normally talking about one's anger helps to settle it. But because she retorted so sharply and insultingly, he could not tell anyone what she had said, so the fury burned so much more fiercely inside him.

Finally, what is the significance of the Gemara's analogy to the small and large pumpkin? *Eitz Yosef* opines that the large pumpkin's leaves at least cover a sizable amount of a person's body. The smaller amount of leaves on the tinier pumpkin reflects the fact that Vashti was even more immodest in her behavior than Achashveirosh. Maybe that is why she suffered her ignominious fate.

MEGILLAH 13A

(see also Megillah 15b; Sotah 12b)

BISYAH, PHARAOH'S DAUGHTER

"And his Yehudiyah (Jewish) wife (Rashi — *her name was Yehudiyah)* bore Yered the father of Gedor, and Chever, the father of Socho, and Yekusiel, the father of Zanoach; and these are the sons of Bisyah, the daughter of Pharaoh, whom Mered married" (Divrei HaYamim I [Chronicles I] 4:18).

*(Rabbi Shimon ben Pazi asked): Why does the verse call her Yehudiyah (*Rashi — *if her name really was in fact Bisyah, the daughter of Pharaoh, as the verse later states)? Because she repudiated idolatry; as it is written,* And the daughter of Pharaoh went down to bathe by the river (Shemos 2:5). *And Rabbi Yochanan said that she went down to wash (purify) herself from the idolatry of her father's house.*

(The verse states that Pharaoh 's daughter bore Yered, Chever and Yekusiel. All three names refer to Moshe.) Did she, in fact, bear Moshe? But she only raised him! This verse teaches us that whoever raises an orphan boy or girl in his house, Scripture considers it as if he gave birth to him.

And these are the sons of Bisyah, (the daughter of Pharaoh), whom Mered married. *But was Mered his name? Was not Caleb his name? The Holy One, Blessed is He, said: Let Caleb come, who rebelled against the plan of the spies, and marry Pharaoh's daughter, who rebelled against the idolatry of her father's house.*

THE MAJOR CHUMASH COMMENTATORS EXPLAIN IN DETAIL THE well-known Biblical stories of Bisyah's discovery of baby Moshe in the Nile, and how she raised him as her own child (*Shemos,* Chapter 2); and the tragic episode of the twelve spies that Moshe sent to scout out Eretz Yisrael, and how Caleb (and Yehoshua bin Nun) were the only two to not speak ill about the land and Hashem (*Bamidbar,* Chapters 13 and 14). It is not the place of this *sefer* to translate and exposit several chapters of the Torah. Also, the Gemara in *Sotah* provides additional details, which we will leave for deeper study there. Suffice it to say that the Gemara equates these two great personages, their actions, and their devotion to Hashem.

Who was Bisyah? Technically, she was the daughter of Pharaoh, but the *Zohar* relates that she was not his biological child. She and her twin sister Tzipporah (Moshe's eventual wife!) were actually foundlings. Bisyah was taken into Pharaoh's palace and raised as his daughter.

Rashi notes that Bisyah (often called in the vernacular Batyah) went down to immerse herself as part of the process of conversion. The commentators point out that this was not technically necessary, as it was prior to the giving of the Torah, and conversion in the true post-Sinai sense did not yet exist. The immersion was more symbolic than it was required, and it represented her total rejection of the idolatrous lifestyle of royal Egypt, and the acceptance of Hashem and the concept of one G-d. She was willing to give up everything to which her high rank entitled her, and to assume the role of a member of an enslaved nation with little prospect for material pleasantries. She was able to see beyond the superficialities of her high society, and risk her life in saving and raising Moshe. Indeed, Moshe had ten names, including his birth name Yekusiel given to him by his biological mother Yocheved, but the only name he goes by in the entire *Chumash* is the name given to him by Bisyah — Moshe — which means she drew him from the water. This name epitomizes the essence of her life, and forever characterizes her as a truly righteous woman of valor. Indeed her own name means the daughter of G-d, and *Derech Eretz Zuta* (at the end of the first chapter) notes that she was one of only nine people to merit entering into Gan Eden while still alive. (Only one other woman in all of Jewish history merited this — Serach, the daughter of Asher, granddaughter of Yaakov — for revealing to Yaakov the wonderful news that Yosef was still alive in Egypt.)

The *Yalkut Shimoni* (*Shemos,* Chapter 166) suggests that she went down to the Nile to immerse herself from a bout of *tzara'as,* a metaphysical skin condition often mislabeled leprosy. When she saw and touched the baby Moshe in the basket, she was miraculously cured of her *tzara'as,* and recognized that this baby was unusual and special.

We also see from this story the tremendous *chessed* that a person performs when he/she raises a child that is orphaned or adopted. Such a person is referred to as the mother (or father) of the child, and there are even various halachic ramifications regarding the saying of *Kaddish*, sitting *shivah*, etc. (see the publication *Al HaDaf, Megillah* 13, for some of the halachic details and references).

MEGILLAH 13AA

(see also Pesachim 117a; Yoma 29b; Megillah 7a; 13a; 14a-b; 15a; 15b; 16a)

THE NAMING OF ESTHER, HER MIRACULOUS DIET AND HER PALACE LIFE

And he (Mordechai) had raised Hadassah ... (who is Esther) (Esther 2:7). *The verse calls her Hadassah (Myrtle) and the verse calls her Esther. (The Gemara brings five different opinions as to why she was known by two names.)*

It was taught in a Baraisa*: Rabbi Meir says: Esther is her name. And why was she called Hadassah? It was according to the designation of the righteous, who are called myrtles.*

And so it says: And he was standing among the myrtle bushes (Zechariah 1:8) *(i.e. the Divine Presence was standing amidst the prophets Chananiah, Mishael and Azariah who are referred to as myrtle bushes). Rabbi Yehudah says that Hadassah was her name. And why was she called Esther? Because she was* מסתרת *(used to conceal) the facts about herself (i.e. not reveal that she was Jewish), as it says:* Esther told nothing of her people (Esther 2:20). *Rabbi Nechemiah says that Hadassah was her name. And why was she called Esther? Because the nations of the world used to call her Esther, which is similar to the word* אסתהר *(the moon). (A play on words —* אסתר *[Esther] sounds like the Aramaic* אסתהר *as if to say she is as beautiful as the moon.) Ben Azzai says: Esther was neither tall nor short, but of average height, like a myrtle (i.e. though her name was really Esther, she was called Hadassah). Rabbi Yehoshua ben Korchah says that (Esther was her true name, but she was called Hadassah because) Esther had a greenish complexion, like a myrtle. And Hashem endowed her with a "thread of grace."*

THE GEMARA EXPOSITS WHAT THE DIFFERENT NAMES OF Esther/Hadassah mean. All are elucidations that show her in a very positive light. Even the last portrayal of Esther where her name is associated with her complexion that was sallow in appearance is favorable. *Eitz Yosef,* quoting the *Vilna Gaon,* writes that she was certainly most beautiful. However, she turned green out of sickness from contemplating having to live with the evil Achashveirosh. Hashem miraculously covered this up though, and all who gazed upon her were enveloped with a spirit of grace. This "thread of kindness" was a gift to Esther and to the Jewish people in that it allowed the ultimate redemption from Haman to unfold.

One could suggest a similar idea regarding the matriarch Leah. According to some commentators, she was the twin of Rachel. Yaakov was therefore unable to tell them apart and thus was capable of being deceived by Lavan. (See this *sefer, Megillah* 13b, for other explanations of this episode.) Thus Leah must have been beautiful, as the Torah relates that Rachel was very lovely (see this *sefer, Megillah* 15a). Yet, the Torah describes her as having "weak," unattractive eyes. Why was Yaakov not able to distinguish the sisters based upon this easily recognizable characteristic? I would like to suggest an explanation. *Chazal* tell us that Leah's eyes were ugly because she was always crying regarding being destined to marry Eisav. She thought that as the older twin sister, she was expected to marry the older twin cousin, Eisav (whereas Rachel would marry the younger Yaakov). She cried and *davened* so much to Hashem that her eyes turned unsightly and homely. Possibly, in the merit of those voluminous tears, however, Hashem also provided her with this "thread of grace," and she appeared comely to Yaakov and to the rest of the world.

In our passage, Ben Azzai explains that Esther was called Hadassah because she was of average height. Because the verse highlights this feature as favorable, *Maharsha* notes that being of average height (not too tall and not too short) must therefore also be a blessing. (See this *sefer*, *Berachos* 31, where this concept is explored in more detail regarding Chana and Shmuel.) *Ben Yehoyada* explains that this is why Purim is a holiday of intermediate length — two days (Purim and Shushan Purim). Not short, like the one day Yom Tov (in Israel) of Shavuos, and not long like the seven days of Pesach or Succos.

Ben Yehoyada opines that the myrtle is known for its beautiful smell. The sense of olfaction is the most spiritual of the physical senses, and it reminds us of Gan Eden where the righteous dwell. (That is why we smell aromatic spices as part of the *Havdalah* ceremony at the conclusion of Shabbos. It is to revive the person from the loss of the special extra "Shabbos soul" that returns to the Heavens when Shabbos is over. Of the five physical senses, the one most capable of assuaging this loss is the sense of smell.) This explains why the prophet Zechariah compares the saintly trio (Chananiah, Mishael and Azariah) to myrtle. Further, the myrtle contains leaves arranged in perfect rows of three. So too Esther was perfect in three ways: thought, words, and actions.

Eitz Yosef (quoting the *Yalkut*) and *Rabbi Yaakov Emden* translate אסתהר as a very bright star. She was as spectacular as such a luminous heavenly sight. The Gemara and commentary below discuss the reasons why Esther hid her origins.

Since she had neither father nor mother... (and when her father and mother had died) (Esther 2:7). *Why is it necessary to restate* and when her father and mother had died *(i.e. the verse already told us she had no father or mother)? Rav Acha said that her father died when*

Esther's mother conceived her and when Esther's mother gave birth to her, her (Esther's) mother died. (Thus the repetition teaches us that Esther never saw her father or mother.)

And when her father and mother had died, Mordechai took her as his daughter *(ibid.). A Tanna taught in the name of Rabbi Meir: Do not read "as his* בת *(daughter)," but rather, "as his* בית *(home)."* (Maharsha *points out that* בית *is often used as an expression for wife, i.e. Mordechai married Esther.) (To prove that daughter can refer to home/wife, the Gemara quotes a verse from* Shmuel II 12:2.*) And similarly it says:* And the poor man had nothing except for one little ewe which he had bought, and he raised her and she grew up together with him and with his children. She would eat from his bread, and she would drink from his cup, and she would lie in his bosom; and she was like a בת (daughter) to him. *Because she would lie in his bosom she was like a daughter to him? Rather, (it intends to mean) as a* בית *(home), (i.e. as a wife who lies in her husband's bosom). So too, Mordechai took Esther as a home (i.e. a wife).*

And the seven maids ... (that were fit to be provided for her from the house of the king) (Esther 2:9). *Rava said: (Esther) would count the days of the week through them (i.e. to know which day was Shabbos).* And he changed her and her maids (to the best of the house of the women) *(ibid.). (Hegai, the custodian of the maidens, did something special for Esther and her maids that he did not do for the other maidens.) Rav said that he fed her Jewish (kosher) food. Shmuel said that he fed her fatty bacon. Rabbi Yochanan said (it was) seeds. And similarly it says (regarding Daniel, Chananiah, Mishael, and Azariah when they went to work as government advisors to Nebuchadnezzar):* And the steward took away their food ... and gave them seeds (Daniel 1:16).

(We will skip ahead to Megillah 13b *to include a statement from there that is more easily discussed here,*

and then return below to Megillah 13a.*)* And the bidding of Mordechai, Esther did (Esther 2:20). *Rabbi Yirmiyah said: She used to show (her) menstrual blood to the Sages to determine if she was a* niddah. Just as she was when she was raised with him *(ibid.). Rabbah bar Lima said in the name of Rav: This indicates that she used to rise from the bosom of Achashveirosh, and immerse herself and sit in the bosom of Mordechai.*

WHY DOES THE *MEGILLAH* NOT COME FORTH AND STATE OUTRIGHT that Mordechai and Esther were husband and wife? Several commentators suggest that since the *Megillah* was a well-known and prominent document in secular circles at the time it was written, it would have been most foolhardy to publicly acknowledge that the queen was married and living with someone other than the king. Thus *Chazal* had to intimate this information in a covert yet decipherable manner for future generations.

What exactly did Hegai do special for Esther, and why was this even necessary? Why did Esther not know which day of the week it was? Esther was given a different maidservant to work each day of the week. *Maharsha* explains that she actually named them after the days of the week; *Benayahu* notes that this was in observance of the *mitzvah* to constantly remember the Shabbos all week long. *Yaaros Devash* and *Anaf Yosef* remark that Esther wanted to keep busy during the week, but was concerned that if she rested on one day (Shabbos) her true identity would be obvious. Thus, by maintaining different maidservants on each day, no one would recognize that her routine was different on Shabbos than it was the rest of the week. The Shabbos attendant would naturally assume she did no work all week long, and similarly, the weekday maids would not notice that she stopped working on Shabbos.

Ben Yehoyada is amazed that Esther could lose track of the days of the week and require this system to keep her dates straight. He postulates that her royal responsibilities or modesty kept her indoors most of the time. Esther was concerned that she might be preoccupied and not realize on Friday afternoon that the sun had already set and that Shabbos had begun. Thus, she had the maidservants begin their workday just *prior* to twilight. In this way she was always certain not to miss the onset of Shabbos. Her seven maids worked in rotation; each one was assigned a specific day of the week. Thus, no matter how wrapped up Esther was in her duties, when the Shabbos maid arrived, Esther knew Shabbos was about to commence.

According to Rav, Esther was served only kosher food. *Ben Yehoyada* queries: How did Hegai know to feed her this diet if she kept her identity a secret from all? He remarks that everyone knew that Esther was raised in the house of Mordechai — it was a well-known fact. Mordechai claimed she was just a foundling, and that he himself did not know her ethnicity or country of birth. Naturally he fed her only kosher as she was raised in his home. Hegai continued to provide Esther with this diet, assuming she was used to it and possibly it was the reason she was so beautiful. *Ben Yehoyada* notes that one of the queens of England maintained a kosher diet as well because she thought it was healthier. This is a commonly expressed belief in modern America as well — kosher food is purer and of superior quality.

According to Shmuel, though, Hegai fed her actual חזיר, non-kosher fatty bacon. *Rashi* explains that Esther ate this only because there was no alternative and she was forced to do so. *Tosafos* remark, "*Chas veshalom,*" Heaven forbid, that the righteous Esther should have partaken of ham. *Maharsha* even adds that her servants did not eat it — they too were righteous! (although the *Rif* in *Ein Yaakov* maintains that the ham was for the maidservants who did eat non-kosher). *Maharsha* further suggests that if the Gemara is to be taken literally that she ate ham, it must have only been by accident.

Many other commentators disagree with *Rashi* as well. Possibly this is because there are many famous stories in the Talmud relating how the righteous are miraculously protected from eating non-kosher foods, so it would be inconsistent to explain that Esther could have failed to be protected in this regard. To wit, baby Moshe would not even suckle from an Egyptian wet nurse. He was supernaturally guarded from the adverse effects that non-kosher items have on the soul. Therefore, *Anaf Yosef* opines that Hegai gave her the bacon for appearance sake only — so she should not look like she was getting different food or preferential treatment compared to the other women. Once alone, he switched her food to kosher food, thereby substantiating both Rav and Shmuel's views.

Ben Yehoyada notes that it was possible that she ate less than one-sixtieth of the ham, and it was thus halachically insignificant compared to the much larger amount of kosher food. Or, possibly, based on the Gemara in *Chullin* (10a), the word חזיר here does not mean pig, but actually refers to a certain fish (*tyucha*) known to have the exact same taste as ham. *Aruch* suggests that the correct text is not חזיר but is really חיזרי, which means lettuce.

However, *Anaf Yosef, Menachen Meishiv Nefesh* and *Ben Yehoyada* provide a most fascinating and incredible alternative explanation. Their source is none other than the Kabbalistic and mystical *Zohar,* and this astonishing answer is attributed as well to the saintly Arizal. *Esther herself never actually had relations with Achashveirosh*! A שד, a supernatural spirit, was conjured up by the pure Esther so that she herself would not to be forced to have relations with Achashveirosh. *Ben Yehoyada* declares: It was this שד that ate the bacon as well! Each time Esther was summoned to have relations with the vile king, she would utter a Holy Name of Hashem at the last possible moment and she would be miraculously replaced by the שד. (Meanwhile, Esther herself would literally become invisible. As the Gemara relates, she would subsequently return to her husband Mordechai after lying with the king. This beautiful insight explains how she was able to leave the palace unnoticed and return unseen.) Esther would only utter the Holy Name when she absolutely had to — when she was under pressure of relations with the wicked Achashveirosh. For other less extreme trials and tribulations with the evil man, she did not resort to using God's Holy Name, out of the concern not to unnecessarily articulate the Ineffable Name.

This explains why Esther went to the *mikveh* after being with Achashveirosh. It would serve no real halachic purpose to immerse herself post forced relations. Rather, she went out of a sense of need to purify herself from the defilement of just being around that evil man. *Yavetz* adds that she performed this immersion so as not to transmit any impurity to Mordechai, in order to remove any spittle or other impurity from Achashveirosh that might have possibly clung to her skin.

We now can better understand how later in the story of the *Megillah*, when she has to voluntarily go to the evil king, she tells Mordechai that now they would be truly lost from each other. Since now she was to go of her own volition to plead with the king to save their people, (and therefore she couldn't send the שד), she would no longer be permitted to Mordechai. [This also explains why Hashem caused Achashveirosh to never desire relations with Esther during the day (as the Gemara below remarks). Esther could not make the שד appear during the daytime!] However, the *Mishnas Yosef* remarks, based upon a careful reading of the verses, that even there Esther indeed did send the שד in her place. And subsequently it was the שד and not Esther who gave birth to their son Daryavesh (Darius)!

Finally, I heard from Rabbi Moshe Meir Weiss *shlita* that the prevalent custom today of eating poppy seed *hamantashen* on Purim is to remind us of the third opinion (of Rabbi Yochanan) that the food Esther was served was seeds.

And Esther found favor (in the eyes of all who saw her) (Esther 2:15). *Rabbi Elazar said: This teaches that she appeared to each and every person as a member of his own nation.*

And Esther was taken to King Achashveirosh into his palace in the tenth month, which is the month of Teves *(ibid.* 2:16*). (The cold winter month of Teves is) the month in which a body derives more pleasure from* *another body (i.e. Achashveirosh would be more likely to desire Esther in such a month) ...*

And the king made a great banquet *(ibid.* 2:18*). He made a feast (in her honor) yet she still did not reveal to him (her origins). He remitted the head tax (in her honor), yet she still did not reveal to him (her origins). He sent gifts (to important people —* Rashi*) (in her honor) yet she still did not reveal to him (her origins).*

And when the maidens were gathered together the second time etc. *(ibid.* 2:19*).*

Achashveirosh went and sought counsel from Mordechai (as to the way to induce Esther to reveal her origins). He (Mordechai) said (to Achashveirosh), "A woman is not made jealous except through the 'thigh of her friend' (i.e. another woman). (Thus, by gathering the maidens again to search for another wife, you will make Esther jealous, and force her to reveal her origins to you.") Achashveirosh followed this advice, and even so, she did not reveal her origins, as it is written: Esther did not tell about her birth etc. *(ibid.* 2:20*).*

WHY DID HASHEM MAKE ESTHER APPEAR TO EVERYONE AS IF SHE was from his or her ethnic group and background? What was the purpose of this seemingly unnecessary additional miracle? *Ben Yehoyada* comments that this gave further veracity to Mordechai's story. He told Achashveirosh that Esther was a foundling, and he was unaware of her true heritage. This extra miracle served to substantiate that claim. Achashveirosh never fully believed Mordechai. He suspected that Mordechai really knew of her origins. Thus, Mordechai himself suggested the second beauty pageant in order to allay Achashveirosh's suspicion that Mordechai knew but was just not telling. Mordechai therefore gave Achashveirosh (what seemed like) the excellent advice to determine the truth from Esther regarding her ancestry. Since Mordechai himself suggested the idea, Achashveirosh no longer suspected that Mordechai was concealing this sought after information. Of course, Mordechai was only too willing to recommend that the wicked king choose a new wife and leave Esther alone!

Why didn't Mordechai want Esther to tell her heritage? *Maharsha* writes that Mordechai was hoping Achashveirosh would assume that her refusal to reveal her origins was tantamount to admitting that she was from simple and probably embarrassing lineage. Thus, Achashveirosh would not take her as his queen. *Eitz Yosef* remarks that Esther maintained this silence even well after they were married. Mordechai only told her to keep her rich royal lineage (Esther was a direct descendant of the first king of Israel, Shaul) a secret so as not to make her more attractive to the king. However, once they were married, there was no longer this reason to hide this information. Yet, Esther maintained the mystery out of a sense of *tznius*, modesty. She did not wish to brag about her lofty ancestry.

I thought as well that the Gemara on *daf* 16a possibly provides another reason. Achashveirosh never directly spoke to Esther *until* she revealed her royal bloodline. It was below his dignity to openly converse with a mere commoner, someone not his sovereign equal. Therefore, he spoke to Esther only through an interpreter. Undoubtedly, this caused a distancing in their relationship, one that Esther was only too happy to maintain.

We gain valuable insight into the complex and absolutely righteous character of Esther, the *tzadekes*, from this glimpse of the Gemara's description of the story of *Megillas Esther*. The next few folios as well describe further details regarding this remarkably courageous and supremely sacrificing woman.

Megillah 13b

Rachel Imeinu—Merciful and Modest

As a reward for the modesty that was exhibited by Rachel she merited that Shaul descend from her. And as a reward for the modesty that was exhibited by Shaul, he merited that Esther descend from him. And what was the modesty exhibited by Rachel? For it is written: And Yaakov told Rachel that he was the brother of her father (Bereishis 25:12). *Now, was Yaakov really the brother of her father? Was he not rather the son of Rebecca, her father's sister? Rather, he said to Rachel, "Will you marry me?" She answered him, "Yes. However, (my) father is a deceiver and you will not be able to outwit him." He said to her, "I am his brother in deceit (i.e. I am a match for him)." She asked him, "Are the righteous permitted to act deceitfully?" He answered her, "Yes. (When others are trying to deceive them)." (As it is written):* With a pure person you act purely and with a crooked person you act crookedly (Shmuel II 22:27). *He asked her, "What is his deceit (i.e. that he would use against me)?" She replied to him, "I have a sister, Leah, who is older than I, and my father will not marry me off before he marries her off. (He will therefore try to trick you into marrying her instead of me." To prevent this from occurring), Jacob gave Rachel "signs," (through which he would be able to identify her as Rachel, thereby preventing Lavan from substituting Leah for Rachel). When the (wedding) night arrived, (and Rachel saw that her father was indeed planning on secretly substituting Leah for her), she thought (to herself) that her sister would be put to shame (i.e. Yaakov will ask her for the passwords and she will not know them). She therefore conveyed the prearranged signs to her (Leah). And thus it is written:* And it came to pass in the morning, and behold, it was Leah (Bereishis 29:25). *Is this to imply that until now it was not Leah? Rather, through the signs that Rachel conveyed to Leah, he (Yaakov) did not know until now (that it was Leah and not Rachel). Therefore, (since Rachel acted modestly* — middah keneged middah), *she merited that Shaul descend from her. And what modestly did Saul exhibit? For it is written:* But of the matter of the kingdom, of which Samuel spoke, he did not tell him (Shmuel I 10:16). *Therefore, he merited that (the modest) Esther descended from him.*

THE *DAAS ZEKEINIM MIBA'ALEI HATOSAFOS* WRITES THAT THE "sign" that Yaakov prearranged with Rachel was *challah* (taking off the priestly tithe from dough), *niddah* (observance of the ritual purity laws), and the lighting of the Shabbos candles. These three *mitzvos* are specifically given to women. The Gemara elsewhere notes — and this statement is included in the Friday night prayers (at the conclusion of *Bameh Madlikin*) in many Ashkenazic shuls — that these are the three sins for which a women can, Heaven forbid, die during childbirth. Possibly Yaakov prearranged these three signs to remind or teach the young Rachel (the Midrash relates she was only 3 years old at the time of their meeting) of the importance of these *mitzvos.*

It is impossible to go into great detail regarding the life and righteousness of Rachel in this *sefer.* We will only discuss the commentators on the *daf* who just scratch the surface.

Ben Yehoyada questions why the Gemara refers to her actions as modest. Wouldn't they more appropriately be called merciful? He answers that in reality, modesty is the correct appellation. After they initially met and had the conversation described above, Rachel and Yaakov acted with perfect modesty towards each other during their long (seven-year) engagement period. She never really showed herself to Yaakov, and thus he was not able to notice any significant difference between her and Leah. Thus it was Rachel's modesty indeed that allowed the conveyance of the signs to work. Others remark that they actually did not see each other for the next seven years! *Iyun Yaakov* writes that Rachel never even told her father Lavan that she met/was engaged to Yaakov. Thus he didn't suspect Rachel would subvert or cause any difficulty with his planned switch. Rachel's modesty permitted the evil Lavan to suspect he could succeed with his deception.

Ben Yehoyada further notes that Lavan planned the wedding for Friday night. He then arranged that some young children came to their private room and they blew out the candles that were lit there. Since it was Shabbos already, Yaakov could not have them relit. In the ensuing darkness, the bride switch was successfully carried out.

MEGILLAH 14A-B

SEVEN PROPHETESSES OF THE TALMUD

The Rabbis learned in a Baraisa*: Forty-eight prophets and seven prophetesses prophesied to Israel ...*

Who were these seven prophetesses? Sarah, Miriam, Devorah, Chana, Avigayil, Chuldah and Esther.

THE GEMARA WILL BRING VARIOUS PROOFS TO THIS STATEMENT. WE will discuss each prophetess separately in the commentary. Obviously, an entire *sefer* could be written about each one of these righteous women. We will only discuss the depiction of each prophetess given by the Gemara and the commentaries on the *daf.*

(see also Megillah 9a-b; Megillah 15a)

Sarah (was a prophetess), as it is written: The father of Milcah and the father of Yiscah (Bereishis 11:29). *And Rav Yitzchak said: Yiscah is Sarah. And why was she called Yiscah? Because she saw with the holy inspiration, as it is written:* All that Sarah tells you, heed her voice *(ibid.* 21:12*). Another interpretation: Yiscah, because everyone gazed at her beauty.*

MAHARSHA (FROM MIDRASH RABBAH) WRITES THAT IN THE VERSE, *All that Sarah tells you, heed her voice*, the word "voice" is seemingly unnecessary and extraneous. *Chazal* therefore derived that the voice is a reference to the Divine Spirit, i.e. her prophecy. *Sifsei Chachamim* adds that indeed Sarah's level of prophecy was even superior to that of Avraham!

Why was Sarah no longer called by the beautiful name of Yiscah, especially since it is such a compliment? *Benayahu* notes that she was only called Yiscah when she was a young girl. Once she grew up and understood the concept of *tznius*, modesty, she never allowed herself to be gazed upon and stared at by others. Thus, she was never again referred to as Yiscah.

Why aren't the other Matriarchs included on this list? *Maharatz Chayes* actually states that Rivkah should be on the list (she prophesied that both her sons, Yaakov and Eisav, would die on the same day). And the *Sfas Emes* quotes *Rashi* in *Chumash* (*Bereishis* 29:34) as stating that all the Matriarchs were prophetesses. *Sfas Emes* opines that the other Matriarchs merited the Divine Spirit only as the wives of the Patriarchs. Thus, they were not included as prophetesses in their own right. Sarah, however, was able to speak with Hashem even prior to marrying Avraham. *Sifsei Chachamim* suggests that only by Sarah is there a *posuk* to prove that she was a prophetess; by the other Matriarchs there is no clear evidence of this from the verse, thus they are not included on the list. Alternatively, *Maharshal* notes that the other three only prophesied about themselves. However Sarah spoke through the Divine Spirit about others as well.

(see also Taanis 9a)

Miriam, as it is written: And Miriam the prophetess, the sister of Aaron, took (Shemos 15:20). *Was she not the sister of Moshe (as well)? Rav Nachman said in the name of Rav: Because she prophesied when she was the sister of (just) Aaron, (before Moshe was born), saying: In the future my mother will bear a son who will save Israel. And at the time he (Moshe) was born, the entire house filled with light. Whereupon, her father rose and kissed her on the head, and said to her, "My daughter, your prophecy has been fulfilled." However, when they cast him (baby Moshe) into the river, her father rose and struck her on her head, and said to her, "My daughter, where is your prophecy?" Therefore, it is written:* and his sister stood herself at a distance to know *(ibid.* 2:4*) — to know what will be with the end of her prophecy (i.e. will Moshe survive and eventually save Israel, as she prophesied).*

E*IN YAAKOV* HAS A SLIGHTLY DIFFERENT VERSION OF THE NARRATIVE. According to his text, her mother, Yocheved, was the person who struck Miriam. *Benayahu* asks what is the significance of the father praising and the mother hitting? *Iyun Yaakov* suggests that a mother takes the "failure" of a child harder than does a father. The father only rejoices over the good, but it is the mother who agonizes more over the children. This is clearly seen as well from the story of Rachel crying during the exile of the Jewish people to Bavel. All of the Patriarchs prayed to Hashem at that time, but were not able to affect the harsh decree. But Rachel's tears over her children had the desired sway.

Iyun Yaakov comments that Miriam of course was eventually proven to have accurately prophesied, as Moshe ultimately led the Jewish people out of Egypt and crossed the *Yam Suf*, the Red Sea. At that time, when she was ultimately vindicated, she led the women in song, as the *Chumash* relates (*Shemos* 15:20,21).

(see also Pesachim 66b; 117a)

Devorah, as it is written: and Devorah, a prophetess, the wife of Lapidos (Shoftim 4:4).

What is (the meaning of) the wife of Lapidos? *She used to make wicks for the Temple. (*Rashi *— the Tabernacle that stood in Shiloh. Other versions actually state "Tabernacle" instead of "Temple.")* And she sat under a palm tree *(ibid.* 4:5*). Why (did Devorah choose to judge*

*Israel while sitting) under a palm tree? Rabbi Shimon ben Avshalom (*Mesoras HaShas *states that the name was Avishalom) said: In order to avoid the prohibition of* yichud*(being secluded alone with a man). Devorah was careful not to transgress the prohibition regarding* yichud. *(*Rashi *— a palm tree has very high branches as compared to other trees. Therefore, a man coming to her would not be considered in seclusion with her, like they would have been had they been inside a house or under a lower branched tree.) Another reason: Just as this palm tree has only one heart, so too, Israel in that generation had only one heart for their Father in heaven.*

M*AHARSHA* EXPLAINS WHY THE GEMARA DID NOT WANT TO FOLLOW the simple translation and say that Lapidos was Devorah's husband. He was obviously less important than she was, and therefore there is no purpose in mentioning him by name. The identification of his name must be coming to enlighten us with a different teaching. *Ben Yehoyada* remarks that her husband was actually the famous Jewish general Barak, who was fearful of entering battle without Devorah at his side. Indeed, this caused him to lose the sole credit he otherwise would have deserved for the stunning victory of his forces over the mightier and better-armored armies of Sisera. I thought that maybe because of this as well, we are not told outright that he was Devorah's husband. He was further punished with relative obscurity for his less than perfect faith in Hashem.

Yavetz writes that the *Bach* states that the word "Lapidos" means fire. Thus, this indicates the connection to the merit Devorah had in making the Temple wicks. *Ben Yehoyada* goes a step further and adds that it was because of this *mitzvah* that she merited receiving the Divine Spirit. *Menachem Meishiv Nefesh* notes that this too is *middah keneged middah.* She increased the light of the Temple, so Hashem increased her light, i.e. Divine revelation.

Anaf Yosef points out that Devorah was very modest and concerned with her public role as a judge. She did not seek out this position, but the populace came to her for her help and advice. *Rabbi Yaakov Emden* adds that there technically should not have been a concern with *yichud*, as the law requires that both parties to a case be present at the time of adjudication. Usually, the presence of two men abrogates the halachic possibility of *yichud*. However, Devorah went beyond the strict legal obligation. She concerned herself with an unlikely technicality that *yichud* might still be applicable if both litigants were evil people, and to satisfy this highly uncommon scenario she sat under the palm tree to avoid any possible impropriety. *Ben Yehoyada* says that her extreme modesty and extraordinary consideration of this problem caused her to merit prophecy.

(see also Brachos 31a-b; Pesachim 66b)

> *Chana, as it is written:* And Chana prayed and said: My heart rejoices in Hashem, my horn is exalted in Hashem (Shmuel I 2:1). *(By using the term) "my* horn is *exalted" and not "my* flask *is exalted" (she prophetically implied) that the reigns of David and Solomon, who were anointed with a horn (of oil), were prolonged; the reigns of Saul and Yehu, who were anointed with a flask (of oil), were not prolonged.*

CHANA HAS BEEN DISCUSSED IN DETAIL ELSEWHERE IN THIS *SEFER* (*Berachos* 31). Many of our *halachos* of *davening* are based upon her prayers for a child. The Gemara here demonstrates that she was a prophetess by her assigning an unbreakable chain of kingship to the Davidic dynasty, while she correctly recognized that the monarchies of Shaul and Yehu were not destined for permanency.

(see also Megillah 15a)

Avigayil, as it is written: And she (Avigayil) was riding on the donkey, and came down by the cover of the mountain" (Shmuel I 25:20). *(Why does Scripture use the expression) "by the cover of the mountain"? It should have said,* "from *the mountain"? Rabbah bar Shmuel said: It (the unusual expression) indicates that Avigayil's meeting with David involved blood* that comes from the hidden parts. *She took* (niddah) *blood and showed it to him (asking David to rule if it rendered her a* niddah). *He asked her, "Do we show blood at night?" (i.e. at nighttime one is not allowed to examine and decide questions regarding blood). She responded to him, "Are capital cases tried at night? (Also certainly not. How, then, can you judge at night my husband Naval and condemn him to death?") David said to her, "He (Naval) is a traitor to the crown, and therefore it is not necessary to judge him (i.e. I can have him killed outright, even at night)." Avigayil replied to him, "Shaul is still alive, and your eminence has not yet spread throughout the world (i.e. you do not yet have the authority to order his death as a rebel against the king)." He (David) said to her, "Blessed be your reasoning, and blessed be you who has prevented me this day from coming to* blood<u>s</u>" *(ibid.* 25:33*).* Bloods, *implying two circumstances (where she saved David. Yet only one was just recorded). Rather, Scripture teaches that Avigayil revealed her leg (and when David saw it) he traveled by its light (*Rashi — *with a burning desire for her) for a distance of three* parsahs. *He said to her, "Listen to me (i.e. have relations with me)." She answered him,* "This *should not be a stumbling block for you" (ibid.* 25:31*).* This *intimates that there will be another (occasion). And what was that? The episode of Batsheva. And in the end it was that way.*

Yet the soul of my master shall be bound in the bond of life *(ibid.* 25:29*). As she (Avigayil) took leave of him*

(David), she said to him, "And Hashem shall deal well with my master, and you shall remember your handmaid" *(ibid. 25:31). Rav Nachman said: It is as the people say: While a woman talks, she spins. (*Rashi — *she was talking about Naval, yet she mentioned that when Naval dies, David should remember her and marry her.) Others say: A goose stoops as it goes, but his eyes peer afar (i.e. she was looking ahead to the future when David would marry her. Thus we see that Avigayil was a prophetess).*

THIS NARRATIVE REQUIRES INTENSIVE ANALYSIS FOR US TO BEGIN TO comprehend the deeper meaning behind the plain words. On the surface, Avigayil's actions seem less than proper. *Tosafos* inquire how such a great and righteous woman could reveal her thigh in David's presence. And what does the Gemara mean when it says that David "traveled by the light given off by her thigh" for a distance of three *parsahs* (twelve *mil*, approximately twelve kilometers!)? *Tosafos* (and *Rashi*, *Rashash*, *Yavetz* and others) reinterpret the pronunciation of the word from "*orah*" (light) to "*oorah*" (desire). *Maharsha* explains that it was at night, and they were not near each other. She uncovered her thigh at a distance from David, unknowing that he would chance to look in her direction at that moment (through Divine intervention). He then had a burning desire to be with her, and raced after her for a distance of three *parsahs*. *Mishnas Yosef* points out that the Gemara in *Berachos* (5b) relates that Rabbi Yochanan revealed his arm and light radiated from it. Apparently some great *tzaddikim* had a certain aura/radiance that was actually physically luminescent and thus visible from a distance. *Ben Yehoyada* argues that it was the Satan that shined a light on her and it was this light that David saw. Finally, *Menachem Meishiv Nefesh* suggests that David came upon Avigayil unknowingly and surprised her. She suddenly became a *niddah* (similar to what occurred to Esther;

see the Gemara on 15b), and it was this blood that Avigayil showed to David for a ruling.

How could she and David discuss marriage and relations while she was still married to Naval?

Menachem Meishiv Nefesh opines that the three *parsahs* alludes to the three prophecies that she was about to relate. One of them was that Naval was about to die. (*Maharsha* says this as well.) Both she and David now knew that they were destined for each other through the Divine Spirit. This was her second prophecy, and therefore, it was not inappropriate for them to discuss such matters. Indeed, David misunderstood her revelation and thought that Naval had already died, thus he sought to consummate their relationship immediately. *Ben Yehoyada* exposits that David did not intend to have relations with her until later when he was certain Naval had died. The *Rif* in *Ein Yaakov* remarks that Naval deserved the death penalty as a traitor to the king, and only after David killed him did David intend to live with Avigayil. Finally, the third prophecy dealt with his eventual marriage to Batsheva and was a warning not to err by taking her as his wife prior to the designated time.

Chuldah, as it is written: Chilkiyahu the priest, and Achikam and Achbor etc. (went to Chuldah the prophetess) (Kings II 22:14). *In a place where Yirmiyahu was (the prophet), how did Chuldah prophesy? The academy of Rav said in the name of Rav: Chuldah was a relative of Yirmiyahu, and so he did not object to her prophesying. But Yoshiah himself, how could he forsake Yirmiyahu and dispatch his agents to Chuldah instead? The academy of Shaila said: Because women are more merciful than men ... (The Gemara provides a second answer as well, that Yirmiyahu was out of the country and thus unavailable.)*

CHULDAH IS A WELL-KNOWN PROPHETESS WHO WAS MARRIED TO THE acclaimed *tzaddik* Shalum. Her husband was a tremendous "*baal chessed*" (doer of kindness), and *Pirkei D'Rebbi Eliezer* actually states that it was because of his acts of charity that Chuldah received prophecy. She primarily prophesied to the women of her generation, and she was a close relative of the Navi Yirmiyahu.

Sfas Emes and *Ben Yehoyada* are perplexed as to why the Gemara implies that Chuldah should have deferred prophesying in this case because Yirmiyahu was available. A prophet is not allowed to conceal a prophecy. To do so is against *halachah* and is a capital crime punishable by death from heaven (Sanhedrin 89a) (e.g. see the Book of *Yonah*). *Ben Yehoyada* suggests that one can receive prophecy only after certain preparations are performed. Thus, she should not have begun the process of prophesying in the presence of a more senior prophet like Yirmiyahu. *Rif* in *Ein Yaakov* remarks that since the subject that Chuldah addressed was clearly one of national concern, it would have been more appropriate to let Yirmiyahu respond. Why didn't she do so?

What difference, though, did it make which prophet addressed the question? Since both were clearly true revealers of Hashem's intent, wouldn't the message be the same regardless? *Maharsha* and *Ben Yehoyada* both explain the Gemara's response that women are more merciful. A male prophet would not be as likely to attempt to intervene with Hashem to change the Divine proclamation (e.g. Eliyahu was famous for the extremely strict standard that he expected the Jews to live up to. When they did not, he requested that G-d punish them severely). Women by nature tend to be far more merciful. Yoshiah therefore went to Chuldah in the hope that if the prophecy was a harsh one, she would quickly intervene with the Almighty on behalf of the nation, and nullify any such decree. Indeed, I have heard from my rebbeim that this could possibly explain why the Torah forbids women to be witnesses. A woman might let her protective instincts and merciful nature color her testimony. Unintentionally, she might give an inaccurate description of what transpired.

(see also Pesachim 117a; Yoma 29b; Megillah 7a; 13a; 13aa; 15a; 15b; 16a)

Esther, as it is written: And it was on the third day and Esther clothed herself in royalty (Esther 5:1). *Scripture should have said that Esther (clothed herself) in royal garments. Rather, Scripture intimates that Esther was clothed in the Divine Spirit. It is written here:* And she clothed, *and it is written there:* And the spirit clothed Amasai etc. (Divrei HaYamim I 12:19) *(i.e. he was a prophet. The similar usage of the word* לבשה *— clothed — is how the Gemara generates the comparison).*

ESTHER HAS ALREADY BEEN DISCUSSED IN GREAT DETAIL ON THE preceding *daf*, and will receive more attention on the next several pages as well. Other proofs directly from the verses themselves demonstrate that Esther was a prophetess.

Rav Nachman said: יהירותא *(prominence —* Rashi*; arrogance —* Menachem Meishiv Nefesh*) is not becoming for women. For there were two prominent women, and their names were repulsive. One's name (meant) bee (i.e. Devorah), and one's name (meant) weasel (i.e. Chuldah). Concerning the bee it is written:* And she sent and called Barak (Shoftim 4:6). *However, she herself did not go to him. Concerning the weasel it is written:* Tell the man (Kings II 22:15). *But she did not say — tell the* king.

M*ENACHEM MEISHIV NEFESH* AND THE *BEN YEHOYADA* BOTH opine that arrogance is not ever becoming for a woman. Not to imply that it is proper for a man! But sometimes, it is a necessary evil for a male king or prophet. The commentators point out that in general, it is good to take the middle ground, and not to sway too much to either extreme. But in regard to haughtiness, our Sages remark: מאד מאד הוי שפל רוח, be *very very* humble (*Avos* 4:4). The double usage of the word *very* teaches us to stay far away from this attribute. As great as the Rabbis tell us these two women were, the Torah and Gemara never hesitate to point out that no one is perfect.

(see also Taanis 5b; Megillah 15a; Zevachim 116b)

Rav Nachman said: Chuldah was a descendant of Yehoshua ... Rav Eina the Elder challenged Rav Nachman (from the following Baraisa*): Eight prophets who were* Kohanim *descended from Rachav the harlot (literally, Targum translates this as "innkeeper"). And these are they: Neriyah, Baruch, Searaya, Machseiya, Yirmiyahu, Chilkiah, Chanamel, and Shalum. Rabbi Yehudah says: Even Chuldah the prophetess was a descendant of Rachav, the harlot ... (Since Chuldah numbered among the progeny of Rachav, how can Rav Nachman say that she descended from Yehoshua?) Rav Nachman said to him: Eina the Elder — and some say (that Rav Nachman addressed Eina) "black vessel" (i.e. a title of respect): "By combining my (statement) and your (statement) the teaching is concluded. Rachav converted (to Judaism) and then Yehoshua married her." (Thus, both teachings were indeed correct. Chuldah descended from both Joshua and Rachav.) But did Yehoshua in fact have any descendants? But it is written:* His son, Nun, his son, Yehoshua (Divrei HaYamim I 7:27). *(Since the recitation of Ephraim's lineage ceases with Yehoshua, the Gemara concludes that Yehoshua did not have children.) The Gemara concludes: He did not have sons, but he did have daughters. (Thus Chuldah and the seven prophets descended from daughters who subsequently married* Kohanim.)

RACHAV HAS BEEN DISCUSSED IN DETAIL ELSEWHERE IN THIS *SEFER* (*Taanis* 5b; see also *Zevachim* 116b). Here, the *Iyun Yaakov, Anaf Yosef* and *Sfas Emes* are all troubled by the same problem. How was Yehoshua allowed to marry Rachav? There is a direct prohibition in the Torah against marrying someone from the seven Canaanite nations, even if they convert to Judaism! They all similarly conclude that since the prohibition against saving her life was removed — through Divine intervention — and the two spies (Kalev and Pinchas) were legally permitted to save Rachav and her family, so too, Hashem gave her permission as well to marry into Israel. Alternatively, she was herself just a sojourner in Israel and did not belong to the Canaanite tribes. Thus the ban on marrying Canaanite women did not apply to her.

Ben Yehoyada points out that the name רחב (Rachav) is a jumble of ח׳ רב, eight Rabbis.

This alludes to her illustrious future progeny. Furthermore, Rachav was a *gilgul* (reincarnation) of the wife of Potiphar who attempted to seduce Yosef (*Bereishis,* Chapter 39). Yehoshua was a *gilgul* of Yosef. This somewhat explains the pure motive that the Midrash ascribes to Potiphar's wife in trying to seduce Yosef. She somehow astrologically "saw" (the Egyptians were known to have various true powers in this realm) that she was destined to bear Yosef's children. Therefore she desired relations with the *tzaddik* to carry his seed. What she did not realize was that her vision was imperfect, and in reality it alluded to a future *gilgul* of her and Yosef. The concept of *gilgul* is well beyond the ken of this *sefer*, and is a subject that remains unclear to even many *gedolim.*

MEGILLAH 15A

(see also Pesachim 117a; Yoma 29b; Taanis 5b and Megillah 7a; 12a-b; 13a; 13aa; 9a-b; 14a-b; 15b; 16a; Zevachim 116b)

FOUR GREAT AND BEAUTIFUL WOMEN: SARAH, AVIGAYIL, RACHAV AND ESTHER

The Rabbis taught in a Baraisa*: There were four women of exceptional beauty* (יפיפיות) *in the world: Sarah, Avigayil, Rachav and Esther. And according to the one who says that Esther was greenish in appearance* (Megillah 13a), *take Esther away and add Vashti.*

The Rabbis taught in a Baraisa*: Rachav inspired immorality by merely mentioning her name; Yael with her voice; Avigayil by remembering her; Michal the daughter of Shaul by her appearance.*

(This next Gemara is copied verbatim from Taanis *5b. The commentary to it can be found there in this* sefer *as well.) Rav Yitzchak said (to Rav Nachman), "Whoever says the name 'Rachav, Rachav,' will immediately 'become impure.'" Rav Nachman remarked back to Rav Yitzchak, "I say it ('Rachav, Rachav') without any concern." Rav Yitzchak replied to him, "I made my remark only regarding someone who knows her and recognizes her."*

THE WORD יפיפיות IS A DOUBLED FORM OF THE WORD יפה (*BEAUTY*). *Maharsha* and *Ben Yehoyada* explain that this doubled form is used to connote exceptional unsurpassed attractiveness. *Ben Yehoyada* further notes that they were unique in their comeliness — no other contemporaries had similar loveliness. Many other beautiful women (e.g. the other Matriarchs, Michal, Yael, etc.) lived at the same time as other exceptionally attractive women, and thus they are not included here. For example, the Torah describes the beauty of Rachel and Rivkah with the same terminology used by Sarah. Why aren't they thus listed by our Gemara? Because the lives of Rachel and Rivkah overlapped, and thus they "canceled" each other out. However Sarah was unique — nobody in her generation approached her beauty. *Chazal* remark that when Sarah died (immediately after *Akeidas Yitzchak*), only then was Rivkah born — thus no overlap occurred. Alternatively, *Ben Yehoyada* suggests that the double language implies beauty that was unchanged with age, a beauty undiminished by the ravages of time. Thus Yael and Michal were excluded from this listing. He also notes that all of the women mentioned by the Gemara did not flaunt their beauty. Indeed, they hid themselves and were exceptionally modest in their behavior. This is a lesson for us to bear in mind, and is the reason the Gemara imparts this seemingly immodest information.

Menachem Meishiv Nefesh points out that Yael was not beautiful in form. Her attractiveness was with her mouth (words). (This is not in any way meant disparagingly. Indeed the Gemara in *Sanhedrin* (105b) equates Yael to the four Matriarchs.) Michal likewise was beautiful in her steps, but not necessarily physically pleasing, and thus they were excluded from the list. *Menachem Meishiv Nefesh* also strongly recommends staying away from women who do not use their beautiful traits and physical attractiveness in a proper manner. They will only lead to sin and trouble. The Gemara is giving us practical advice — if they are not like these four — beware!

Tosafos ask a very strong question. Why wasn't the mother of all living beings, Chava, included in the Gemara? the Gemara in *Bava Basra* (58a) clearly states that Sarah, compared to Chava, was like a monkey! Certainly then Chava should have been mentioned? *Tosafos* therefore write that only women born of a woman are enumerated. But Chava, who was fashioned by Hashem directly from Adam, was not considered.

Ben Yehoyada quotes the *Chida* as writing that Adam was far more handsome than Chava — she paled in comparison to his beauty! But *Ben Yehoyada* refers to other *Chazal* that remark that Chava was so much prettier that Adam could not bear to gaze at her. He reconciles the two antithetical approaches though by suggesting that she was prettier before the sin of eating from the tree of knowledge in Gan Eden; but subsequently she lost some of her beauty due to the sin.

Finally, *Maharsha* substantiates and supports the Gemara's description of the various traits of these women with *pesukim* from *Tanach*.

> And the cavity of the queen's body loosened (Esther 4:2). *What does "and the cavity loosened" mean? Rav said: She suddenly began to menstruate. And Rabbi Yirmiyah said: Her bowels loosened (i.e. she had diarrhea) ...*
>
> Go and assemble all of the Jews, etc. *until* (then I will go to the King) which is not like the custom (and if I am lost, I am lost) *(ibid.* 4:16*). Rabbi Abba explained: It was not like the custom" means until now every day (when I went to Achashveirosh) it was against my will (i.e. I was forced), but now, it is by my own free will.*
>
> ... and if I am lost, I am lost *(ibid.). Just as I am lost from my father's house, so too will I be lost from you ...*
>
> *"And it was on the third day and Esther clothed herself in royalty" (ibid.* 5:1*). Scripture should have said that Esther (clothed herself) in royal garments. Rabbi Elazar said in the name of Rabbi Chanina: This teaches us that Esther was clothed in the Divine Spirit. It is written here:* And she clothed, *and it is written there:* And the spirit clothed Amasai etc. (Divrei HaYamim I 12:19) *(i.e. Amasai was a prophet. The similar usage of the word* לבשה *— clothed — is how the Gemara generates the comparison).*

BEN *YEHOYADA* EXPLAINS THE SIGNIFICANCE OF THE *MEGILLAH* teaching us the details of Esther's adverse reaction to the frightening news of the evil decree. This further demonstrates the magnitude of the miracle Hashem wrought on our behalf. When a person has diarrhea or is menstruating, they are not necessarily at the peak of their attractiveness. Yet, it was precisely at this time that Esther went to visit Achashveirosh without an invitation, and yet she appeared to him to be exceptionally beautiful and full of grace. She was willing to put her life on the line — it was potentially a capital crime should Achashveirosh be so inclined — therefore, this was an even greater demonstration of Divine intervention.

Why didn't Esther send the שד (the supernatural spirit Esther conjured up by uttering a Divine Name) so as not to be forced to have relations with Achashveirosh? (See this *sefer*, *Megillah* 13aa for a more complete discussion of this idea.) *Ben Yehoyada* remarks that Esther herself needed to speak directly with Achashveirosh to plead for the Jewish people's lives. The שד would be incapable of doing so. Esther therefore had to personally go this time. However, the *Mishnas Yosef* remarks, based upon a careful reading of the verses, that even here, Esther indeed did send the שד in her place. And subsequently it was the שד and not Esther who gave birth to their son Daryavesh (Darius)!

Tosafos ask why Mordechai didn't divorce Esther prior to her visitation. This way she would not have been technically married at the time of her relations with Achashveirosh, and she would have remained permissible to Mordechai. *Tosafos* maintain that for a legal divorce to be halachically binding, it would have entailed witnesses. They were afraid that the possible resultant publicity would have revealed to Achashveirosh their secret, with the immediate death of both Esther and Mordechai. The approach of the *Ben Yehoyada* complements this argument perfectly. No one was aware that Mordechai and Esther were together because, as stated above (*Megillah* 13aa), Esther became invisible when the שד took her place. Her leaving Achashveirosh to be with Mordechai was never divulged to anyone. If divorce witnesses were now to be made aware of their marriage, it would be far too risky.

Rashba, however, questions this *Tosafos*. According to Torah law, a handwritten divorce delivered by Mordechai to Esther without witnesses would have at least accomplished divorce on the Torah level. Wouldn't that have been better than nothing? *Menachem Meishiv Nefesh* provides a different technical reason why the divorce wouldn't have been effective.

The entire subject of Esther and her relationship with Achashveirosh, its permissibility and the halachic ramifications of her actions are the subject of intense discussion in the Gemara, the commentators, and the *poskim*.

Megillah 15b

(See also Pesachim 117a; Yoma 29b; Megillah 7a; 13a; 13aa; 14a-b; 15a; 16a; Sotah 12b)

Queen Esther and Bisyah— "Stretching" to the Limit

And when the king saw Queen Esther ... *(*and the king extended the golden scepter to Esther*)* (Esther 5:2). *Rabbi Yochanan said: Three ministering angels appeared for her at that time. One that raised her neck; one that drew a thread of* chessed *upon her; and one that stretched the scepter (towards her). And how much (did it stretch)? Rabbi Yirmiyah said it was two* amos *long and the angel fixed it to twelve; and some say it was (elongated) to sixteen; and some say twenty-four; (some versions also add twenty-eight). In a* Baraisa *it was taught that it was extended up to sixty amos. And likewise it was found by the* אמתה *(arm) of Pharoah's daughter (Bisyah) (that it was unnaturally stretched to sixty* amos*) ... Rabbah bar Oofran said in the name of Rabbi Eliezer who heard from his rebbi, and whose rebbi heard from his rebbi: two hundred ...*

(The Gemara then further discusses several ideas and statements from the Megillah attributed to Esther. In keeping with the theme of this sefer *to discuss stories of the women in the Gemara, and not necessarily to discuss every detail of women mentioned in* Tanach, *we will skip these derivations.)*

B*EN YEHOYADA* RELATES THE SIGNIFICANCE OF ALL OF THE NUMBERS described above by the Gemara. Furthermore, they are not mutually exclusive — indeed all are correct. The scepter first extended ten additional *amos*, then four more (sixteen total) etc., until it reached its final state. The six stages represent the six orders of the Mishnah (*Iyun Yaakov* only lists five and says they represent the five Books of Moshe).

Three different angels were required because a single angel is capable of doing only one action. The commentators also note that the three actions are related. Esther was weak from fasting, and thus her head was drooped and required raising. This fasting as well made her ill appearing and necessitated the thread of charm. Finally, as she had never before sinned with Achashveirosh (according to the theory posited on *Megillah* 13aa and 15a that a שד took her place until now), she was now literally frozen in place (from fasting and fear) and the angel had to extend the king's scepter to reach her.

The commentators in *Chumash* differ as to the meaning of the word אמתה. Some say it literally meant her arm, and it is to this opinion that our Gemara refers. (Others, however, translate אמתה as maidservant, and state that she sent them out to fetch the baby Moshe.) According to our version, which implies that the baby Moshe was well out in the middle of the river, what purpose was served by Bisyah extending her hand out to reach the boy? After all, she was so far away she could never reach him. I heard an interesting insight from my rebbeim. Our job is to always do what is right. We need to attempt to do this against any odds, no matter what public opinion says, and no matter how impossible it seems to be. If we do what we are supposed to do, if we make the initial effort, then we can rely upon Hashem to make sure that we will be able to reach even seemingly impossible goals!

Megillah 16a

(see also Pesachim 117a; Yoma 29b; Megillah 7a; 13a; 13aa; 14a-b; 15a; 15b)

THE LADIES IN HAMAN'S LIFE

And (Haman) proclaimed before him (Mordechai): Such shall be done for the man whom the king especially wants to honor (Esther 6:11). *(This* posuk *relates the sequence of events in the* Megillah. *Achashveirosh told Haman to parade Mordechai, dressed in the king's clothing, throughout the city on the king's horse. This was done to publicly display the king's affection to Mordechai for uncovering the assassination plot and saving Achashveirosh's life.)*

As he (Haman) was leading Mordechai through the streets near Haman's house, Haman's daughter, who was standing atop the roof (of their house), presumed that the rider was her father, and the one leading him was Mordechai. She took the bathroom chamber pot and dumped it on the head of the one she thought was Mordechai (it was actually her father). Haman raised his eyes upwards (looking to see who so degraded him) and she saw it was her father. She thereupon fell from the roof to the ground and died. And thus it is written: And Mordechai returned to the king's gate (and Haman hurried to his house mourning and with his head covered in filth) *(ibid.* 6:12*). Rav Sheishes said:* ... and Haman hurried to his house mourning and with his head covered in filth: *"Mourning" — for his daughter; "with his head covered with filth" — because of what transpired to him.*

Ben Yehoyada queries: how was it possible that Haman's daughter did not recognize her own father? And even if she was too far away to get a glimpse of his face, why didn't she recognize his voice? He was constantly yelling, "Such shall be done for the man whom the king especially wants to honor!"

Ben Yehoyada notes that Haman was yelling this verse all day along the parade route. By the time he reached his neighborhood, his voice was hoarse; and thus it was either inaudible or it sounded quite different than usual. Indeed, that was exactly why she assumed it definitely was not her father! In addition, Haman specifically kept his face down (out of embarrassment and shame). And thus she could not catch a good look at his features. Mordechai too was not easily visible. After all, he was still fasting regarding Esther's unsanctioned visit to Achashveirosh. His head was bowed from weakness and hunger. Thus Mordechai also was not readily recognizable to somebody on top of the roof.

Haman's daughter was obviously formed from the same mold as her cruel and wicked father. To throw refuse on top of any person, especially one giving honor to (what she assumed was) her father, is a classic example of chutzpah and brutality. Her ultimate fall — either suicide, or secondary to being weak-kneed from shame — is an appropriate ignominious demise for a vile woman.

Zeresh, Haman's wife, advised Haman to run away at this point. It was clear to her that he was in a calamitous downward spiral. She tried to remove him from further danger. However, the plans of the Almighty are not so simply thwarted. *Iyun Yaakov* remarks that Hashem sent court officers to bring Haman immediately to the palace for the second party with Achashveirosh and Esther — before he could follow through on Zeresh's advice. Indeed the *Rif* in *Ein Yaakov* points out that they came so quickly, Haman did not even have time to bathe and cleanse himself from the refuse before he was abruptly summoned to the party.

And King Achashveirosh said, and he said to Esther the Queen (Esther 7:5). "Said, and he said" — *why the repetition (of the word said)? Initially, (Achashveirosh would speak with Esther only) via an interpreter. But when she told him she was from the (royal) house of Shaul, immediately,* and he said (directly) to Esther.

(Achashveirosh asked, "Who is this person who wants to kill you and your people?") And Esther said, "An adversary and an enemy — this wicked Haman" *(ibid.). Rabbi Elazar said: This teaches that she (Esther) was pointing to Achashveirosh (when she said these words). But an angel came and turned her hand toward Haman.*

B*EN YEHOYADA* COMMENTS THAT IT IS LUDICROUS TO SUGGEST THAT previously Achashveirosh never spoke to Esther directly. They were husband and wife, and were frequently totally alone with each other. He thus writes that only in public did he address her through an interpreter, whereas in the privacy of the inner palace he of course spoke directly to her.

Ben Yehoyada also notes that Esther was willing to give up her life for the safety of her Jewish brethren. She wanted to point at Achashveirosh and tell him he was the real cause behind all of their troubles. She knew of his wickedness and quick temper and assumed he would immediately have her beheaded, like he did to Vashti. There existed a rule that if a senior government official (e.g. the queen) is killed, a royal decree automatically is revoked. By pointing at Achashveirosh, Esther wanted to guarantee the future well-being of the Jews, even though it would mean sacrificing her own life. Hashem of course did not want this, and the angel saved Esther.

Megillah 18a

(see also Eruvin 53b; Rosh Hashanah 26b; Moed Katan 17a; Kesubos 104a)

Legendary Maidservant of Rebbi

The Gemara is in the midst of a series of linguistic forays that are based upon the understanding of certain pesukim. *The maidservant of the great Rebbi, Rabbi Yehudah the Nasi, explains four such complex translations to the Rabbis. As their derivation is technical, we will not list the actual Gemara here.*

The famous maidservant of Rebbi was obviously an accomplished linguist and is described in the Gemara (*Eruvin* 53b) as being quite clever and verbally adept [literally: she spoke in the language of wisdom]. The Rabbis clearly respected her, going so far as to accept her placing a person under a Rabbinical ban for three years (*Moed Katan* 17a). Her devotion and admiration of Rebbi are also legendary, as described in *Kesubos* 104a.

Megillah 25a-b

Illicit Relationships

The Mishnah and Gemara discuss various halachos *regarding the reading and translating of certain chapters and verses in the* Tanach. *The escapades of many famous Biblical female figures are alluded to by the Gemara. As the Gemara does not really discuss any of them, but just mentions them in regard to a specific* halachah, *we will also not discuss them in this* sefer. *The reader is referred to the Chapter in* Tanach *and the Biblical commentators for the complete details. (Other narratives from the Torah are described by the Gemara as well; only those involving women are listed here.)*

> *Reuven and Bilhah* (Bereishis *Chapter* 35);
> *Tamar and Yehudah (ibid. Chapter* 38*);*
> *Amnon, Tamar and David* (Shmuel II *Chapter* 13)*;*
> *Lot and his two daughters* (Bereishis *Chapter* 19)*;*
> *the concubine and the town of Givah* (Shoftim *Chapters* 19-20).

All of the scenarios discussed in the Gemara involve what may appear superficially to be less than stellar behavior on the behalf of many saintly individuals or great people. Some deal with illicit relationships or immorality that is difficult to understand without extensive investigation. However, based on what my rebbeim have taught me over the years, I believe there is an underlying theme and unifying purpose to these stories. The Torah, the Gemara and *Chazal* are never afraid to vividly demonstrate to us the foibles of even our greatest Biblical figures.

No one is infallible. All of us constantly contend with our *yetzer hara*, and the outcome of the battle is not always ideal. Nevertheless, the Talmud does not hesitate to relate these issues in great detail. Often, one can discover more from the fall and subsequent climb back up of a great *tzaddik* or *tzadekes*, than one learns from simply reading about how perfect they were. It is very difficult to emulate a figure that never errs; it is near impossible to identify with someone who knew *Shas* by heart at 6 and never spoke a harsh word about anyone ever in their life. But when we recognize that even the righteous are rocked by the same daily trials and tribulations that we face, we can hopefully use their example as a way to improve ourselves.

Megillah 27b

Rabbi Zakkai's Mother

The disciples asked Rabbi Zakkai (who lived a very long time) to what did he attribute his long life span? He told them (The Gemara lists several reasons. We will only discuss the one dealing with the story of a woman.) ... that he never neglected to recite the Kiddush *of the day (i.e. Shabbos* Kiddush*). He had an elderly mother. One time, (when he had no money for wine) she sold the hair covering that she had on her head and brought him (wine for) the* Kiddush *of the day. We learn in a* Baraisa*: When she (Rabbi Zakkai's mother) passed away, she left him with 300 barrels of wine. When Rabbi Zakkai died, he left his son 3,000 barrels of wine.*

*Rav Huna girded himself with a grass belt (*Rashi, Bach*) and stood before Rav. He (Rav) said to him, "What is this (grass belt — what happened to your regular belt)?" He (Rav Huna) replied, "I did not have* Kiddush *(wine —* Bach*), so I gave my belt as collateral (to borrow money) and I brought wine for* Kiddush*." He (Rav) said to him, "May it be the will (of Hashem) that you become covered in silk (i.e. that you become wealthy)." At the time that Rabbah his son (of Rav Huna —* Rashash*) got married — (as an aside, the Gemara now relates that) Rav Huna was a short person — he was sleeping on a bed. His daughters and daughter-in-law took off their silk garments and threw them on top of him (*Mishnas Yosef *— they did not see him lying there) until he was covered in silk (i.e. literally fulfilling the blessing of Rav) ...*

EITZ YOSEF QUOTES *RASHI* (FOUND IN THE *EIN YAAKOV* IN *SOTAH*) that the students wanted to know which special *mitzvah* or action their rebbi had performed that resulted in his unusual longevity. *Yavetz* adds that normally we say that the reward for a *mitzvah* is not given in this world. So too, the disciples recognized that something unusual must have transpired to cause their rebbi to live so long.

Meiri, Rashba, Maharsha and others all point out that Rabbi Zakkai went beyond the expected requirement to fulfill the dictum to bless the Shabbos (i.e. make *Kiddush*) because he specifically made *Kiddush* over wine. The *halachah* is that if one is too poor to afford wine, it is permissible to make *Kiddush* on the two loaves of *challah*. Rabbi Zakkai, however, was especially scrupulous and strict in his observance of this precept. Therefore, *middah keneged middah*, Hashem so to say likewise "went out of his way" to lengthen Rabbi Zakkai's life beyond the normal span. *Tosafos* add that the Gemara in *Shabbos* (23b) promises that anyone who is zealous regarding *Kiddush* will merit having much wine.

Rabbi Zakkai's mother (grandmother) epitomizes the archtypical self-sacrificing Jewish woman of valor. Throughout the centuries, Jewish women have willingly and eagerly given up their basic physical and material needs to allow their children/husbands to learn Torah and perform *mitzvos*. Even at her death, she made sure that her son could continue to perform his *mitzvah*, as she left 300 barrels of wine for him in her will. Undoubtedly, she could have used the money in her lifetime. By the fact that her son inherited her, she therefore must have been widowed, and money was clearly quite scarce in their family. Yet, she gave up her own material needs for Torah observance. It is only because of such women that *Klal Yisrael* is able to accomplish what it does. The *Rif* in *Ein Yaakov* points out that Rabbi Zakkai saw how his mother went above and beyond what was expected, and he learned this trait from her.

Anaf Yosef brings down the *Sefer Yuchsin,* which claims that our Rabbi Zakkai was the father of the famous Rabbi Yochanan ben Zakkai, the well-known Tanna who lived at the time of the destruction of the Second Temple. He, however, questions this, as the appellation rabbi is missing from Rabbi Yochanan ben Zakkai's father, and thus it might be referring to someone else.

Ben Yehoyada queries why the story of the mother of Rabbi Zakkai is even brought down at all. He posits that this narrative not only illustrates the greatness of the mother, but also of the son. After all, she saw how determined her son was to always make *Kiddush* specifically over wine. To spare him the pain and suffering he would feel if he could not get any wine, she was willing to sell her own hat. This also explains the seemingly unnecessary mentioning that his mother was old. The Gemara tells us this in order to explain how Rabbi Zakkai could accept the gift from his mother. After all, how could he let her go with her hair uncovered? Thus the Gemara lets us know she was old, and therefore didn't leave the house. Alternatively, he suggests that she was old and therefore cared less about her appearance than a younger woman would, and she went out with a less glamorous head cover. The Schottenstein Edition, Megillah 27b (note 33) suggests that the old lady was really his grandmother.

Finally, *Ben Yehoyada* notes that the Talmud adds the extraneous information that she sold the hair cover *that was on her head.* Where else would the hat be? *Ben Yehoyada* states that the Gemara is further praising the mother. Don't think that the mother took an extra hat she had in the house and sold it. No, she took the one she was wearing, the one she needed, and was willing to give that up to help her son perform a *mitzvah* perfectly.

What is the significance of the number three (hundred or thousand) in the story? *Ben Yehoyada* says that this is an allusion to the three meals of Shabbos. Quoting from the Arizal, he says that even though there is no *Kiddush* at the third meal (*shalosh seudos*), nevertheless there is still a *mitzvah* to drink wine then. Also, the number three illustrates that they performed the *mitzvah* perfectly — complete in thought, words and action.

In the second story about Rav Huna, *Rashi* (in *Ein Yaakov*) comments that Rav Huna became very well off and could now clothe his daughters and daughter-in-law in rich silk. *Mishnas Yosef* quotes the *Chazon Ish* pointing out a Gemara (i.e. *Taanis* 20b) that demonstrates how wealthy Rav Huna became. He also comments that the blessing of a great *tzaddik* can even be seen to continue in the children of the person blessed, as illustrated by the daughters/daughter-in-law wearing silk. We should always take the blessings of a great person very seriously.

Ben Yehoyada provides further insight. Rav Huna mortgaged the value of the entire belt, even though he could have purchased wine for less than this amount. Rav Huna purchased the best wine possible — he didn't skimp at all! — and therefore he was rewarded with tremendous wealth. Similarly, since he sold an article of clothing, he was blessed with (silk) garments, another illustration of *middah keneged middah*.

Yavetz comments as to why the Gemara makes the incongruous remark that Rav Huna was short. He notes that the Gemara relates that Rav subsequently became upset that upon hearing the blessing which Rav conferred upon him, Rav Huna did not immediately respond and return the prayer and declare, "And I, too, bless my rebbi, as well!" It was obviously an opportune moment for a *berachah*, and Rav wished that Rav Huna had blessed him in return. Why, in fact, didn't Rav Huna do so? Because Rav blessed Rav Huna that he be covered in silk. Rav Huna was very short, and the Gemara elsewhere says that Rav was very tall. Thus, if Rav Huna had said, "I bless rebbi, as well," Rav would have been only partially blessed. Rav Huna did not want to give only a half-hearted *berachah*, so he did not say anything at all.

מסכת מועד קטן

MOED KATAN

Moed Katan

Moed Katan 8a

THE WOMAN AND THE EULOGIST

Rav Kahana said in the name of Rav Yehudah who said in the name of Rav: There was an incident with a certain man who collected money for the festival pilgrimage to Yerushalayim. However, along came a eulogist and stood at the entranceway to the house, and the man's wife took (the festival pilgrimage) funds and gave them to the eulogist. (Now, without money), the man refrained and did not go up to Yerushalayim. At that time they (the Rabbis) said: A person should not hire eulogists for his dead thirty days prior to the holidays.

IT WAS COMMON CUSTOM IN THE PERIOD OF THE GEMARA FOR professional eulogists to circulate throughout Israel and inspire lamentations for recently deceased people. The practice was to hire and pay such professionals to increase the fervor and mourning for the departed. However, as a result of our narrative, the Rabbis restricted this practice. Funds designated for festival use should not be utilized for less holy purposes. As it was usual to start securing monies for the festival pilgrimage thirty days prior to the holiday (based upon the well-known dictum of studying the laws of the holiday thirty days before their occurrence), the Sages instituted this restriction only during this period.

This story demonstrates the innate tender female nature. The Gemara does not inform us where the husband was when the eulogist came, but it is possible that a man might not have reacted in the same fashion. While there are many exceptions to the rule, women in general are more sensitive and empathetic to such emotions than are men.

Moed Katan 9b

Rav Chisda's Wife

(The Gemara is in the midst of a discussion regarding certain activities and their permissibility on the intermediate festival days — Chol HaMoed. The Mishnah stated that women may apply make-up on these days.)

*The wife of Rav Chisda was adorning herself (applying make-up, etc.) in front of her daughter-in-law. Rav Huna bar Chinana was sitting before Rav Chisda, and he was sitting and he said, "They (the Rabbis of the Mishnah) only taught (this halachah permitting applying make-up on Chol HaMoed) regarding a young girl but not for an elderly woman." He replied to him, "By G-d! (This is the halachah) even for your mother, and even for your mother's mother, and even if she is standing over her grave (i.e. is very old and at death's door)." For people say: A 60-year-old woman is like a 6-year-old girl — they run to the sound of the bells. (*Rashi, Ran, Meiri — *Just as a 6-year-old enjoys the music at a wedding and runs to hear it, so too does a 60-year-old woman. This pleasure is independent of age. So too, regarding the application of make-up. One is never too old to desire to affix it, and thus it is permissible for women of any age to apply it on Chol HaMoed.)*

R*ASHI* POINTS OUT THAT THE GEMARA INFORMS US THAT SHE APPLIED make-up *in front of her daughter-in-law* to provide us with her approximate age, i.e. that she was at least old enough to have a married son. *Rashash* comments that the Gemara in

Kiddushin (29b) writes that Rav Chisda got married at the young age of 16. It is quite possible that a son of his also got married at a tender age. Mrs. Rav Chisda (the daughter of Rav Chanan bar Rava, granddaughter of the illustrious Rav) might therefore have only been in her late 20's/early 30's at the time of this story. *Rashash* thus suggests that all of Rav Chisda's very famous sons (the Gemara elsewhere lists seven great Rabbis as his children) were actually born to him very late in life. Later in our *mesechta* (*Moed Katan* 28a) we are told that Rav Chisda died at 92 years of age, so he had plenty of time to raise his sons even if they were born well after he was married. I would just add that *Bava Basra* (141a) quotes Rav Chisda as remarking that girl children are preferable to boys. Indeed, *Tosafos* there state that his two daughters married great men (Rava and either Rami bar Chama or Mar Ukva bar Chama), and they undoubtedly played a major role in the leadership of the Jewish people.

The Gemara in *Kesubos* (85a) states that Rav Chisda took halachic advice from his wife regarding certain questions of Jewish law. It states that he trusted her advice even more than the great Rav Pappa!

(see also Shabbos 80b)

Rav Bibi had a daughter whom he anointed with lime, limb by limb (in order to remove excess hair and to beautify her complexion; he did not apply it all at once because that would be too dangerous). He was so successful in making her attractive, that he received for her (from a prospective suitor — Rashi*) 400* zuzim *(a very large amount of money). (Upon seeing this), a Cuthite who lived in the neighborhood who also had a daughter, applied lime to her (but he anointed her entire body) simultaneously, and the daughter died. The gentile neighbor declared, "Bibi killed my daughter." Rav Nachman stated: In Rav Bibi's house, beer (which causes excessive and dark hair growth —* Rashi*) is frequently drunk, thus there is a need for smearing girls with lime. However, for us who do not drink beer, lime application is unnecessary.*

THIS NEAR IDENTICAL GEMARA IS FOUND ON SHABBOS 80B, AND IS fully discussed there in the commentary.

MOED KATAN 16B

THE SCHOLAR AND THE WOMAN IN "SHAMTA"

(The Gemara is in the midst of describing the different levels and durations of Rabbinical excommunication.)

*There was a certain woman who was sitting along the roadway. She stretched out her leg [while] she was winnowing hulled barley seeds (*Rashi *in* Sanhedrin 27a*). Subsequently, a young Talmudic scholar came and passed by, but she did not humble herself before him (i.e. did not withdraw her leg to let him pass easily). He (the scholar) said, "How brazen is this woman!" The woman then went before Rav Nachman (to inquire whether that statement constituted a formal halachic excommunication or not). He (Rav Nachman) said to her, "Did you hear the word '*shamta*' (a specific expression of excommunication) from his mouth?" She replied that she had not heard that formula. He said to her, "Go and conduct yourself for one day as a '*nizufa*' (minor form of rebuke/excommunication)."*

M*AHARSHA* SAYS SHE WAS REMOVING THE SHELLS FROM THE barley.

Shitas Rivav (in *Ein Yaakov*) notes that Rav Nachman asked her if she actually heard the young scholar state *shamta* because the *halachah* would then require her to ask forgiveness from him before the *shamta* could be lifted. Thus, Rav Nachman was inquiring for a very practical purpose — does she need to seek him out after the day of *nizufa*? *Ben*

Yehoyada wonders: Since she acted improperly by not allowing the Talmudic sage to pass easily, why didn't Rav Nachman himself excommunicate her on the spot (even if the young scholar hadn't)? He answers by stating an important principle — a person does not have the ability to make him/herself into a legally defined wicked person. Meaning, we are not permitted halachically to accept her words and judicially act upon the admission that she acted improperly. She can, and should, follow the recommended suggestion of Rav Nachman that she treat herself as a *nizufa* for the day. But Rav Nachman had no authority to actually excommunicate the woman solely based upon her own admission.

(The gemara subsequently discusses several historical figures [King Shaul, Tzipporah, King Chizkiyah, the Jewish nation] referred to as Cushites. The Talmud is bothered by the fact that Tzipporah is referred to by Miriam as a woman of Cushite extraction, when indeed we know she was a Midianite. Miriam spoke lashon hara *about her brother Moshe regarding his wife Tzipporah. Miriam questioned why Moshe was different than all other prophets and felt he had to divorce his spouse. She did not realize that Moshe was constantly "on-call" to Hashem and thus could not maintain a normal husband-wife relationship.)*

Similarly, the following is said, "regarding the 'Cushis' (Cushite) woman that he took" *(*Bamidbar 12:1*). And is* Cushis *her name? But Tzipporah is her name! Rather, just as a Cushite person is unusual in his skin, so too, Tzipporah was unusual in her deeds.*

CUSHITES OR *CUSHIS* ARE PEOPLE WITH A DARK COMPLEXION. IT IS a term often used to describe black-skinned individuals, and it is also used to characterize the people and/or the country of Ethiopia. A dark-skinned human is a relatively unusual visage in the Biblical/Talmudic literature. Indeed, the Gemara in *Berachos* relates that upon seeing such a person, a special blessing is recited, because of the uniqueness of the individual! Thus, by specifically describing her as a *Cushis*, the *posuk* is obviously teaching us a certain lesson. *Ben Yehoyada* points out that a person's skin color is immediately noticeable and recognizable. So too, when the Gemara describes a trait of an individual as being *Cushis*, it is informing us that this person possesses a character feature that is clear, obvious and stands out to all onlookers.

Maharsha notes that the verse cannot possibly be describing a second wife of Moshe, because the definitive article <u>the</u> *Cushis* is used to describe her, implying <u>the</u> wife of Moshe, i.e. his only, previously mentioned, wife. However, *Rashbam* (quoted in the *Iyun Yaakov*) states that Moshe actually took a married Cushite queen as his wife, but never had relations with her. (Various Midrashim relate that Moshe was a Cushite king for a forty-year period of time between his initial flight from Pharaoh at the age of 20 [some say 40], and until his return to Egypt at the age of 80. After abdicating his throne, Moshe journeyed to Midian where Yisro, his future father-in-law, initially threw him in a deep pit/dungeon for ten years! Moshe only survived because of the kindness and great courage that Yisro's daughter, Tzipporah, displayed. She surreptitiously brought him food, at great personal risk, during his entire ten-year imprisonment.) *Middah keneged middah*, Moshe was now being punished for this "sin" of taking the Cushite queen by having to divorce Tzipporah.

What character feature made Tzipporah so unusual? The *Talmid Rabbeinu Yechiel MiParis* writes that she was especially *tzanua* (modest) in her actions. *Benayahu* points out that you might have thought that Moshe wanted to divorce her because she was a convert, so the Gemara tells us that her deeds and actions were superior and far more righteous than those of most other Jewish women.

The *Ein Yaakov* add the words "and she was unusual in her deeds and her beauty" to the text of our Gemara. The *Kosev* writes that she was prettier than all other women. Indeed, the *Sifri* (*Behaaloscha* 99) formulates that her name Tzipporah, צפרה, is a contraction of צפו וראו, *gaze and see* (how beautiful she is). Why is she not listed therefore in *Megillah* 15a among the most beautiful women ever? Indeed, *Midrash HaGadol* (*Bamidbar* 12:1) writes that she was beautiful in her youth and old age, one of the criterion mentioned by *Ben Yehoyada* as necessary for eligibility on this list. Possibly, I would suggest, it is because her sister Bisyah (see this *sefer, Megillah* 13a) also lived at the same time, and unless one's beauty was unique in her generation, one was not eligible for inclusion.

MOED KATAN 17A

(see also Eruvin 53b;
Rosh Hashanah 26b; Kesubos 104a)

REBBI'S MAIDSERVANT

(The Gemara is in the midst of a story regarding whether a ban of excommunication can be lifted if the original scholar [Rav Yehudah] who placed the ban has died. As part of that discussion, the following argument is brought.)

Rabbi Shmuel bar Nachmani rose to his feet and said: In the case of the maidservant of Rebbi (Rabbi Yehudah HaNasi), the Sages did not treat her ban of excommunication lightly for three years (i.e. the ban stood in place for three years). Therefore, how much more so, for (the great Amora, Rav) Yehudah our friend, (should we not treat his ban seriously)? ...

What is the story of the ban of Rebbi's maidservant? The maidservant of Rebbi saw a certain man who was striking his mature son (i.e. usually referring to a child above bar mitzvah *age;* Rashi [kesiv yad] *— the oldest son). She said, "Let that person be in '*shamta*' (a type of excommunication) because he transgressed the verse:* Do not place a stumbling block before the blind (Vayikra 19:14)*." For it was taught in a* Baraisa: Do not place a stumbling block before the blind *— this verse refers to one who strikes his mature son.*

REBBI'S MAIDSERVANT IS MENTIONED IN SEVERAL PLACES IN *SHAS* IN a very positive light. She was a well-known personality with great merits. Here we see how the Rabbis were very much aware and cognizant of her elevated status. The *Raavad, Ran, Rosh, Ritva, Nimukei Yosef* and others all ask what was the reason that the ban of Rebbi's maidservant lasted for three years? If she died, why didn't the Sages lift the ban sooner? And even if she was still alive, why didn't the leading scholars remove the excommunication? These commentators point out that a *shamta* has no specific time duration, unlike other bans that are specified for a designated duration. Thus, this father was obviously not repentant and appropriately contrite for hitting his son, and thus he was left in *shamta* for three years until he finally asked forgiveness. *Rosh* and others add that since Rebbi's maidservant was a woman of such unusual "extra" wisdom and "fear of sin," no other rabbi was willing to take it upon himself to overrule her ban of excommunication while she was around. *Shitas Rivav* further notes that even the *Nasi* wouldn't do this, because of concern that she was superior to him, and it would be inappropriate to overturn her decision. Thus we clearly see the great respect and lofty status conferred upon this unusual woman.

Rashi explains that if a parent hits a child, and should that child then strike or curse the parent back (a capital punishment), the parent would have indirectly caused the child to sin. This is what the Gemara refers to as a stumbling block. *Ritva* says that this rule applies even for selected minor children (below *bar mitzvah*) who are capable of understanding the *halachah*. This is not the *psak* of the *Rama* (*Shulchan Aruch Yoreh Deah* 240:20), who rules that a father is not subject to this ban even if he strikes his child up until the age of 22 or 24.

This Gemara is not to suggest that hitting children is necessarily an appropriate or effective means of punishment. Indeed, the *Piskei Tosafos* (cited in the glosses of *Rabbi Akiva Eiger,* quoting from the *Maharikash,* in *Yoreh Deah* 240:20) writes that striking a child more than necessary is grounds for excommunication! Whether it is ever acceptable to hit a child is a very controversial and potentially dangerous issue; the potential for parental abusive behavior should not be minimized. Under the appropriate setting, and with the appropriate controls and guidelines, it may be acceptable (halachically and psychologically) to occasionally use some form of corporal punishment. I once heard an interesting story from one of my rebbeim about a *gadol* of a previous century. His son did some sort of egregious mischief around the house, resulting in significant damage to an important item. The father did nothing at the time, but two weeks later he called the son into his study and gave him an unexpected "*potch.*" The puzzled son asked what he did to deserve the *potch*. The father replied that it was for his behavior two weeks earlier. The father explained, "Until today, I was still angry with you, and I could not strike you without my own emotions getting in the way. It is only now, that I have complete control of my reaction, that I can properly assess the situation and determine the appropriate response. You deserve a *potch*, and now I can give it with exactly the appropriate strength (not one bit extra!) that you deserve!"

Why does the Gemara only state the *halachah* regarding a son, but does not mention a daughter? *Iyun Yaakov* says that the law is the same for both. However, girls are far less likely to hit their parents, or even fight with their parents at all, and thus there was no need to discuss such a rare occurrence. Plus, the father is required to teach his son Torah and a profession. One might think, therefore, that the son would feel indebted to his father and not hit him back even in anger. Therefore the *halachah* is brought down specifically regarding a son to negate this possible misunderstanding, but he suggests that it applies even more so to a daughter. Alternatively, it was unusual in those days for a 12-year-old girl to still live at home; the situation thus rarely came up where a father had the opportunity to hit his post *bas-mitzvah*-age daughter.

MOED KATAN 23A

THE REMARRIAGE OF YOSEF HAKOHEN: A FUNERAL "PROPOSAL"

(The Gemara is in the midst of a discussion regarding the appropriate time a person must wait after the death of a close relative or of one's spouse before remarrying. The Gemara states that if a husband is unable to raise the young children then he may immediately remarry.)

It once happened that the wife of Yosef HaKohen died, and he said to her (his wife's) sister in the cemetery, "Go and care for your sister's children (i.e. marry me and raise them)." Nevertheless, he did not have relations with her until a much later time. What is a much later time? Rav Pappa said: After thirty days.

THIS GEMARA IS BROUGHT DOWN IN SLIGHTLY DIFFERENT VERSIONS IN the Yerushalmi (*Yevamos* 28b; Chapter 4, *Halachah* 11), and in *Maseches Semachos* (Chapter 7). The basic story is ascribed as either occurring to Yosef HaKohen (alternatively referred to as Rav Yosef HaKohen) and/or Rabbi Tarfon. Interestingly, both are *Kohanim*.

On the surface, Yosef HaKohen (and/or Rabbi Tarfon) can be mistakenly thought of as callous and indifferent. To essentially propose to one's sister-in-law at the actual funeral — when burying her sister/one's wife — is difficult for us to understand or comprehend. However, we must remember that this was prior to the days of modern comforts and economic advantages that we take for granted. There was no day care, no 24-hour a day convenience stores and no refrigeration. And in our particular case, there were absolutely no alternative family or friend care providers. The *Talmid Rabbeinu Yechiel MiParis* further comments that men in those days were simply incapable of providing care for young children. We are therefore dealing almost with a case of "*pikuach nefesh*" (danger of loss of life) and the unusual actions of Yosef HaKohen (and/or Rabbi Tarfon) must be understood in that light. Indeed, the *halachah* reflects this concern, and actually permits one to get married if there is no alternative child-care provider once the seven-day *shivah* period is concluded. However, consummation of the marriage is only permitted after the thirty-day *sheloshim* mourning duration is finished (*Rosh; Ran; Shulchan Aruch Yoreh Deah* 382:2). Our version of *Tosafos* actually states that if marriage is permitted, then relations are allowed as well, but *Rabbi Akiva Eiger* (in the *Gilyon HaShas*) remarks this is a printing error.

Tosafos explain that Yosef HaKohen did not actually marry his sister-in-law at the cemetery, even though that is what the words literally suggest, because this would be prohibited. Indeed, the text in *Maseches Semachos* records the encounter with the sister-in-law as taking place during *shivah*, not at the cemetery. Likewise, the *Ritva*, and the *Shiltei HaGiborim* (quoting *Ramban*) remark that the word <u>immediately</u> in the Gemara is a relative term. As opposed to the normative rule that a man must wait until three festivals have passed before remarrying, here "immediate" implies a lesser wait, i.e. until after the *sheloshim* period has passed. (Incidentally, the ruling is more lenient for a widowed woman. She must only wait a period of ninety days — to guarantee that the true biological father will be recognizable if a child is conceived immediately in the new marriage.)

Alternatively, *Rosh* expounds that he just <u>proposed</u> to her in the cemetery, but they actually got married after *shivah* (*Shach*, based on *Bach,* brings this down as the *halachah*. One can propose a *shidduch*, even on the day of the burial). *Riva* (in *Tosafos*) and the *Ritva* suggest that the wife died on *erev* Pesach (as described in *Zevachim* 100a). *Shivah* was uprooted by Pesach and in fact ended the very day it began. Therefore, the

Gemara is really telling us that they got married after the *shivah* was over, albeit that very same day. (Since formal *shivah* ends before the start of Pesach, the prohibition to marry during *shivah* as well is uprooted prior to the close of the day.)

Tosafos in *Yevamos* (43b) helps us further understand the rationale behind Yosef HaKohen's actions. If a sister-in-law agrees to the marriage, we permit it to occur right away because of the needs of the poor orphans. The Rabbis realized that the most perfect substitute mother for these distressed children would be the person who would show the most compassion and love for them — their maternal aunt. *Sfas Emes* adds that even if the children were not those of the deceased wife — i.e. they were from a previous marriage — the *halachah* remains the same.

Finally, as a last demonstration of the purity and holiness in which the Rabbis involved in our story conducted themselves, I suggest that the reader refer to the Yerushalmi (*Yevamos* 29a, Chapter 4, *Halachah* 12) and the *Tosefta* in *Kesubos* (5:1). In a time of great famine and poverty, Rabbi Tarfon, who was a *Kohen* with apparently significant stores of *terumah*, took it upon himself to marry 300 young girls to permit them to eat *terumah*. (Normally, non-*Kohanim* are forbidden [with a punishment of death] to eat *terumah*. However, the non-*Kohen* wife of a *Kohen* is allowed to eat *terumah*.) The Sages debate the *halachah* there. Is a full marriage (*nisuin*) required for a bride of a *Kohen* (who was not a *Kohen* herself) to eat *terumah*, or is only *erusin*, the first stage of marriage, necessary? Rabbi Tarfon held the latter view — only *erusin* without consummation of the marriage is required. Thus, he assumed this tremendous financial obligation to feed these impoverished starving young women out of pure charity and righteousness, and not *chas veshalom* out of any prurient personal physical satisfaction (i.e. full marriage). So too, in our Gemara, his sole concerns were for the welfare of his tiny orphaned young babies. He did not consummate the new marriage until an appropriate later date. (We should also keep in mind the Rashbam in Pesachim who states that the gemara uses the number 300 as an exaggerated amount — it means simply a large number).

MOED KATAN 27B

A MOTHER'S MOURNING

And Rav Yehudah said in the name of Rav: Anyone who "hardens" (excessively mourns his dead; Mesoras HaShas *— binds himself) more than appropriate will ultimately cry over another deceased person. There was a certain woman who lived in the neighborhood of Rav Huna. She had seven sons. One of them died, and she cried excessively for him. Rav Huna sent her (the following message): Do not do so (i.e. do not mourn excessively). She did not pay attention to him. He sent her (a second message): If you listen to me, everything will be good. And if not — make provisions for another one (i.e. prepare a second set of funeral shrouds for another death). A second son then died. (She did not try to stop her excessive grieving.) Subsequently all of her (seven) sons eventually died. She continued to cry. (These four words are added from the* Ein Yaakov. Rashi *there comments — she continued to mourn excessively.) At the end, he (Rav Huna) said to her: Prepare provisions for yourself. She then also died. (The Gemara then brings verses from the Book of* Yirmiyahu *to support the concept of not mourning excessively.)*

IT IS NOT CLEAR FROM THE GEMARA OVER WHAT PERIOD OF TIME THE tragic loss of the women and her seven sons occurred. Obviously though, it must have been within her power to stop excessively mourning, or it would have been unfair to punish her. In addition, for Hashem to deal with her in such an exacting fashion (as is normally the rule only for the righteous), she must have been on a very high spiritual level. G-d judges such individuals much more strictly than He does a common person. It is also crucial to point out that this Gemara deals exclusively with excessive inappropriate grieving — what we term medically "pathological mourning." This is neither spiritually nor psychologically healthy. But the Gemara is certainly not discussing legitimate halachically required grieving, which fulfills both religious and psychological purposes.

Rashi (*kesiv yad*) writes that if one lets himself be drawn into excessive sorrow and suffering, then sorrow will follow and consume him. *Nimukei Yosef* explains that excessive mourning means observing *shivah* and mourning longer than the proscribed or required period of time. *Chazal* knew that observing mourning for the proper duration would ultimately lead to appropriate fear of Hashem's judgement and prevent transgressions. Apparently a longer period would have been counterproductive. *Rabbi Shlomo ben HaYasom* (cited in the Schottenstein Edition of Talmud Bavli, *Moed Katan* 27b note 30) states that excessive grieving refers to one who magnifies the pain beyond its true extent. The *Ritva* notes that this appears as if one has not lovingly accepted Hashem's decree and is rebelling against the heavenly decision. Indeed, the Gemara in *Berachos* and other places describes how one must make a blessing with the same fervor and love over a horrible tragedy as one does at a time of great gladness and happiness. Finally, *Iyun Yaakov* alludes to the Gemara in *Taanis* 29a. The Jewish people inappropriately cried then, upon hearing the slanderous words of the spies on their return from investigating Eretz Yisrael. G-d therefore declared: "You cried for naught on this day, I will give you something to cry about forever." That day was Tishah B'Av, a day of infamy and tragedy throughout Jewish history.

The *Rif* in *Ein Yaakov* reminds us though that it is praiseworthy to constantly feel the loss of the positive influence that the righteous person had on those left behind. He cites several examples from the *Tanach* illustrating this point. One is permitted to "excessively" mourn this aspect of "lost guidance" and/or the "shining example" that is now missing from one's life. Furthermore, we see by Avraham Avinu that he mourned Sarah in different ways and for different durations. *Chazal* explain that the letter כ' in the word לבכתה (and to mourn her) is written smaller than the other letters of the Torah. This symbolizes the various stages that Avraham grieved. We are not permitted to excessively mourn the physical loss. Only a relatively short time is spent mourning that. A longer duration is spent remembering the person's good deeds and influence.

Contrast the actions of the unfortunate and tragic lady in our story with those of other righteous women blessed with seven sons. (The stories of Kimchis (*Yoma* 47a) and Hilni (*Succah* 2b) are described elsewhere in this *sefer*.) *Chazal* tell us the unbelievable tale of Chana (not the Chana who was the mother of the Navi Shmuel). She lost all seven of her sons (and all were below *bar-mitzvah* age!) to a wicked tyrant who demanded that they bow down to an idol. Each son adamantly refused, and each son was killed before her very eyes. She did not protest or grieve excessively, but told Hashem, "Avraham only prepared to sacrifice his son Yitzchak, but did not actually have to do so. I have willingly brought you seven holy offerings."

Why didn't the poor woman in our Gemara realize what she was doing after the second, third or even fourth child's death? Why couldn't she control herself? I heard an answer from my rebbeim, attributed to Rabbi Yaakov Kamenetsky *zt"l*, in regard to a similar idea. The Midrash relates that the second plague (*makkah*) in Egypt, the *makkah* of numerous frogs disseminating all over Egypt, began when one large frog emerged from the Nile. The Egyptians immediately attacked it. However, each time they hit it, the frog divided into two. But they kept on striking the frog till there were hundreds of thousands of creatures. Why didn't they stop after they saw the initial disastrous results? Human nature. They were so embroiled in what they were doing, so caught up in their emotions and anger, that they did not comprehend the true reality. Possibly, the same explanation can apply in our narrative. The woman was so inordinately engrossed in her own pain and suffering that she could not comprehend the tremendously negative connotations of her actions. Despite Rav Huna's repeated careful admonitions, each subsequent death further solidified her defiance, and ultimately led to her own demise and family destruction. We must always remember the big picture — our purpose in this existence, our *raison d'etre.* And that is to serve Hashem, no matter what cards we are dealt.

Moed Katan 28a

(see also Taanis 9a; Megillah 14a-b)

Miriam's Death — A Kiss from Hashem

Rabbi Elazar said ... And Miriam died there and was buried there (Bamidbar 20:1). *The burial took place immediately after her death. And Rabbi Elazar said: Miriam also died by means of a "kiss" from Hashem. He determines this based upon the comparing of the same word "שם — there" which appears in our verse, and again in* Devarim 34:5 *in reference to the burial of Moshe. (This method of derivation is called a* gezeirah shavah *— equivalent word comparison. In certain places we have a Sinaitic tradition that words of a similar nature are compared to each other to derive certain laws or teachings. The* posuk *specifically relates that Moshe died via the "kiss" of Hashem. Through the* gezeirah shavah *"there" "there" we can derive the same for Miriam.) And why does the Torah not openly state "by the mouth of Hashem"? Because it is improper to use this language (regarding a woman). Rav Ami said: Why is the story of the death of Miriam juxtaposed to the narrative of the Red Cow? To teach you that just as the Red Cow provides atonement, so too, the death of the righteous provides atonement.*

Miriam is the only woman (amongst five men — the three Patriarchs, Aharon and Moshe) listed in the Gemara in *Bava Basra* (17a) who was brought up to Heaven directly via the hand of Hashem (i.e. through the "kiss" of G-d), and not through the advent of the Angel of Death. *Mishnas Yosef,* quoting the holy *Zohar,* states that this form of death is the highest possible spiritual form of departing from our world. Our Gemara explains that it would be indelicate to actually describe Hashem as "kissing" Miriam. Thus, it is only indirectly alluded to through Biblical exegesis. I believe this is yet another illustration of the principle we have discussed several times already in this sefer — כל כבודה בת מלך פנימה — loosely translated as the honor of the King's daughter is in private. Women in Judaism are specifically kept out of the public eye for reasons of modesty.

Menachem Meishiv Nefesh asks: How do we know that Miriam's death and immediate burial were because she was so righteous — maybe it was due to purely physical considerations? Maybe she had an impure discharge that rendered her ritually impure — e.g. a *zavah* — and as a result they buried her immediately so as not to risk defiling anything pure that would come into contact with her. Or, maybe she died immediately prior to nightfall, and thus she was buried right away because of the requirement not to let a dead body remain overnight if at all possible. *Menachem Meishiv Nefesh* answers that since we are told that she died via the "kiss" of Hashem, these other possibilities would have to be dismissed. If she were a *zavah* at the time of death, then Hashem would not have "kissed" her, as this would result (so to say, as if it were possible) in G-d becoming defiled. Likewise, only one who dies at the hands of the Angel of Death must be buried right away and not wait overnight. This requirement does not apply to one who dies at the hands of Hashem.

Tosafos notes that the Red Cow provided special atonement to the Jewish nation. The laws of the Red Cow are too numerous and detailed for us to discuss here. Suffice it to say that these laws can not be understood by our limited human minds; they are Divine decrees from Above. However, *Tosafos* bring down the well-known Midrash that explains specifically why a mother cow was chosen to provide atonement for us. A human king will tell his maidservant whose young child has carelessly dirtied and soiled the king's palace to go and clean up her son's mess! So too, Hashem declares: Let the mother cow "clean up" the mess of her child, i.e. let the Jewish people receive atonement for the sin of the Golden Calf via the mother cow. *Ben Yehoyada, Mishnas Yosef* and *Eitz Yosef* all write that the righteous are referred to as the mother of the Jewish people. It is thus very appropriate that the deaths of such saintly individuals serve as atonement for the entire nation.

Moed Katan 28b

The Women of Shechnatziv

(The Gemara is in the midst of a section where various eulogies are described. Rava states seven terse, pithy and profound elegies attributed to and recorded from the women of Shechnatziv. As the true meaning and specific explanation of their cryptic and puzzling statements is not easily understood, and it is not relevant to the theme of this book, we will not actually enumerate them here).

WHO WERE THESE WOMEN OF SHECHNATZIV? *RABBEINU CHANANEL* describes them as "lamenters" (elegy chanters) who were very wise. *Iyun Yaakov* remarks that we learn from these women the proper way to speak and converse. We should always answer in a concise fashion, and not talk in a slanderous manner.

Rabbi Yaakov Emden in his *Hagahos Yavetz* writes that Rebbi gave his sons four pieces of advice on his deathbed (see *Pesachim* 112b). The first one was not to live in the town of Shechnatziv because its populace was full of mockers; if one were to reside there, the citizens would draw him into their mockery and hypocrisy. How then does our Gemara proceed to quote seven maxims of Shechnatziv's townsfolk if they were people of ill repute? *Hagahos Yavetz* therefore suggests that only the men were mockers, but not the women. Since Rava quotes the women extensively in our Gemara, they were obviously meritorious, and not the type of people that Rebbi instructed his sons to avoid. *Hagahos Yavetz* alternatively posits that one can learn good things even from bad people. As Ben Zoma teaches us in *Pirkei Avos* (4:1): *Who is the wise man? One who learns from every man.*

I would like to suggest another simple reconciliation between Rebbi's admonition to his son, and our Gemara. The exposition of Rebbi took place many years prior to Rava — the populace might have changed dramatically for the better during the centuries, undoubtedly from the influence of great scholars such as Rava and the righeous women who influenced their spouses and children to become better individuals.

מסכת חגיגה

CHAGIGAH

CHAGIGAH

CHAGIGAH 4B-5A

MIRIAM (MARY), BRAIDER OF HAIR

When Rav Yosef came to this verse — And there is one who succumbs without justification (Mishlei 13:23) *— he cried. He said (*Rashi *and* Tosafos *delete "he said" and substitute instead — the Gemara queries): Is there anyone who leaves not at his time (i.e. does anyone die before their appropriate time)? (The Gemara answers): Yes, it is similar to what happened to Rav Bibi bar Abaye. He regularly visited with the Angel of Death (i.e. he regularly conversed with him). Once (Rav Bibi heard that) the Angel of Death said to his agent, "Go and bring to me Miriam* מגדלא שיער נשיא, Miriam, the braider of women's hair. *The agent went, however, and brought Miriam* מגדלא דרדקי, Miriam, the one who raised young children. *The Angel of Death said to his messenger, "I told you to bring me Miriam, the braider of women's hair!" The agent replied to the Angel of Death, "If so, I will return her (i.e. I will restore the life of Miriam the one who raises young children)." The Angel of Death responded to his agent, "Since you already brought her, let her be numbered amongst the dead." (*Menachem Meishiv Nefesh *has the text: Let her be included in the count of the dead.) Rav Bibi asked the Angel of Death, "But how were* *you able to take her (if it wasn't her time)?" The Angel replied, "She was holding a spit (a poker) and extended it (into the oven), and she was cleaning/sweeping out the oven. She then removed the (now hot) spit and (accidentally) placed it on her foot and burned herself." (Alternatively,* Menachem Meishiv Nefesh *writes that the agent of the Angel of Death pushed it onto her leg and charred her. Her* "mazal" *("luck" — fortune) was thus worsened, and she was able to be brought to her death. Rav Bibi bar Abaye asked the Angel of Death, "Do you have permission to do so?" He replied to him, "Isn't it written:* And there is one who succumbs without justification?" *Rav Bibi asked the Angel of Death, "But it is written:* A generation goes and a generation comes (Koheles 1:4), *(i.e. no person can be taken before his allotted time is up)?" The Angel responded, "These souls stay with me until they have completed their generation (allotted time), and only then do I deliver them to* Dumah *(the guardian of the dead —* Rashi*)." Rav Bibi replied, "But in the very end, nevertheless, what do you do with the extra years (the years the person never actually lived because they were taken prematurely)? (The total count of all the years people live must still be exactly as preordained. What happens to those extra years not utilized by the person who died too early?") He answered, "If there is a young Talmudic scholar who is especially forgiving in nature to other people, I add those years to him as a replacement for the prematurely deceased person."*

THIS IS A VERY DIFFICULT GEMARA TO TRULY ELUCIDATE, AS IT DELVES into the *modus operandi* of Hashem in running this world. Even Moshe Rabbeinu, when he asked Hashem to permit him to understand His ways, was told that it is impossible — it is beyond the comprehension abilities of mere mortals. However, suffice it to say that, of course, nothing transpires or happens to any individual without Hashem's direct involvement. We must always remember that even if we do not understand how something works, we can and must still learn and benefit from it. The Torah is a guide to the workings of this world, a blueprint or instruction manual. Even if we don't begin to comprehend the how and why of Divine judgment, we continue to study the rules of the "game" by analysis of the Torah and the Talmud. If a person dies prematurely, it is solely because that accords with the Divine plan of Hashem.

Rabbeinu Chananel and *Benayahu* understand our Gemara as a dream. *Rabbeinu Chananel* adds that Rav Bibi was involved in attempting to see "demons" and his words are not to be relied upon in this case. Most commentators though, accept the Gemara literally.

Tosafos note that the Angel of Death was relating stories from the past to Rav Bibi. This narrative actually occurred during the Second Temple period, whereas Rav Bibi lived many years after its destruction. The woman referred to as "Miriam מגדלא שיער נשיא, Miriam, the braider of women's hair" was none other than Mary (Miriam!), the mother of אותו האיש, "that man," Jesus of Nazareth!

Tosafos cite the Gemara in *Shabbos* 104b as proof for this amazing statement. Yet, the standard Vilna edition of the Talmud Bavli on that folio has no such description of Mary/Miriam, nor is there even mention of her name. Is *Tosafos* in error? Certainly not. The fact is, various non-Jewish authorities have censored the Talmud over the years. Many small sections have been changed or entirely deleted and removed in this manner. Some citations are lost forever, while others are retained only as seemingly inexplicable references in commentaries on the Talmud. Indeed, many such passages, including this missing passage, can be found exactly on the appropriate *daf*, in the *sefer Chesronos HaShas* (Missing Sections of the *Shas*). (For this particular segment, one can also see the Steinsaltz edition of *Maseches Shabbos*.) There, the Gemara clearly discusses the married mother of אותו האיש/ Miriam מגדלא שיער נשיא. I have heard from my rebbeim that it is possible that the word מגדלא is related to the word (Mary) Magdalene.

Benayahu further explains how the agent of the Angel of Death erred. When the Angel of Death asked the agent to bring the woman, he said, "Bring Miriam מגדלא." The messenger, however, mistakenly brought a different woman with that name, and hence the mix-up. *Rabbeinu Chananel* actually has the names reversed in his text. The Angel requested "Miriam מגדלא דרדקי, Miriam one who raises young children," but received instead Miriam מגדלא שיער נשיא.

The "guardian of the dead," *Dumah*, is mentioned in the *Hallel* prayer. *The dead do not praise You, nor do those who descend to "Dumah"* (*Tehillim* 115:17). The word *Dumah* literally means "silence." The dead no longer can praise Hashem; they are under the domain (guardianship) of silence.

Chagigah 5a

(see also Eruvin 65a; Moed Katan 9b; Yevamos 34b; Bava Basra 12b)

Rava's Wife

> *Rava said: This (i.e. another example of an improperly performed good deed) refers to one who sends his wife "uncut meat" on* erev *Shabbos. But Rava (himself) sent such uncut meat to his own wife? The daughter of Rav Chisda (Rava's wife) was different. Rava knew she was expert in these laws (and would not err).*

"Uncut meat" is meat not fully koshered. It contains various forbidden cuts still physically attached to the kosher sections. (An example would be the forbidden *gid hanasheh* [sciatic nerve tissues] together with the surrounding kosher *filet mignon.*) *Rashi* explains that sending such meat containing kosher and non-kosher parts very close to Shabbos could easily lead to preparing and ingesting non-kosher food. Everyone is so busy *erev* Shabbos that one might assume the meat is fully ready to cook, and therefore inadvertently prepare forbidden sections as part of the meal. Kosher and nonkosher meat cooked together in this fashion is prohibited even if the nonkosher parts are subsequently removed, because, by means of the cooking, their essence is absorbed into the other cuts. *Iyun Yaakov* adds that the wife would presume that her husband removed any forbidden pieces, and she therefore would not bother to check this herself. *Meiri* comments that she would not necessarily be able to recognize whether the meat had been properly *kashered*. *Maharsha* notes that it is this potential for error that makes an otherwise meritorious act (i.e. preparing expensive meat for Shabbos) into an inappropriate deed.

Rav Chisda's daughter was a unique individual — she had a different status than the average person. She was very knowledgeable in the laws of *kashrus* and *kashering*, and thus her husband, Rava, was not concerned that she would err in any way in this matter.

Rava cared very dearly for his wife. The Gemara in *Berachos* 56a relates a fascinating series of dreams that Rava had. He went to a well-known dream interpreter, Bar Hedya, who favorably interpreted dreams *if the price was right*. The Gemara there explains that under certain circumstances, a dream's true interpretation and its subsequent realization can be determined by the way it is interpreted. (This is a very complicated subject that is mostly inapplicable today and will not be delved into here.) Rava was unaware of this, and was also unaware that Bar Hedya charged for a "positive" interpretation. Bar Hedya consistently portrayed Rava's dreams in a negative manner. After his interpretations were all unfortunately borne out (including many severe personal and financial tragedies), Rava discovered Bar Hedya's secret. He told Bar Hedya, "I could forgive you for all the tragic outcomes you portended, except for one — the death of my wife, the daughter of Rav Chisda."

Their marriage itself is an interesting story. The Gemara in *Bava Basra* (12b) relates that as a little girl, Rav Chisda'a daughter sat on her father's lap. He asked her which of the two Torah scholars present at the time (Rami bar Chama and Rava) she would like to marry. She responded that she wished to marry both of them. Rava quickly remarked that if so, he wanted to be the second one to marry her (i.e. she would marry Rami first, and then when he dies, she would marry Rava). And so it transpired, as the young girl's words were prophetically true. She grew up and married Rami bar Chama, who subsequently died. Only many years later, after Rava's first wife also passed away, did she finally marry Rava. In the intervening years, she turned down many other marriage opportunities, as the Gemara in *Yevamos* 34b describes, to wait for her intended new spouse, Rava.

Chagigah 6a

(see also Berachos 31a-b; Pesachim 66b; Megillah 14a-b)

CHANA, MOTHER OF SHMUEL

(The Gemara is in the midst of a discussion regarding who is exempt from the obligation of going up to Yerushalayim for the three festivals. Beis Shammai's opinion is that parents are exempt from bringing a child so young that he is incapable of riding on his father's shoulders. Beis Hillel holds that only children capable of walking while holding onto their father's hand are obligated; younger children are not).

Rebbi objected on behalf of Beis Hillel to Beis Shammai. And Chana did not ascend (to the Tabernacle in Shiloh) because she said to her husband (Elkanah), "Until the child (Shmuel) is weaned — then I will bring him" (Shmuel I 1:22). *But Shmuel was capable of riding on his father's shoulders? (i.e. the age of weaning in those days was two years. But even before then a child could be carried. Thus Beis Shammai is incorrect in stating that riding on one's father's shoulders is the minimal age of obligation). His (Rebbi's) father replied to him (Rebbi), "According to your reasoning, Chana herself poses a problem. Wasn't she obligated (in the mitzvah of) rejoicing (on the holidays)? (Why did she not go up to Shiloh?) Rather, Chana saw that Shmuel was a very fussy baby, and she was concerned that he would become seriously ill from the journey." (Thus Shmuel was exempt only because of unusual circumstances, and one cannot bring support to the opinion of Beis Hillel from this case.)*

CHANA IS DISCUSSED IN GREAT DETAIL IN THE GEMARA ELSEWHERE in this *sefer*; she is one of the most important female Biblical figures. She dedicated her son Shmuel at the age of 2 to the service of Hashem. The initially barren Chana prayed fervently to Hashem to have this child. She *davened* passionately to save his life (*Berachos* 31a-b); and in order to protect her son, she selflessly gave up going with her husband to the Tabernacle. Yet, she willingly sent him away for tutelage (to the Tabernacle under the aegis of the *Kohen Gadol* Eli) when he was just 24 months of age. Chana is the prototypical Jewish mother, raising her child solely for the purpose of glorifying Hashem's Name. Coupled with her overriding concern for his spiritual growth, was a maternal concern for his physical health. She was very willing to miss out on "עילת רגל" (the mitzvah of going up to the Sanctuary for the Holidays), to personally sacrifice her own spiritual development, in order to care for her son. I believe this is on of the essential reasons why women are not obligated in certain time-dependent commandments. It is a function of "העוסק במצוה פטור מן המצוה". One who is involved in a mitzvah, is exempt from performing another mitzvah. The supremely important mitzvah of nurturing and raising healthy God fearing children exempts women from performing certain Jewish rituals. For a women therefore to change these priorities simply for her own "personal growth" (at the expense of her family's), is to essentially state that she knows better than God what is best for her and her family.

CHAGIGAH 15B

PROMISE UNFULFILLED: ACHER'S DAUGHTER

The daughter of Acher (Elisha ben Avuyah) came before Rebbi. She said to him, "Rebbi — (please) support me." He said to her, "Whose daughter are you?" She replied to him, "I am the daughter of Acher." He said to her, "Are there still descendants of his in the world? But it is written (regarding the wicked): He will have neither child nor grandchild amongst his nation, and no survivor in his dwelling place" (Iyov 18:19). *She said to him, "Remember his Torah, but do not remember his deeds." Immediately, a fire descended (from Hashem) and seared the bench of Rebbi. Rebbi cried, and said, "And what, for those who disgrace it (i.e. their Torah) are so defended, how much more so (will Hashem defend) those who praise it (the Torah)!"*

ACHER — "THE OTHER ONE" — IS THE APPELLATION THE RABBIS USE throughout the Talmud to describe the Tanna Elisha ben Avuyah. He was originally a well-respected and highly regarded *talmid chacham,* who tragically left the path of Torah after misunderstanding various images and visions to which he was privy in the lofty spiritual heights he reached in the Heavens. His tragic story is detailed in our Gemara (earlier on this *daf*), as well as in several places in the Talmud Bavli and Yerushalmi. *Tosafos* on 15a summarizes the various underlying reasons why he went astray. He was named Acher, the other one, based on a story in our Gemara (15a). After his spiritual downfall, he transgressed many Torah prohibitions. Once, he desired to cohabit with a harlot. She was surprised, and wondered, "Aren't you the great Rabbi Elisha ben Avuyah?" He violated a Biblical Shabbos law in her presence, and she remarked, "This must be *another (person)*." Hence he became known as Acher — "the other one."

Rebbi was amazed that Acher should have a living descendant. The *posuk* in *Iyov* suggests that ultimately a wicked person will leave behind no living legacy, and that all his progeny will die. *Maharsha* notes that there are far worse sinners than Acher who have many offspring who have survived. Why was Rebbi so surprised? *Maharsha* explains, based on the Yerushalmi, that Acher's sin of blasphemy was especially egregious, as he should have known better. He was a renowned Torah scholar, a person who literally and/or figuratively traveled to the Heavens and saw amazing wonders and sights that no other person could imagine. And yet, he erred in thinking that there was an aspect of dualism running this world. For him to believe or think that there could be anything else besides the One God was an especially deviate and horrendous transgression.

Why was fire specifically sent from above to singe Rebbi's bench? *Maharsha* posits that fire is an allusion to the Torah, as illustrated in *Devarim* 33:2, where the Torah is referred to as אש דת, a law of fire. *Ben Yehoyada* explicates that this hints to the fires of Gehinnom that were purifying Acher. This is likewise alluded to in Acher's real name — אלישע — a jumble of the words עלי אש, which means "raised by fire." Originally, a Divine decree ordained that Acher would remain forever in a limbo-like state. He would not be punished because his tremendous Torah scholarship would protect him from the fires of Gehinnom. However, at the same time, this lack of chastisement would result in permanent banishment from Heaven. His devoted disciple, the great Rabbi Meir, succeeded in eventually bringing Acher into Heaven. Rabbi Meir prayed that Acher's judgment be completed by suffering in Gehinnom. Acher ultimately was punished for many years in those fires, but this led to his eventual spiritual salvation.

What was the significance of the bench in particular getting scorched? *Ben Yehoyada* writes that this refers to the idea that the souls of the righteous are "stored under the Chair of Honor" of Hashem. Rebbi was being sent the message: Do not be so quick to write off Acher. It is never too late to do *teshuvah*. Indeed, *Tosafos* quote the Yerushalmi that states that Acher did repent on his deathbed (see below).

Why did Rebbi ask the woman whose daughter she was? What difference should it make? I thought that possibly Rebbi was interested in seeing if he could help her out on a long-term basis. If he knew her family and/or her background, he might be able to intervene more effectively on her behalf, and not simply provide her with temporary financial relief. The Schottenstein Edition of the Talmud Bavli (*Chagigah,* 15b note 14) suggests that depending on her lineage, she might have been eligible for a higher priority in receiving charity funds (*Horayos* 13a). Alternatively, if she came from a higher socio-economic status, she would be entitled to increased *tzedakah* funding (*Kesubos* 67b).

The Talmud Yerushalmi (*Chagigah* 2:1, 9b) has a slightly different version of this story. After his death, Acher's daughters went to Rebbi to ask for *tzedakah*. Rebbi, however, quoting *Tehillim* 109:12 (which discusses David HaMelech and the wicked men of his generation who mocked him), declared: *"May none extend chessed upon him; and may none be merciful to his orphans."* The daughters replied to Rebbi, "Do not look at his actions; instead look at his Torah." At that moment Rebbi cried and decreed that they should be supported. He stated, "Even though this one (Acher) toiled at Torah without the proper heavenly intent, look at what he has established. How much more will be accomplished by one who toils at Torah with the proper intent!" The *Korban HaEidah* asks what was Rebbi referring to that Acher "established"? It refers either to his establishment of Rabbi Meir, the teacher of Torah to all of Israel, and/or it connotes the daughters Acher raised who were very wise.

The Gemara in *Kiddushin* (39b) relates to us that one of Acher's daughters had a son, Rav Yaakov, who was an outstanding *talmid chacham.* Ironically, the Gemara there relates that he correctly understood an incident that was partially responsible for his grandfather Acher veering off the Jewish path. Both saw (at separate times) a father ask his son to climb up a tree, send away a mother bird, and bring back the baby birds to him (the father). The son obediently followed his father's command, but upon shooing away the mother bird and taking the babies, the son fell out of the tree and died. Acher was shocked into disbelief, because both of these *mitzvos* (listening to and honoring one's parents, and the obligation to send away the mother bird before taking the eggs or the young) are commandments for which the Torah specifically promises the reward of a long life to those who observe them. Thus, how was it possible for this young boy, who simultaneously performed both precepts, to die at such a tender age?! Acher therefore questioned and doubted the veracity of the Torah. His grandson Rav Yaakov, however, understood the correct interpretation and was not misled. The Torah's promise of a long life does not mean in this world. This world cannot truly contain the phenomenal reward one will receive for performing *mitzvos.* The *posuk* actually pledges a long life in the World to Come.

Finally, the Gemara remarks that one should stay away from a Torah scholar whose "inside is not like his outside," i.e. his actions and deeds are in opposition to the Torah knowledge he has acquired. The risk of going astray outweighs any potential benefit that might accrue from studying Torah from such a person. Yet, Rabbi Meir was able to remain Acher's disciple. He threw away the shell (Acher's external sins) and was able to harvest the sweet fruit inside (the Torah) because of his extraordinary righteousness and sagacity. I would suggest that the same applies to Acher's daughter(s). She clearly demonstrated great respect for the Torah and the Rabbis, despite having grown up and learning daily from her father. She realized that her father's actions and deeds were evil, yet she told Rebbi to recognize and remember only his Torah. Thus, she too must have been able to discard the bad and keep the good, as did the great Rabbi Meir. Indeed, the proof can be seen from the very *posuk* that Rebbi quoted in our Gemara. Since Acher did indeed have children and grandchildren who were righteous, he could not have been totally evil. Instead, truly righteous individuals were able to take his good qualities and discard the wickedness. The Yerushalmi concludes the discussion of Acher with the following note. On his deathbed, Acher was visited by Rabbi Meir. Rabbi Meir quoted to him various verses stating that it is never too late to do *teshuvah*. Acher cried, and died. Rabbi Meir remarked, "It appears to me that he died while doing repentance." The Gemara ultimately relates that Rabbi Meir, and subsequently Rabbi Yochanan, were able to bring Acher into Heaven.

Chagigah 20a

Halachic Incidents

The Gemara discusses three stories mentioning women and various halachos *regarding whether certain garments in question had acquired* tumah *(ritual impurity).*

(1) Two women unintentionally had their clothing exchanged in a bathhouse.

(2) A woman wove a garment in purity, but did not expressly intend to set her mind and to guard the garment from ritual contamination.

(3) A woman weaving a certain article of clothing initially moistened its thread with her saliva.

The Gemara then provides the p'sak halachah *and explains the rationale.*

These stories are not delved into deeply in this *sefer* because they involve complicated laws of ritual purity that do not apply today. Furthermore, the mentioning of women in these stories is only incidental to the point in each case. The *halachah* is no different in these cases for either men or women, and no significant additional insight is obtained by the fact that these stories involved women. The main reason these narratives cited women was because they were real life occurrences, with real life halachic decisions. As women were more frequently involved in the weaving of clothing, it is not surprising that these cases were used to demonstrate the *halachah*.

INDEX

N

P

R

S

T

V

W

Y